/\.\.\ CONTENTS

PREFACE

Bronislaw Malinowski was already in the United States when the Second World War broke out, and he accepted what was at first a temporary, and later a permanent post, as Professor of Anthropology at Yale University. Naturally he needed a considerable amount of the manuscripts, notes, and books which he had left at the London School of Economics on leaving for the United States for his sabbatical leave at the end of 1938; and after accepting the Yale appointment he made a careful selection of these, to be sent to him at New Haven, while the greater part of his books and papers were stored away in the London School of Economics for the duration of the war. In New Haven, part of this material was kept at his home, and the rest was kept in his office at the Yale Graduate School.

In May 1942, Malinowski died suddenly of an entirely unpredicted heart attack. One of the first people to come to New Haven on hearing the bad news was Dr. Feliks Gross, friend and former student of Malinowski's, who offered to help in the special task of sorting and ordering Malinowski's books and papers, beginning with the contents of the Graduate School office. While this work was going on, Dr. Gross suddenly telephoned me from that office, asking if I knew of the existence of a smallish thick black notebook which he had just found, containing a diary of Bronislaw Malinowski, written almost entirely in Polish in his handwriting. Dr. Gross brought the notebook straight over to me and translated a few entries chosen at random which referred to his field work in Southern New Guinea. Malinowski had never mentioned to me the existence of this diary; I kept it carefully and took it with me to Mexico when I moved there permanently in 1946.

Sometime after the end of the war, Malinowski's books and papers were taken from their storage place in the London School of Economics, and about 1949 this considerable mass of manuscripts, notes, and books was sent to me in Mexico; among these I found two envelopes containing notebooks, one marked "Early Polish Diary" and the other "Diaries." All of these small notebooks were written in Polish. I put these with the first notebook found at Yale, with the idea of having them translated and possibly published at some later date.

The diaries remained, therefore, locked away until the end of 1960, when I made a visit to New York. There I spoke of the diaries to one of Malinowski's publishers; and we decided on their publication. Mr. Norbert Guterman was kind enough to undertake the translation from Polish, which he rendered in a very direct manner. In correcting the proofs I have tried to assure the closest possible adherence to Malinowski's personal use of English words and phrasing, in which language in the latter part of his life he expressed himself with such freedom. A few extremely intimate observations have been omitted, the omissions being indicated by dots. The early Polish diary has not been included because it antedates Malinowski's anthropological career.

I have always felt a desire—even a need—to know something of the life and personality of any painter, writer, musician, or scientist whose work has profoundly interested or moved me.

I feel that the psychological and emotional light shed by diaries, letters, and autobiographies not only give one a fresh insight into the personality of the man who wrote certain books, developed a certain theory, or composed certain symphonies; but that through this knowledge of that man as he lived and felt, one is often brought into a closer contact and a greater comprehension of his work. When there exists, therefore, the diary or autobiography of an outstanding personality, I feel that these "data" regarding his daily and inner life and his thoughts should be published, with the deliberate aim of revealing that personality, and linking up this knowledge with the work left behind.

I know that some people will think that a diary is of a basically private nature and that it should not be published; and those who hold this point of view will probably be severely critical of my decision to publish my husband's diaries. But after seriously weighing the matter, I reached the conclusion that it is of greater importance to give to the present and future students and readers of Malinowski's anthropological writings this direct insight into his inner personality, and his way of living and thinking during the period of his most important work in the field, rather than to leave these brief diaries shut away in an archive. I am, therefore, solely responsible for the decision to publish this book.

VALETTA MALINOWSKA

Mexico
May 1966

INTRODUCTION*

This diary by Bronislaw Malinowski covers only a very brief
period of his life, from early September 1914 to the beginning
of August 1915, and from the end of October 1917 to mid-July
1918—about nineteen months in all. It was written in Polish, as a
private document, and was never intended for publication.
What then is its significance? Malinowski was a great social
scientist, one of the founders of modern social anthropology,
and a thinker who tried to relate his generalizations about human nature and human society to the issues of the world around
him. The diary refers to that very critical period of his career
when, having equipped himself theoretically for empirical studies,
he began to carry out field research in New Guinea. The first
section covers his apprenticeship period among the Mailu; the
second, after an unfortunate gap of two years, covers most of
his last year in the Trobriands. Nowadays it is recognized that
while the personality of a scientist may not necessarily have a
direct bearing upon his selection and treatment of problems, it
must influence his work in other more subtle ways. Although

* I am grateful to Audrey Richards and Phyllis Kaberry, friends of
Malinowski, and to Józefa Stuart, his eldest daughter, for advice on this
Introduction. They have, of course, no responsibility for the opinions ex-
pressed here.

chronologically very brief, and although giving no great amount of detail on professional matters, the diary does indicate vividly how Malinowski thought about issues and about people—or at least how he expressed himself when he was writing only for himself as audience.

Malinowski came to be in New Guinea through his association with British anthropology. What led him to this move so far from Poland, his native country, is not now fully known. But despite his often unkind comments upon England and English gentlemen, he seemed always to have a basic respect for the English intellectual tradition and the English way of life, and it seems likely that even at that early period of his career he was attracted to both. (Note his revealing description of Machiavelli in this diary as "very like me in many respects. An Englishman, with an entirely European mentality and European problems.") He himself has told us how, when at the (Jagiellonian) University of Cracow, he had been ordered to abandon for a time his physical and chemical research because of ill-health, but was allowed to follow up a "favorite sideline of study" and so began to read Frazer's *The Golden Bough* in the original English version—then three volumes only.* Malinowski had obtained his Ph.D degree in 1908 in physics and mathematics, and after two years of advanced study at Leipzig he came to London and began his systematic studies of anthropology with C. G. Seligman and Edward Westermarck, at the London School of Economics and Political Science. He also

* For this and other details see B. Malinowski, *Myth in Primitive Psychology*, London, 1926, pp. 5-6; also Raymond Firth in *Man and Culture*, London, 1957, pp. 2-7; Konstantin Symmons-Symonolewicz, "Bronislaw Malinowski: Formative Influences and Theoretical Evolution," *The Polish Review*, Vol. IV, 1959, pp. 1-28, New York. A few further facts appear in "A Brief History (1913-1963)" of the Department of Anthropology of the London School of Economics, published in the departmental programme of courses, session 1963-64 and succeeding years.

made contact with A. C. Haddon and W. H. R. Rivers of Cambridge—all of whom are mentioned in the diary. His first major publication, a documentary study of *The Family Among the Australian Aborigines*, was published in London in 1913. Another book, in Polish, on *Primitive Religion and Forms of Social Structure*, completed early in 1914, was published in Poland in 1915. Influenced especially by Seligman and Haddon, Malinowski had prepared for field research in the Western Pacific, after an unsuccessful attempt by Seligman to get funds for him to work in the Sudan. Money for field research in anthropology was then much more difficult to obtain than it is nowadays. Malinowski was helped through scholarship funds and a grant from Robert Mond, the industrialist, obtained primarily through Seligman's energies. An attachment as Secretary to R. R. Marett, who was Recorder of Section H—the Anthropology Section—of the British Association, which was meeting in Melbourne in 1914, gave him a free passage to Australia. Malinowski's situation, with exiguous field resources, was complicated by the outbreak of war, since he was technically an Austrian national. But through the help of his friends, the Australian authorities proved themselves very understanding by allowing him to proceed to carry out his field research in New Guinea. Their liberality was also shown in supplementing his finances by a grant from the Home and Territories Department of the Commonwealth. After traveling to Port Moresby, Malinowski spent the greater part of six months in the Mailu area in the south of New Guinea. A brief visit to the Trobriand Islands off the northeast coast stimulated his interest more and he returned there on two subsequent expeditions of a year each, 1915–16 and 1917–18.

One of Malinowski's outstanding contributions to the development of social anthropology was the introduction of much more intensive and much more sophisticated methods of field re-

search than had previously been current in his subject.* The
many references to his ethnographic work in his diary show his
industry. The day after his arrival in New Guinea he had con-
tacted an informant (Ahuia Ova), and the next day he began
collecting field data on social structure. Only a fortnight later
he noted two basic defects in his approach—he did not observe
the people enough, and he did not speak their language. Both of
these he tried hard to correct, and his endeavor was the clue to
all his later work. The ethnography of the diary consists of
references to subjects of talk or observation—taboo, burial rites,
stone axes, black magic, dancing, procession with pigs—rather
than development of ideas about field questions or theoretical
problems. But an occasional note shows these behind the scene.
"I asked about the division of land. It would have been useful to
find out about the old system of division and to study today's as
a form of adaptation." This is an early indication of an interest
in social change which later developed into a major theme in his
work. What the first diary does show is Malinowski's keen desire to get his early material written up as soon as possible for
publication, and in fact his report on *The Natives of Mailu* was
ready before the middle of 1915.† One is led to infer that it was
in the course of writing up this material ("in fact as I worked
out my notes") that Malinowski came to perceive the significance of many points of field method which he later developed
and incorporated into his treatment. The Trobriand account is
more vivid—the choosing of the site for the tent, the meeting
with old acquaintances, including the chief To'uluwa, and the
man "who used to bring me eggs, dressed in a lady's nightgown";

---

* See Phyllis Kaberry, in *Man and Culture*, 1957, pp. 71-91.

† See bibliographical reference in introduction to Index of Native Terms
infra. Malinowski's preface was dated June 9th, 1915, from Samarai, when
he had already begun his second expedition to New Guinea. (He received
the D.Sc. degree from the University of London in 1916 for this publication together with *The Family Among the Australian Aborigines*.)

the making of village plan and census; the amassing of information about *baloma* and *milamila*, about *gimwali* and *sagali*. The references to the *kula* are fascinating to anyone who has followed his analysis of that complex system of exchange of shell tokens of social status, with its economic, political, and ritual overtones.

What an anthropologist may miss particularly in the diary is any detailed account of how Malinowski arrived at the choice of his field problems, why he selected one topic rather than another for investigation at a particular point of time, and whether fresh evidence led him to reshape a hypothesis. Some evidence there is—as when he notes that reading Rivers drew his attention to "problems of the Rivers type," presumably those of kinship. But on the whole such methodological issues are not pursued in this daily record of his thoughts. Of more interest are Malinowski's occasional flashes of theoretical observation, such as his remarks on language as a system of social ideas, both instrument and objective creation or on history as "observation of facts in keeping with a certain theory." These give sign of his concern with issues which were then relatively novel but later became part of the general talk of the academic market place. But if the diary does not dwell either on field methodology or on problems of anthropological theory, it does convey most keenly the reactions of a field anthropologist in an alien society. There he must live as recorder and analyst, but as such he cannot completely share the customs and values of the people, admire or dislike them as he may. The feeling of confinement, the obsessional longing to be back even if for the briefest while in one's own cultural surroundings, the dejection and doubts about the validity of what one is doing, the desire to escape into a fantasy world of novels or daydreams, the moral compulsion to drag oneself back to the task of field observation —many sensitive fieldworkers have experienced these feelings on occasion, and they have rarely been better expressed than in this diary. Some emotions, no doubt, have been expressed more violently by Malinowski than they would be felt—or at least stated—by other anthropologists. Most fieldworkers at some time have been bored by their own inquiries, and have been conscious of frustration and exasperation against even their best friends in the field. Few may have been willing to admit this even to themselves. Few perhaps except those as highly strung as Malinowski have cursed the people they were studying as heartily as he did. Yet this revelation of a darker side of the relation of an anthropologist to his human material should not mislead us. Malinowski often used equally violent language about other groups and persons, European and American. He had to explode to get his irritations out of his system and it was almost a point of honor with him not to repress his feelings or curb his tongue. This also should not obscure from us Malinowski's own appreciation of his Trobriand friendships, of which the diary also makes mention. Few anthropologists too would be prepared to write with Malinowski's freedom, even as he did for his own eyes alone, of their sensual lusts and feelings, or to engage in, much less set down, such ribald gestures as singing to a Wagner melody the words "Kiss my ass" to chase away flying witches!

As an ethnographer, Malinowski stood somewhat apart from the government officials, missionaries, and traders who constituted the white society in New Guinea at that time. Consequently, we get from him new and sometimes unexpected shafts of light, though only in passing, upon personalities known usually to us only from more formal literature. His thumbnail sketch of the now almost legendary figure of Sir Hubert Murray, the lieutenant governor and apex of the official pyramid, seems to me very apt, though his remarks about some other acquaintances, including Saville, the missionary who helped him, may be less just. It is significant that Malinowski's capacity for seeking out meaningful experiences led him as much to the company of some of the pearl buyers in the Trobriands, particularly Raffael Brudo with whom he later stayed in Paris, as to the more official sectors of the white society. Though scanty, his comments on conditions in New Guinea half a century ago are very useful sociological evidence. But it is as a human document rather than as a scientific contribution that Malinowski's diary should be evaluated.

A diary in the ordinary sense can be a simple chronological record of day-to-day events. This is what many people keep, or try to keep, as a kind of *aide-mémoire* to their recollections or as a kind of justification to prove to themselves that the days that have gone by have not been completely wasted. An extension of this kind of diary, seen in the memoirs of generals, ambassadors, and other public figures, may provide interesting, perhaps critical, evidence on the shaping of public affairs. In revealing the doings and sayings of prominent people the record may be all the more attractive to the world at large if the issues mentioned are controversial or touched with scandal. But another kind of diary, much more difficult to write with sincerity, is the expression of a personality through day-to-day commentary on events at least as much in the world or the self as in the world outside. The great diaries of history, if not notable for the light they throw on public events, illumine those private aspects of a personality which can be interpreted as having a general meaning for the student of human character. Their significance lies in the interplay of temperament and circumstance, in the intellectual, emotional, and moral struggles of men or women striving to express themselves, to preserve individuality, and to make headway in the face of the challenges, temptations, and flatteries of the society in which they live. For such a diary to have meaning and impact, literary skill may be less important than force of expression, modesty is probably

less effective than vanity, weakness must be displayed as well as
strength, and a kind of brutal frankness is essential. If it is ever
published for the common reader to see, the writer must incur
criticism as well as appreciation; in justice too he should be
given understanding if not compassion.

By these criteria, while this diary of Malinowski's in its
purely ethnographic sense cannot be ranked as more than a
footnote to anthropological history, it is certainly a revelation
of a fascinating and complex personality who had a formative
influence on social science. In reading it, one must bear in mind
its purpose. I think it is clear that its object was not so much
to keep a record of Malinowski's scientific progress and intentions, or to set down the daily events of his studies in the field,
as to chart the course of his personal life, emotional as well as
intellectual. In the earlier section it would seem that he regarded
the periodic chronicle of his thoughts and feelings as a way of
helping to organize his life, and to realize its deeper meaning.
But in the later section he meant it as an instrument as well as a
reference work; he saw it as a means of guiding and indeed rec-
tifying his personality. Part of the reason for this intensified
emphasis of the diary as discipline was clearly the relationship
he had entered into with the woman who later became his wife.
What he writes of E. R. M.'s qualities of character in this diary
those who knew her later would confirm, and what shines out in
these pages is the depth and sincerity of his love for her and the
efforts he continually made to avoid sullying what he tried to
keep as a pure emotional bond. What it meant to him then and
as far as one can judge all through their later years is beautifully expressed in the phrase that for him she had "treasures to
give and the miraculous power to absolve sins." There seems to
have been little that he did not confess to her; in the later diary
his relation with her was partly at least responsible for its
frankness. To be honest with her as well as with himself was one
of Malinowski's prime aims. Yet he did not pursue it consis-

tently, and it was his emotional link with another woman from whom he had not completely broken which accounts for so much of his self-questioning and self-accusation.*

The vividness of some of the descriptions in the diary is very striking, revealing Malinowski's perceptive eye for the color of the New Guinea landscape, and his love of the sea and of sailing. It is very interesting to have these sidelights on his personality. But how far his innermost personal feelings should be exposed must always remain a question. Whatever the answer be it is amply clear that this diary is a moving, human document written by a man who wished to leave himself with no falsity of illusion about his own character. Some passages in it illustrate his emotions, while others mock at them. Some passages show his hypochondria, his continual quest for health, through the pursuit of a mixture of exercise and medicaments. Other passages again may even nowadays offend or shock the reader, and some readers may be impressed as much by the revelation of elements of brutality, even degradation, which the record shows on occasion. My own reflection on this is to advise anyone who wishes to sneer at passages in this diary to be first equally frank in his own thoughts and writings, and then judge again. Malinowski's was a complex personality, and some of his less admirable characteristics come through perhaps more clearly in this diary than do his virtues. If so, this is what he intended because it was his faults and not his virtues which he wished to understand and make clear to himself. Whether or no most of us would wish to emulate his frankness, we should concede its courage.

RAYMOND FIRTH

London
March 1966

* As I understood it much later from him, it was Baldwin Spencer's knowledge and misunderstanding of the overlap in this relation and inept attempt to intervene which led to the breach between him and Malinowski. E. R. M., when Malinowski's wife, apparently shared his views though she spoke of Spencer, who had been an old friend of hers, in more forgiving terms.

SECOND INTRODUCTION 1988

It is intriguing after twenty years to look back upon the reception by the anthropological profession of a controversial work such as Malinowski's *Diary*. So I have accepted the invitation of the publisher to write this new Introduction, partly as a reflection on what has seemed to be the effect of this work upon other anthropologists, and partly to review my own earlier impressions of it.

I wrote the original Introduction somewhat unwillingly, at the request of Valetta Malinowska, Malinowski's widow, who was determined to publish these private diaries. I thought then that I might help to explain the significance of this revealing, egocentric, obsessional document, with its mixture of stimulus, dullness, pathos and outrageousness, to those who had never known that protean character that was Malinowski. I had also hoped, mistakenly, to draw some of the teeth of the criticism that would be levelled at portions of the work.

Malinowski wrote his field notes concerning the Trobriands in English and Kiriwinian; his diaries were written in Polish. They were clearly meant as a private record, a confession to himself, a kind of purgation and guide to personal correction, almost certainly for his own eyes alone. In

one sense the publication of the diaries was an act of betrayal –
not so much because it exposed Malinowski's weaknesses
without his knowledge, as that it assumed that his weaknesses
could be part of a commercial property to be exploited. I have
not altered my view that publication of the diaries was an
invasion of privacy, even though their author was dead. I do
not believe that "the public has a right to know" the more
intimate details of any person's life. Nor do I believe, as some
of my colleagues appear to do, that anything written down,
however personal and private, is ultimately even if subconsciously destined for public attention. But once publication was
in hand, it seemed to me that a preface which tried to give
some perspective and interpretation for the diaries was
justifiable.

My original introduction drew adverse comment from
friends of mine who had also known and admired Malinowski,
and felt strongly about the impropriety of publication and the
damage it might do to Malinowski's reputation. Hortense
Powdermaker, for instance wrote sadly to me "I, and many
other anthropologists, do not understand how you could have
given implicit consent to the publication of the *Diary* by
writing an Introduction to it" (3/11/67), and parallel sentiments
were expressed by others, such as Phyllis Kaberry and Lucy
Mair.

The initial reception of the book was mixed. The *Times
Literary Supplement*, in an anonymous review (26/10/67), was
very dismissive – "a very boring repetition of banalities".
Those who had worked with Malinowski tended to be strongly
critical. Ian Hogbin wrote: "In my view the volume holds no
interest for anyone, be he anthropologist, psychologist, student
of biography or merely a gossip." (*American Anthropologist* 70,
1968 : 575). Edmund Leach was more reflective, but still
decidedly censorious. He wrote that it was to the discredit of

all concerned that the diaries had now been committed to print. But he did point out that once in print such private documents of fieldworking anthropologists should be read as devices for retaining a grip on reality in traumatic situations, a kind of catharsis, and should never be interpreted as a balanced record of the writer's inner personality. He also stressed the absurdity of translating *nigrami* as "niggers" instead of "the blacks", and so putting Malinowski into a racist category. (*Guardian* 11/8/67).

A close friend and counsellor of the Malinowski family, Audrey Richards, gave a further analytical appraisal. She had heartily disapproved of the publication of the book, and found it disappointing from an ethnographical point of view. Under the title of "In Darkest Malinowski" (*The Cambridge Review*, 19 January 1968) however, she did her best to elucidate the meaning of this intensely personal document. She saw Malinowski, with his varying moods of hope and despair as "the hero, or the anti-hero" of the book – "anti-hero because no man was ever more brutally frank about his own failings." She pointed out how the striving anxious figure of the *Diary* was a very different creature from the witty, apparently cynical teacher of renown. She discussed in some detail Malinowski's negative attitude towards his informants, contrasting this with the much more positive reactions he displayed towards them in later talk with his students. Characteristically, also, Audrey Richards used this review of Malinowski's field diaries as a peg on which to hang some interesting general observations of her own on the role of the anthropological research worker in the field. But Richards, like Malinowski's other friends, had been worried about the unpleasing impression which the diaries might give to people who were already antagonistic to him. She had written to me at an early stage, in her vivid style : "I gather from Hortense that Americans are already howling with delight – not at any sex improprieties which really do not seem to matter much, but at the use of the word 'nigger' and the constant reference to his dislike of his informants and the amount of time he spends with Europeans" (5/4/67).

But serious American reviews were in fact very different. Adamson Hoebel, though dubious about the justification for publication, and finding the book hard to appraise, was conscious of its unique character. Beautifully descriptive in some parts, flat, dull, cryptic in others, the *Diary* was best seen, so Hoebel wrote, as "a device of naive self-therapy", a recurring refrain of rather pathetic and immature strivings. Yet he noted that critical as Malinowski was about people, in these diaries he was never so hard on others as on himself. And he stressed that none of the defects of the self that Malinowski belaboured in the diaries have shown in his anthropological masterpieces (*Minnesota Tribune* (approx. May 1967). In a lengthy essay-review George Stocking was impressed by the evidence of cultural marginality and ambiguous relation to things English which ran through the book. Struck by an analogy with Joseph Conrad's *Heart of Darkness*, Stocking saw Malinowski "alone with his instincts" in the field situation, though these had to do with sex rather than with the notion of power as in Conrad's novel. Be this as it may, Stocking found it hardly surprising that Malinowski's attitude towards "natives" was ambivalent and often aggressive, and interpreted even his occasional violent outbursts as no clear proof of lack of empathy with the people he was among. Indeed, the cathartic function of writing the diary may have helped to make Malinowski's empathy more possible, Stocking argued. He was very willing to generalize Malinowski's response to his field situation, and was very interested in Malinowski's "extended personal psychological crisis whose aura pervades the diaries". Stocking saw the diaries as having methodological significance in the history of anthropology, but only if interpreted in the context of the body of Malinowski's ethnography. In contrast to most reviewers, he found the book "fascinating reading" and recommended it highly to anthropologists (*Journal of the History of the Behavioral Sciences* vol. IV, no. 2, 1968: 189–94).

An extensive review by Clifford Geertz (*New York Review of Books*, 14 September 1967) was more restrained and rather clearly disparaging of Malinowski. Geertz called the book "a very curious document" and saw in it a chronicle of Malinowski working with enormous industry in one world (New Guinea) while living with intense passion in another (an imagined Australian and European setting). The book depicted "a sort of mental tableau whose stereotyped figures – his mother, a boyhood friend with whom he has quarrelled, a woman he has loved and wishes to discard, another he is now in love with and wishes to marry – are all thousands of miles away, frozen in timeless attitudes which, in anxious self-contempt, he obsessively contemplates". In this florid account, Geertz stressed two main themes, each marked by contrast. One was the contradiction between the empathy conventionally attributed to anthropologists in respect of the people they study, and Malinowski's seemingly detached, often brutal attitude in writing of the Kiriwinians. "The value of Malinowski's embarrassing example is that, if one takes it seriously, it makes difficult to defend the sentimental view of rapport as depending on the unfolding of anthropologist and informant into a single moral and emotional universe." The second theme was that Malinowski achieved salvation from "an emotional swamp" of nostalgia and despair by hard work. "Not universal compassion but an almost Calvinist belief in the cleansing power of work brought Malinowski out of his own dark world of oedipal obsessions and practised self-pity into

Trobriand daily life." Though the review made shrewd points, it was over-written, and left an impression of distortion on those who had known and worked with Malinowski. To portray the archetypal fieldworker as "a crabbed self-preoccupied, hypochondriacal narcissist" seemed a travesty. So Hortense Powdermaker and Ashley Montague, for example were moved to protest against Geertz's imperceptive view that Malinowski was apparently unable to make human contacts – a view, they insisted, which was belied by Malinowski's own evidence in *Argonauts* and other writings and by his relations with students (*New York Review of Books*, 9 November 1967). What Geertz's review illustrated, it seemed, was the danger which Leach had indicated of taking the intensely personal, private outpourings of the *Diary* as clues to the whole character of the author.

One of the most perceptive and sympathetic reviews was by an anthropologist who had never known Malinowski, but who had had much experience of the New Guinea scene. Anthony Forge found no difficulty in interpreting Malinowski's basic mode of expression as a response comparable with that of a modern anthropological fieldworker. Under the heading of "The Lonely Anthropologist" (*New Society* 17 August 1967) he remarked that while one learns little of field method from the *Diary* it illustrates very well the dilemma of every anthropologist in the field – that of retaining his/her own identity while being as much as possible involved in the affairs of the local society. The loneliness of the anthropologist is of a special kind – "surrounded by people whom you like and who like or at any rate cheerfully tolerate you, but who have no conception of who you are, what sort of person..." Longings for a remote idealised civilization are frustrating, and letters disappointing; "there is only one person who can start to understand how you feel, and that is yourself." Hence, for

those who are articulate on paper, a diary is a valuable
catharsis. "This is the function of a diary under these
conditions, a place to spew up one's spleen, so that tomorrow
one can start afresh." But as Forge points out, perhaps too
strongly, fieldworkers' diaries are meaningless to anyone except
themselves, the product of a sort of suspended state between
two cultures.

In the light of all this early diversity of opinion, where
does the *Diary* now stand? And do the opinions expressed in
my initial Introduction still hold?

After twenty years, the shock waves generated by the
publication of this intimate document have died down. Few
anthropologists who knew Malinowski are still alive. The
diaries have come to be judged from a rather different
perspective. They can be accepted as part of the literature of
the history of anthropology. Old-fashioned, eccentric, often
irrelevant but giving insight if only in part into the complex
personality of one of the founders of modern social anthropology, they have helped to throw light upon the problem of
what it means to be a working anthropologist engaged in the
study of human social material. When Hortense Powdermaker
chided me for writing the Introduction, part of my reply was :
"When I read the Diaries I found them fascinating because I
knew Malinowski well. Other people who did not, now find
them bewildering, boring, or good ammunition against the
myth of Malinowski. What strikes me is that when all the dust
has settled and we are gone they may, with the ancillary
materials of review and comment, help to elucidate a bit
further for future generations of anthropologists some aspects
of Malinowski's complex character. This may have more
meaning in the future than it does today, although already
there is a distinct trend towards trying to understand what an
anthropologist produces by reference in part to his own

personality and his relations with the people. What has still to be worked out is that an anthropologist need not – though he often does – *like* 'his' people in order to good work" (7/11/67).

Now, I think that both my original Introduction and the opinions expressed in that letter are still broadly valid. But what I tended to overlook in the original Introduction was the value of the *Diary* in an analogic sense. I had seen it primarily as a clue to the interpretation of Malinowski's personality, and hence his work. But I had not realised that for younger anthropologists unacquainted with Malinowski the interest of the book could be in what they themselves drew from it as help or reassurance in understanding their own position in confronting field problems. This is where Anthony Forge's review seemed to catch the meaning of the diaries. The modern vogue for "reflexive anthropology" may sometimes seem to turn ethnography into autobiography. But there is a much clearer recognition nowadays that the position of an ethnographer is not simply that of a recorder of the life of a society, but is also that of someone who both affects that life and is affected by it. Earlier ethnographers were not unaware of this. But at that stage of the study, the major job of description and analysis of the alien institutions by which we were faced seemed more important than expatiating upon our perception of our own roles in the situation.

There has perhaps been another element also in the reception of the *Diary*. The relative lack of information about the personal reactions of the early anthropologists in the field tended to give an air of Olympian detachment to the published accounts – the anthropologist came, saw, recorded and retired to write up the material, apparently untouched by his or her experiences, with at most an introductory chapter of comment upon relations with the people and their effect upon the fieldworker. With the publication of Malinowski's *Diary* this stereotype was destroyed. Fieldworkers too turned out to be human – all too human. Even the doyen of the discipline' had been exposed to temptation, had displayed the frailties of boredom, malice, frustration, longing for his own kind, and gave his most petty miseries full expression. It may have been with something of relief that some younger anthropologists discovered the "feet of clay" of the most eminent of elder practitioners. The more tolerant interpretation of the *Diary* may well have been strengthened by a realization that not only among anthropologists, but also more generally e.g. in the literary field, a loosening of attitudes about publication of intimate details of personal life had come to be accepted.

In the light of this it is interesting to consider a couple of recent appraisals of the work of Malinowski, including the Diary. One of the more intriguing features of some modern analyses is the authoritative tone of statements about Malinowski by people who never knew him. Leaving this aside, a feature which stands out in modern estimations of the Diary is the problem of its validity as evidence in the dilemma of translating field experience into written systematic ethnography. The idiom of discussion has been coloured by recent foci of interest in the field of literature. Clifford Geertz has devoted a section of a book on the anthropologist as author (*Works and Lives. The Anthropologist as Author*. Stanford Univ. Press 1988) to Malinowski. His treatment is milder and more analytical than in his review of the Diary twenty years before, though still prone to exaggerated expression. He is concerned primarily with Malinowski's texts. The Diary "presumably not written to be published" now poses not a psychological but a literary problem. It is "a literary product genre-addressed to an audience of one, a message from the self writing to the self reading". In it and his other enthnographic writings, Malinowski – according to Geertz – tried to project two antithetical images of himself – on the one side the empathetic Absolute Cosmopolite with fellow feeling for the savages he studies, and on the other the Complete Investigator (Geertz's terms), dispassionate, rigorously objective. "High Romance and High Science . . . uneasily yoked" (pp. 78–79) says Geertz, in a magnificent over-simplification.

James Clifford ('On Ethnographic Self-fashioning: Conrad and Malinowski' in *Reconstructing Individualism: Autonomy, Individuality and the Self in Western Thought.* ed. Thomas C. Heller, Morton Sosna & David E. Wellbery. Stanford Univ. Press 1986 : 140–62) takes a different but still literary-oriented line. As others have done, Clifford has compared *The Heart of Darkness* with Malinowski's Diary and *Argonauts of the Western Pacific*. Clifford's judgement, fairly enough, is that Malinowski was a Zola rather than a Conrad – "a naturalist presenting 'facts' plus heightened atmosphere." Clifford sees the Diary as an inventive polyphonic text, and a crucial document in the history of anthropology because it reveals the complexity of ethnographic encounters. But in a lapse of critical skill he treats the Diary and *Argonauts* as "a single expanded text". He ignores not only the time span between them – four years or so – but also the fact that the Diary was written, not for publication, day by day in the Trobriands, as a bachelor, in a time of great stress; while the *Argonauts* was written, for publication, as a unified work, in the Canary Islands, as a happily-married man, in a time of relative tranquillity. Of course they are poles apart. But to regard them in effect as two sides of Malinowski's *contemporary* complex personality is straining at the argument. Moreover, Clifford has become fascinated by the notion of *fiction* and tends to treat any text with an element of personal subjectivity in it, as fictional. It is not clear what he understands as 'fiction'. But for him the Diary is a fiction of the self for Malinowski, and the *Argonauts* the fiction of a culture – though "realistic cultural fictions", whatever they may mean. (In some contexts, Clifford seems to equate 'fiction' with 'construct'.) In his zeal for literary interpretation, Clifford even is tempted to propose ethnographic comprehension – coherent sympathy and engagement with the people studied – as best seen as a creation of ethnographic *writing* than as a quality of ethnographic *experience* (p. 158 – his italic). But though one may not accept all of Geertz's or Clifford's interpretations, their serious treatment of the Diary and suggestive commentaries show that the work has now an established place in anthropology.

So in this second Introduction to the *Diary* I would modify one judgement in the first Introduction. Though the book is undoubtedly lacking "in its purely ethnographic sense" I would no longer rank it as "no more than a footnote to anthropological history". The concept of ethnography has altered and widened, and the book has accordingly moved over to a more central place in the literature of anthropological reflection. It is not merely a record of the thinking and feeling of a brilliant, turbulent personality who helped to form social anthropology; it is also a highly significant contribution to the understanding of the position and role of a fieldworker as a conscious participator in a dynamic social situation.

RAYMOND FIRTH

NOTE

The problems involved in producing a faithful text from the
original handwritten manuscripts have made certain editorial
devices necessary. In some cases the handwriting was illegible,
and this has been indicated by ellipses in brackets [. . .]; such
passages seldom involve more than a word or a short phrase. In
other cases, where words or spellings could not be entirely made
out, brackets have been used to indicate conjectured readings.
Brackets have also been used for ordinary editorial additions
for the sake of clarity—as on the first page of text: [Fritz]
Gräbner [German anthropologist]; or where abbreviations
might not be readily understood—as in H[is] E[xcellency].
Parentheses in all cases are the author's. Editorial omissions
are indicated in the usual way by ellipses.

As the introduction to an Index of Native Terms explains,
the original manuscripts contain many words and phrases from
the many languages Malinowski was familiar with. As a matter
of added interest, his use of foreign languages has been indicated
by printing in the original language in italics all passages not
in Polish (including passages in English), with translations
supplied in brackets where this seemed necessary.

The detailed maps (of the Mailu area, the *kula* district,

and the Trobriands) are based on maps published in Malinow-ski's early works under his supervision. Some of the place names are not in agreement with current maps (particularly in or-thography), but it seemed preferable to show these areas as they were during the period covered by the diaries.

PART ONE

/\.\/\ 1914–1915 /\.\/\

/.\/.\/.\

Port Moresby, September 20, 1914. September 1st began a new epoch in my life: an expedition* all on my own to the tropics. On Tuesday, 9.1.14 I went with the British Association as far as Toowoomba. Met Sir Oliver and Lady Lodge.† I chatted with them and he offered his assistance. The falseness of my position and Staś's attempt to "set it right," my taking leave of Désiré Dickinson, my anger with Staś‡ which became a deep resentment that persists even now—all this belongs to the previous epoch, the trip to Australia with the British Assoc. I went back to Brisbane alone in a parlor car reading the Australian *Handbook*. At Brisbane I felt quite deserted and had supper alone. Evenings with [Fritz] Gräbner [German anthropologist] and

* Malinowski's report on this expedition is *The Natives of Mailu: Preliminary Results of the Robert Mond Research Work in British New Guinea, Transactions of the Royal Society of South Australia*, XXXIX, 1915.

† Sir Oliver Lodge, a prominent English physicist, was also interested in religion and psychical research and had published several works attempting to bring together both the scientific and the religious point of view. Since 1900 he had been the principal of the University of Birmingham.

‡ Stanislaw Ignacy Witkiewicz (1885-1939), son of the renowned Polish poet and painter and an artist in his own right, who was a close friend of Malinowski's from boyhood.

Pringsheim, who hope to be able to go back to Germany; we talked about the war. The lobby of the Hotel Daniell, its cheap furniture, its staircase in full view, are closely bound up with my recollections of this period. I recall morning visits to the museum with Pringsheim. Visit to Burns Phelp; a visit to the goldsmith; a meeting with [A. R. Radcliffe-]Brown. . . . On Thursday night I went to see Dr. Douglas,* to say good-by to the Goldings and to give Mrs. Golding a letter for Staś. I returned books to her.

It was a cold moonlit night. As the streetcar went up, I saw the suburb low at the foot of the hill. Afraid I might catch cold. I went for a walk with the doctor's sister, a plump blonde. Then the Goldings arrived. Because I missed the British Assoc., I treated them with a warmth which was not, however, reciprocated. . . . I had a much friendlier evening at the Mayos. Night; rain; after supper I went to the ferry. Still, calm night, the ferry boat suddenly lit up when the moon came out from behind the clouds. I walked to the foot of the hill and lost my way; it began to rain and Mayo came to meet me with an umbrella. Talk about the possible resignation of Seymour, plans for the summer, chance of spending our vacations together, etc. They are immensely charming people. I went back to the tram. Conductor reminded me of Litwiniszyn. Many drunks. All in all I didn't feel well in Brisbane. Strong fear of the tropics; abhorrence of heat and sultriness—a kind of panic fear of encountering heat as terrible as last June and July. I gave myself an injection of arsenic, after sterilizing the syringe in the kitchen.

On Saturday morning (election day) I went to the museum to present a book to the director; then bought medicines (cocaine, morphine, and emetics) and sent a registered letter to Se-

---

* Probably the Hon. John Douglas, who had been special commissioner for the British Protectorate of New Guinea, 1886-1888.

ligman* and a number of letters to Mother. After paying the exorbitant hotel bill I boarded the ship. Several persons came to see me off. . . . The Mayos stood on the shore; I watched them a long time through binoculars and waved my handkerchief—I felt I was taking leave of civilization. I was fairly depressed, afraid I might not feel equal to the task before me. After lunch I went out on deck. Sailing down the river reminded me of the excursion with Désiré and the other "Assoc's." Eurypides is situated below the gigantic slaughterhouse. Talked with *fellow* passengers. The flat banks of the river broaden suddenly. There were hills all around; land to the west and south; islands to the east. To the northwest, the strange, picturesque forms of the Glasshouse Mountains rise from a plain. I looked at them through binoculars; they reminded me of the Saturday excursion to Blackall Ranges. . . . Earlier I had watched the ship sail beyond the island; the sea got rougher and rougher, the ship pitching more and more. . . . I went to my cabin after dinner and fell asleep after an injection of Alkarsodyl. The next day was spent in my cabin, dozing with a bad headache and general numbness. At night I played cards with Lamb, the captain, and Mrs. McGrath. The next day was better; I read Rivers† and Motu grammar.‡ Got chummy with Taplin and danced with Mrs. McGrath. This state of things persisted. There was a lovely green sea, but I could not see the full sweep of the [Great Barrier]

* G. C. Seligman, the British anthropologist, Malinowski's mentor and author of *The Melanesians of British New Guinea* (1910).

† W. H. R. Rivers, English anthropologist and physiologist, founder of the Cambridge school of experimental psychology. He administered psychological tests to the Melanesians, and developed a method of recording kinship data which became the most important method for collection of data in field work. His work was influential on all field work, including Malinowski's. His *History of Melanesian Society* was published in 1914.

‡ Motu, the language of the Motu (around Port Moresby) and *lingua franca* of the South Massim. Malinowski used a grammar and vocabulary by Rev. W. G. Lawes (1888), the only published work on the language at that time.

Reef. Many little islands along the way. Would have wanted to learn the principles of navigation, but feared the captain. Marvelous moonlit nights. I enjoyed the sea very much; sailing became enormously pleasant. In general, as we left Brisbane, an awareness that I am somebody, one of the more notable passengers aboard. . . .

We left Brisbane Saturday, 9.5.14, arrived Cairns Wednesday, 9.9. The bay was lovely seen in the morning half-light—high mountains on both sides; the bay between cuts deep into a broad valley. The land was flat at the foot of the mountains; at the end of the bay, thick green mangrove forests. Mountains in fog; sheets of rain kept moving down the slopes into the valley and out to sea. Ashore, it was damp with sultry tropical heat, the town small, uninteresting, its people marked with tropical self-conceit. . . . I walked back to the sea and along a beach facing east. A number of quite nice little houses with tropical gardens; enormous purple hibiscus flowers and cascades of bougainvillaea; different brilliant shades of red set against shiny green leaves. Took a few pictures. Walked slowly, feeling very sluggish. [Saw] a camp of aborigines, a mangrove thicket; I talked with a Chinese and an Australian from whom no information whatever could be obtained. . . . That afternoon I read Rivers. At night a bunch of drunks. Visited a drunken Russian and a Pole. Medical consultation at the Russian's. The Russian smuggles birds of paradise. Went back to wait for the "Montoro." Lamb was drunk. I got to the shore with Ferguson and waited there. The "Montoro" came in very slowly. Saw the Haddons,* Balfour,† Mme. Boulanger, Alexander, Miss Crossfield, and Johnson. Once again I was vexed

---

* Alfred Cort Haddon, English anthropologist and ethnologist, a major figure in anthropology at the time.

† Henry Balfour, F.R.S., British anthropologist and curator of the Pitt-Rivers Museum at Oxford.

and emotionally disappointed. We talked a quarter of an hour, they said good-by, and turned in. I did too. Oh yes, that was the time I made the mistake of reading a Rider Haggard novel. Slept badly that night, and felt rotten on Thursday. The sea was very rough—threw up my breakfast, went to bed and threw up twice more. I spent the evening on deck with the whole company, singing English songs in the dark. Friday, 9.11, the same —couldn't manage anything, not even the Motu grammar. That night I did some packing.

On Saturday, 9.12, arrival in New Guinea. In the morning the mist-covered mountains appeared in the distance. One very high ridge behind the clouds with a number of other ridges below it. Rocky cliffs down to the sea. The wind was quite cold. Off shore a coral reef, the *wreck* of the "Merry England" * to my right. A hill behind which lies Pt. Moresby. I felt very tired and empty inside, so that my first impression was rather vague. We came into the harbor and waited for the doctor, a fat and unpleasant dark-haired man. I left my things in the cabin and went ashore with Mrs. McGrath. Called on Mrs. Ashton, then on Mr. [H. W.] Champion [secretary to the Papuan Government]— telephoned the Governor [Judge J. H. P. Murray, lieutenant governor of British New Guinea]; then Jewell; then Stamford Smith† from 12 to 4; got part of my stuff off the ship and that night turned in very early and slept a long time, though poorly.

Sunday morning, went to Stamford Smith Institute and

---

* "Merrie England," a government steam yacht which in 1904 had been used in a punitive expedition to the island of Goaribari to avenge the cannibalistic murder in 1901 of two missionaries and ten Kiwai islanders.

† Probably Miles Staniforth Cater Smith, who in 1907 was director of agriculture and mines and commissioner for lands and surveys in Port Moresby, in 1908 was appointed administrator of Papua, and later became the director of agriculture and mines, commissioner for lands and surveys, and dormant administrator. In 1910-1911 he led an exploratory expedition into the area between the Purari River and the Fly-Strickland River system, for which he was awarded the Royal Geographic Society medal.

read Reports there, getting down to work fairly energetically. At 1 o'clock I took a boat to Government House, where the crew of fuzzy-headed savages in government uniforms gave me very much the "sahib" feeling. My over-all mood of the first hours: exhaustion from the long spell of seasickness and the minor heat wave. Rather depressed, barely able to drag myself up the hill to Mrs. Ashton's place. Pt. Moresby struck me as just the kind of place that you hear a lot about and expect a good deal of, but that turns out utterly different. From Mrs. Ashton's veranda, a view straight down a steep slope to the shore, which was covered with pebbles and meager, dried grass and was littered with refuse. The sea has cut out a deep circular bay with a narrow entrance. It lay there calm and blue, reflecting a sky that was at last clear. On the opposite side lay chains of hills, not too high, varied in shape, scorched by the sun. On the near shore, a cone-shaped hill stands at the entrance of another inlet which extends deep inland in twin bays. On the right, the hill close by cuts off the view of the native villages and of Government House, which to me were the most interesting features of the landscape, its quintessence. Along the shore there runs a fairly broad path —past the wireless station, through palm groves, across the narrow beach on which a few clumps of mangrove grow here and there—leading to the native villages. I did not go out there at all my first day. . . .

Sunday the 13th I went (*ut supra*) to Government House. The Governor's nephew met me halfway. The path runs through coconut palms, past a gigantic fig tree; then it turns and bypasses the old Government House to the new one. Governor Murray is a tall, somewhat stooped, broad-shouldered man; very much like Uncle Staszewski. He is pleasant, calm, and a bit stiff, does not come out of his shell. Two half-naked boys served lunch. Afterward, I talked with the Governor and Mrs. De Righi, a kindhearted, horsy Australian woman who treated me with the deference of a socially inferior person. H[is] E[x-cellency] gave me a letter to O'Malley and I called on him in his little house surrounded with palm trees, down below Govt. House. A fat, rather small man, clean-shaven, reminded me a little of Lebowski, only more *en beau*. He sent for Ahuia.* The Governor and Mrs. De Righi joined us and the three of us set out for the village. It was my first sight of it. We all went into Ahuia's little house. A couple of women wearing only short grass skirts. Mrs. Ahuia and Mrs. Goaba wore dresses of mohair cloth. Murray and I talked with Mrs. Ahuia, and Mrs. De Righi with Mrs. Goaba; we examined gourds with lime for chewing betel. Mrs. Goaba gave one to Mrs. De Righi as a present. The four of us walked the length of the village; I caught sight of the *dubu*† built [. . .] in 1904 in Hododae and a few entirely new little houses made of tin, crammed between the old huts. . . . Took leave of the Gov. and Mrs. D. R. The boys from the boat caught up with me. I returned by the boat and tipped them 2/-. It was dark already when I got to the Pratts.‡ Oh yes, the day before at Ryan's§ hotel I had met Bell, who asked me to supper on Monday. Evening at the Pratts'; Bell,‖ Stamford Smith, Mrs. Pratt, and the two Pratt daughters. Talk about the young ladies' excursions, about the *boys*, etc.

* Ahuia Ova, a native informant trained in ethnology by Seligman, later carried on his own ethnological work. See F. E. Williams, "The Reminiscences of Ahuia Ova," in *Journal of the Royal Anthropological Institute,* LXIX, 1939, pages 11-44; and C. S. Belshaw, "The Last Years of Ahuia Ova," in *Man,* 1951, No. 230.

† Explanation of native terms can be found on pages 306 to 315.

‡ Mr. and Mrs. A. E. Pratt. He was a surveyor who had accompanied the Smith expedition.

§ Henry Ryan, assistant resident magistrate, who in 1913 explored the area Smith had intended to explore.

‖ Leslie Bell, inspector of native affairs and one of the four European members of the Smith expedition.

On Monday the 14th I went to see Judge Herbert* and borrowed Ahuia for a whole day. Went out with Ahuia and Lohia around 11 o'clock and gathered some information. Then I went to Govt. House and waited a very long time for lunch. Not until about 3 did I get back to the village. There, in Ahuia's house, the old men had gathered to give me information. They squatted in a row along the wall, fuzzy heads on dark torsos, dressed in torn old shirts, patched-up jaegers, and pieces of khaki uniform, while under these civilized clothes peeped out *sihis*, a kind of belt that covers the thighs and adjacent parts of the body. The bamboo pipe circulated rapidly. A little intimidated by this conclave, I sat down at the table and opened a book. Got information concerning *iduhu*, genealogy, asked about the village chief, etc. At sundown the old men left. Lohia and Ahuia stayed. I walked as far as Elevala. It was dark when I got back. Marvelous sunset; it was cold and I was feeling rested. Felt not too distinctly or strongly but surely that a bond was growing up between myself and this landscape. The calm bay was framed in the curving branches of a mangrove tree, which were also reflected in the mirror of the water and on the damp beach. The purple glow in the west penetrated the palm grove and covered the scorched grass with its blaze, slithering over the dark sapphire waters—everything was pervaded with the promise of fruitful work and unexpected success; it seemed a paradise in comparison with the monstrous hell I had expected. On Monday evening, Chignell, a good-natured missionary with absolutely no understanding of the natives but on the whole a likable and cultured person.

On Tuesday I worked with Ahuia at Central Court in the morning; in the afternoon we went to the village. I was given my first coconut drink. . . .

* Judge C. E. Herbert, acting administrator of the Territory of Papua at the time of the Smith expedition.

[On Wednesday] morning I hung around the *duana*. Evening dancing at the McGraths'. Thursday at home with Ahuia. On Friday I went to the village with Ahuia and we planned an excursion into the interior for Saturday. . . . By then I was tired. Went back home, [washed], and spent the evening at the Governor's. Very boring. Old Mrs. Lafirynd and young Miss Herbert, who monopolized Murray.

On Saturday morning I was fairly tired. On horseback to the village. Disappointed by nonappearance of a guide Ahuia had agreed to get for me. Went to see Murray, and he sent for Douna, the missing guide. We rode past villas at Kanadowa, then through a few gardens belonging to the inhabitants of Hanuabada and entered a narrow little valley covered with burned grass and thinly scattered pandanus and small trees of the Cycas species. Here and there very strange trees. Feeling of sheer delight at being in so very interesting a part of the tropics. We climbed fairly steeply. Sometimes the mare would not advance a step; in the end I walked to the top, which gave a lovely view of the interior. . . . I rode down past fenced-in native gardens and along a little valley, turning into a transverse valley, with grass higher than my head on horseback. We met Ahuia, saw women with netlike bags; a few naked savages with spears. La Oala, chief of Wahanamona *iduhu*. Fires had been kindled in a few places. Marvelous spectacle. Red, sometimes purple flames crawled up the hillside in narrow ribbons; through the dark blue or sapphire smoke the hillside changes color like a black opal under the glint of its polished surface. From the hillside in front of us the fire went on down into the valley, eating at the tall strong grasses. Roaring like a hurricane of light and heat, it came straight toward us, the wind behind it whipping half-burned bits into the air. Birds and crickets fly past in clouds. I walked right into the flames. Marvelous—some completely mad catastrophe rushing straight on at me with furious speed.

The hunt achieved no results whatever. [On the way to] Ahuia's garden at Hohola I saw native gardens up close for the first time. They were surrounded with fences of sticks; bananas, sugar cane, and taro leaves and [. . .]. There were a few handsome women, particularly one in a violet caftan. I toured Ahuia's garden with him and visited the interiors of the houses. I was sorry I had not brought along tobacco and candy, for it made it harder to make contacts with the people. On my way back I passed natives cutting up a wallaby. Rode through a wood that greatly reminded me of the Australian bush. Occasional eucalyptus trees and cycas amid burnt grass. After several miles I got very tired and my left leg went numb. I made it to the road and was annoyed to learn how far I still was from the town. I could not enjoy the landscape the rest of the way, though it was certainly lovely. The road wound along the hillside amid bushes and palm trees, past some civilized native houses (Malays, Polynesians?). Took it easy back to town (galloped along the beach). At Govt. House I watched tennis and drank beer. Back home on foot, very tired. That night I stayed in and started this diary.

Sunday, 9.19 [*sic;* Sunday was the 20th], I slept late and wrote letters. After dinner, tired, I slept two hours. More letters, and took a short walk down the road to the village. In the evening the devil persuaded me to call on Dr. Simpson. I went in a bad humor and completely torpid, and climbed slowly up the hill. The music there reminded me of many things: some *Rosenkavalier,* some tangos, the "Blue Danube." I tangoed (not too well) and waltzed with Mrs. McGrath. At moments was assailed by blackest depression.

Today, Monday, 9.20.14, I had a strange dream; homosex., with my own double as partner. Strangely autoerotic feelings; the impression that I'd like to have a mouth just like mine to kiss, a neck that curves just like mine, a forehead just like mine (seen from the side). I got up tired and collected myself slowly. Went to see Bell with whom I talked about native labor. Then Ahuia at Central Court. After lunch again with Ahuia. Then I reported to O'Malley, with him to McCrann. Back home I wrote to Mother and Halinka. Went up the hill. . . .

Sunday, 9.27. As of yesterday have been here two weeks. I cannot say that I have felt really fit physically. Last Saturday I got overtired on the excursion with Ahuia, and haven't quite recovered since. Insomnia (not too marked), overtaxed heart, and nervousness (especially) seem so far the symptoms. I have the impression that lack of exercise, caused by an easily overtired heart, combined with fairly intensive intellectual work, is at the root of this condition. I must get more exercise, especially in the morning while it is still cool, and in the evening after it gets cool again. Arsenic is indispensable, but I must not exaggerate the quinine. Fifteen *grains* every 9 days should be enough. As for what I am doing, my ethnological explorations absorb me a great deal. But they suffer from two basic defects: (1) I have rather little to do with the savages on the spot, do not observe them enough, and (2) I do not speak their language. This second defect will be hard enough to overcome although I am trying to learn Motu. The extreme beauty out here does not affect me so strongly. In fact, I find the region right around Port Moresby rather dismal. The veranda of my house has a [rattan curtain] around it for 4/5 of [the way], so that my only view of the bay is at the two ends. The ground is stony and pitted, littered with all kinds of refuse. It looks like a dump sloping down to the sea. The houses are surrounded with trellised verandas with openings here and there. However, the sea and the hills around the bay are marvelous. The effect is extraordinary, particularly on the road to the village where the view is framed by a few palm and mangrove trees. In the morning everything is wrapped in a light mist. The hills can scarcely be seen through it; pale pink shadows projected on a blue screen. The lightly rippled sea shimmers in a thousand tints caught briefly on its continuously moving surface; in shallow spots, amid the turquoise vegetation, you see rich purple stones overgrown with weeds. Where the water is smooth, unruffled by the wind, sky and land are reflected in colors ranging from sapphire to the milky pink shadows of the mist-enveloped hills. Where the wind churns up the surface and blurs the reflections from the depths, from the mountains, and from the sky, the sea glistens with its own deep green, with occasional spots of intense blue. A little later the sun or the wind scatters the mists, and the outlines of the mountains can be seen more distinctly; then the sea turns sapphire in the deep bay, and turquoise along the shallow coast. The sky spreads its blue over everything. But the fantastic shapes of the mountains continue to blaze in full pure colors, as if they were bathing in the azure blue of sky and sea. Not until afternoon do the mists entirely disappear. The shadows on the mountains turn to deep sapphire; the mountains themselves take on a strange ghostly expression, as if some pitch-darkness held them in thrall. They contrast vividly with the perpetually serene sea and sky. Toward evening the sky is covered with a light mist again, diversified by the patterns of feathery clouds which are kindled by the purple glow of the setting sun and arranged in marvelous designs. One day at noon, the smoke of some distant fire saturated the air and everything took on extraordinary pastel shadows. I was terribly tired and could not feast my eyes on the spectacle as much as I wanted to, but it was extraordinary. In general, the character of the landscape is more desertlike than anything else and brings to mind views in the Suez isthmus. It is a mad orgy of the most intense colors, with I can't say just what strange character of festive, overrefined purity and distinction—the colors of precious stones sparkling in the sunshine.

My life these last few days has been rather monotonous. Tuesday the 21st [*sic*] Ahuia was busy at court all day. I got Igua* to help me unpack. Tuesday evening I felt rotten and had not the slightest desire to go see Dr. Simpson. Wednesday morning, A. was busy from 11 on. In the afternoon I called on O'Malley, who didn't actually have anything interesting to tell me. I met the beautiful Kori whose skin and tattooing I found delightful; a glimpse *des ewig Weiblichen* [of the eternal female] framed in a bronze skin. Thursday morning I spent with Ahuia; in the afternoon I went to the village; very tired. In the evening Bell came and we discussed the *natives*. On Friday morning I met Mr. Hunter,† lunched with him, and in the afternoon we talked; I was frightfully tired and couldn't do a thing. Oh yes, on preceding nights I had developed some photographs; today even this tires me. On Saturday morning Hunter came; once again he was very helpful; then an hour with Ahuia, and after that I went to see Bell, invited myself to lunch at the Governor's, and after lunch I read Tunnell and did some Motu grammar. In the evening I took a walk on Pago Hill—felt a bit stronger; talked with Stamford Smith. Went to bed early. . . . The political events don't bother me; I try not to think about them. I have far-reaching hopes that Poland's lot will improve. As for homesickness, I suffer little enough from it and very egotistically at that. I am still in love with [. . .]—but not consciously, not explicitly; I know her too little. But physically

* A Motuan "cook boy" from Elevala, who went with Malinowski to Mailu and acted as his interpreter.

† Probably Robert Hunter, who had accompanied the Armit-Denton expedition in the 1880's.

—my body longs for her. I think of Mother [. . .] sometimes [. . .].

Mailu, 10.21.14 [*sic*]. Plantation, on the river; Saturday
[10.24].
    Yesterday a week had passed since my arrival in Mailu.
During that time I was much too disorganized. I finished *Vanity
Fair*, and read the whole of *Romance*. I couldn't tear myself
away; it was as though I had been drugged. Did some work,
however, and the results are not bad for only a week, consider-
ing the terrible working conditions. I don't care for life with
the missionary, particularly because I know I'll have to pay for
everything. This man disgusts me with his [white] "superiority," etc. But I must grant that English missionary work has
certain favorable aspects. If this man were a German, he
would doubtless be downright loathsome. Here the people are
treated with a fair amount of decency and liberality. The missionary himself plays cricket with them, and you don't feel that
he pushes them around too much.—How differently a man imag-
ines his life from the way it turns out for him! The island is
volcanic, surrounded by coral reefs, under an eternally blue sky
and in the midst of a sapphire sea. There is a Papuan village
right next to the shore, which is strewn with boats. I would
imagine life amid palm groves as a perpetual holiday. That was
how it struck me looking from the ship. I had a feeling of joy,
freedom, happiness. Yet only a few days of it and I was es-
caping from it to the company of Thackeray's London snobs,
following them eagerly around the streets of the big city. I
longed to be in Hyde Park, in Bloomsbury—I even enjoy the
advertisements in the London newspapers. I am incapable of
burying myself in my work, of accepting my voluntary captivity
and making the most of it. Now for the events of these past
weeks.

Port Moresby. My last entry was Sunday, 9.27. I was under the spell of Tunnell, whom I had been reading for hours on end. I promised myself I would read no novels. For a few days I kept my promise. Then I relapsed. The most important thing that week was my expedition to Laloki [a village near Port Moresby]. Invited by the Governor to dinner on Tuesday—Miss Grimshaw and Mrs. De Righi were there. We planned to leave Thursday, or rather Friday. All that time I had little opportunity to work with Ahuia, for he was busy with the trial of Burnesconi who had hung up a native for five hours. I have no clear recollection of those days; all I know is that I was not concentrating very well. Oh yes, I recall: on Wednesday, dinner at Champion's; before it, visit to the missionary. The Sunday before I went to lunch at the Governor's, Captain Hunter was there and I read Barbey d'Aurevilly. Ahuia was not at home. I went to see O'Malley; then to the missionary, who took me to the town in a boat. I remember that evening; night was falling on the village; the engine churned and groaned unsteadily under us; it was cold and the fairly heavy sea splashed a good deal. On Wednesday I felt poorly; I took an injection of arsenic and tried to get some rest. Thursday morning Murray sent me a horse with Igua and Douna, who met us in the village; I rode out behind the mission station through a valley covered with gardens, past numerous groups of natives working in the fields or on their way back to the village. Near the spring is a pass from which a beautiful view stretches back to the sea. I rode down the valley—at the foot of the hill a little *clump* of trees with marvelous shade; I felt a longing for tropical vegetation. Then on, down the valley in a raging heat. The same dry *bush;* little cycas trees and pandanus—the former resemble woody ferns, the latter with fantastic fuzzy heads [. . .]—they relieve the far from exotic monotony of the dried-up eucalyptus trees. The grass is dried up, bronze-colored. The strong light seeps in ev-

erywhere, giving the landscape a strange starkness and sobriety
which in the end becomes very tiresome. Here and there spots of
greener green whenever you approach moisture—a dried-up
creek—or come to better soil. Vaigana *Creek* winds through the
scorched plain like a green snake, cutting a swath of luxuriant
vegetation. Lunch; Ahuia gave me some information about the
boundaries of the various territories. We rode on (after taking
two photographs) across the plain. Ahuia showed me the demar-
cation line, the boundary between two territories; it runs in a
straight line, without any natural basis. We rode up a hill. I
went to the top with Ahuia and drew a map—he made a sketch.
Before me was the plain traversed by Vaigana Creek, to the
right dried-up swamps, behind them the Baruni Hills. In the
distant background, a range of hills extending right down to
Port Moresby bay. Had a hard time getting the map right. We
rode down along a narrow valley. To the left were fields of tall
bronze grass that kept turning crimson and violet, waving and
shimmering in the sun like velvet caressed by an invisible hand.
Ahuia organized a little hunt. We entered the thicket of Agure
Tabu—a murky little river dragging on sluggishly between the
trees; I saw a sago for the first time. A. told me that a prayer is
said on such occasions, and that it is dangerous to drink this
water or to eat the fruit of the sago or the other plants that
grow here. We came to a jungle that extends in a narrow strip
on both sides of Laloki. There were monumental *ilimo* trees—on
their very broad bases they rise to tremendous heights—and
magnificent climbing plants. . . . We forded a river with tall
rushes. Then on the other side we rode along a path lined with
tall trees, climbing plants, and bushes. To my right was the
river; to my left gardens were visible now and then. A little set-
tlement on the riverbank with four little houses around a clearing of smoothed, dried earth. In the middle was a little tree with
purple berries turning into a marvelous vermilion. A few na-

tives; children roaming in the square among pigs. We walked through a garden where bananas, tomatoes, and tobacco were growing, and back to the river. There A. was stalking an alligator—in vain. I picked my way back along the bank, the sharp spikes of loxa cane tearing my shoes. At home, I sat and talked with Goaba and Igua.

Next day (Friday) I got up early, but too late to hear the speech and cry marking the beginning of the hunt. Went with A. to the other side of the river, where natives from Vabukori were sitting. Oh yes, I had been there the previous evening. On a platform, wallabies were being smoked over a fire. Bed of dried banana leaves, sticks on supports for head rests. Women boiled food in petroleum cans. The hastily built platforms that serve as pantry and storeroom are interesting. I took a picture of some platforms with wallabies. The Governor arrived. Photographs of hunters with nets and with bows and arrows. We walked across a garden, then through grass, around the village, through the woods, past a pond with violet lotuses. We stopped at the edge of the woods; I went right over toward the nets and sat down with two natives. The flames were not as beautiful as in the hunters' fire I had seen earlier; not much of it could be seen, mostly a great deal of smoke. The wind blew in front of the fire, and there was a strong crackling noise. One wallaby ran into the net, overturned it, and fled back into the woods. I didn't manage to get a picture. One was killed to our right. A. killed a *boroma*. We went back through the scorched area. Monstrous heat and smoke. Lunch with the Governor and Mrs. D. R.; conversation about sports. They left early, at 2. I stayed. Then to bed. . . .

Next morning (Saturday) I got up fairly late and went with Goaba and Douna out to the gardens. I observed the digging and wrapping of banana trees, then pursuit of a [deer]. Siesta under a mango tree; I took pictures of some women. Had lunch (papaya); slept. Afterward I bathed in the river—very pleasant—then walked in the woods. Marvelous secluded spots and natural bowers. One enormous tree trunk had supports like flying buttresses—an *ilimo* tree. We came to a clearing where a group of natives sat around cutting up wallaby meat and roasting it. First they cut open the belly and throw away the [viscera]; then they roast it skin and all. Yellow smoke rose in the air and made its way into the woods. We went back, heard wallabies running away. A. already back. We had a talk (the day before we had a talk about children's games, but unfortunately I didn't take notes).

On Sunday we got an early start back, returned the way we had come, as far as the ford, then cut across Agure Tabu and went on foot over a fairly long stretch of plain, as far as a tall mound covered with ashes, a little like a [*wall*]. At the foot of it we made another turn where we could see plantations where they grow Mexican hemp (*sisal*). I made another sketch from a little hill. Lovely view of the mountains, Hornbrow Bluff and Mt. Lawes. Suddenly I felt very tired. I rode on, dozing quietly. A. shot and killed a wallaby. When we reached Hohola I was very tired. Terribly annoyed by the fact that N & G apparatus was out of order. We took statements from the bailiff of Hohola (chief of Uhadi *iduhu*) about conditions that formerly prevailed among the Koitapuasans. Rest of the way home as before. At Pt. Moresby I found an invitation to tea from Mrs. Dubois whose husband (a Frenchman) strikes me as intelligent and pleasant; we talked about the Motu language. Spent the evening at home.

Monday, 10.5., I worked with A. and telephoned Murray. Did not go to see him until Wednesday (?). Moments of severe moral collapse. Once again I read. Fits of dejection. For instance, when reading Candler about India and his return to London, I was overcome with a longing for London, for N., how I lived there the first year in Saville St. and later in Upper Marylebone St. I find myself thinking about *T*.* often, very often. The break still seems to me extremely painful, a sudden transition from bright sunlight to deep shadow. In my mind's eye, I go over and over the moments at Windsor and after my return, my complete certainty and feeling of security. My serious plans, made several times, for living with her permanently. The actual break—from Saturday, 3.28, until Wednesday, 4.1, and then my vacillation—Thursday night, Friday, Saturday, going round in circles—all this keeps coming back, painfully. I am still in love with her. I also keep remembering the later times after I came back from Cracow.

I rarely think about the war; the lack of detail in the reports makes it easy to take the whole thing lightly. From time to time I take up the art of dancing, trying to instill the tango into Miss Ashton's mind and heart. Beautiful moonlit nights on the veranda at Mr. and Mrs. McGrath's—I am filled with dislike for these ordinary people who are incapable of finding a glimmer of poetry in certain things which fill me with exaltation. My reaction to the heat is varied: sometimes I suffer a great deal—never as much as on the "Orsova" † or in Colombo and Kandy. At other times I bear up very well. Physically I am not very strong, but intellectually I am not too dulled. I sleep well as a rule. I have a good appetite. There are moments of exhaustion, the same as in England; still I feel decidedly better than that hot summer, at the time of the coronation.

A typical day: get up late in the morning and shave; go to breakfast with a book in my hand. I sit opposite Vroland and Jackson. I get ready and go to C[entral] Court; there with Ahuia, to whom I give cigarettes. Then lunch; siesta; then to the village. Evening at home. Never have been to Hanuabada in the

---

* These initials in the manuscript are actually an *n* and a *t* in a circle. Italic initials are used throughout to denote this symbol.

† Perhaps a reference to his voyage to Australia, via Suez and the Red Sea, in the summer of 1914.

evening. Back over the hills, through the palm trees, the sea and the sky blazing with red reflections, in the midst of sapphire shadows—this is one of the more pleasant moments. Dream of settling permanently in the South Seas; how will all this strike me when I'm back in Poland? I think of what is going on there now. Of Mother. Self-reproach. Occasionally I think of Staś, with increasing bitterness, missing his company. But I am glad he is not here.

Friday, 10.9, toward evening I went out for a short walk— I wanted to call on Dr. Simpson, when the "Wakefield" sailed in. Had to pull myself together and get ready for my departure. (Oh yes, I also failed to mention the large amount of time I have wasted dabbling in photography.)

On Saturday I went to lunch at Govt. House, where I discussed letter to be written to Atlee Hunt.* Afternoon in the village.

Sunday 11. Packed; did not get to Ahuia's until late, and with him I went to the missionary; came back on foot. Monday spent the whole day packing, sending things down to the "Wakefield," seeing the banker, writing letters, etc. In the afternoon I went to Govt. House, where I again saw Gov: Murray. I called on the missionary. Then back home with Igua. Finished packing. Night on the "Wakefield."

Tuesday, 10.13. Departure in the morning. The air was not too clear, and the distant mountains appeared only in silhouette. At close quarters the landscape more distinct. Villages: Tupuseleia, etc. At Kapakapa I went ashore. Throughout the trip I felt a bit uncertain and I kept my nose buried in Maupassant's short stories. The little houses of Kapakapa stand far out in the sea, on a great many stout pilings. The roofs make a continuous

---

* Atlee Hunt, C.M.G., secretary of the Home and Territories Department of the Commonwealth of Australia, who was instrumental in getting money from his department to help Malinowski in his field work.

line with the walls so that the form of the houses is the same as in villages like Mailu. Each clan occupies a separate group of houses. On shore I enjoyed the sight of the open sea, beyond the reef, which I missed so much at Pt. Moresby. We sailed on—plains grown with pandanus and dry jungle—from a distance I saw clumps of coconut trees—Hulaa. We dropped anchor; marvelous sunset, forlorn feeling. The second morning I did not get up until we reached Kerepunu. The estuary is lovely, with a vast panorama of mountains deep inland. On both sides a sandy beach with lovely palms. A few people came on board; a half-blind old man, a local trader, urged me to visit it some day. We sailed past the coral reef. Choppy sea; I felt rotten. Not until we arrived in Aroma did I begin to feel better. I went ashore there and looked at the little village. The houses were incomparably better constructed than at Hanuabada; the platform is made of strong wide boards. The house proper is entered through a hole in the floor. The village is inclosed by a fence or rather a palisade.—Beyond Aroma we enter the rainy zone. Approaching Vilerupu (or was it Belerupu)—a marvelous region with bright, intensely green mangrove vegetation, deep bays with jutting fjords, the village very prettily situated on a hill, farther back high mountains—all this forms a magnificent whole. I went ashore with the trader, crossed over to the other side in a native boat. There I talked with a policeman [afflicted with *sepuma*] who knew nothing about anything. The village is entirely new; it has come into being under the influence of the whites. The children ran away and kept at a distance. I drank coconut milk and went back to the ship. The evening was beautiful. Next day we left the fjord. The trip was fairly calm; I read Miss Harrison* on religion. This part of the trip reminds me most

* Jane Ellen Harrison, English archaeologist and classical scholar, author of *Prolegomena to the Study of Greek Religion, Ancient Art and Ritual,* and other widely influential works.

strongly of cruising on the Lake of Geneva: shores lined with luxuriant vegetation, saturated with blue, leaning against a great wall of mountains. I was unable to concentrate amid this landscape. Not at all like our Tatras [mountains in the Carpathians] at Olcza, where you'd like to lie down and embrace the landscape physically—where every corner whispers with the promise of some mysteriously experienced happiness. Out here the marvelous abysses of verdure are inaccessible, hostile, alien to man. The incomparably beautiful mangrove jungle is at close quarters an infernal, stinking, slippery swamp, where it is impossible to walk three steps through the thick tangle of roots and soft mud; where you cannot touch anything. The jungle is almost inaccessible, full of all kinds of filth and reptiles; sultry, damp, tiring—swarming with mosquitoes and other loathsome insects, toads, etc. *"La beauté est la promesse de bonneheur"* [*sic*].

I don't remember the scenery between Belerupu and Abau. Abau itself is marvelous—a fairly high, rocky island with a view on a broad bay, a lagoon, surrounded on every side by mangroves. Farther on, mountainous walls tower up one behind the other, higher and higher, and the principal range dominates them all. Armit [the resident magistrate of Abau] is genial, casual, not too refined, a trifle backwoodsy. I talked with him first in his house. We climbed the hill and then talked with prisoners. . . . I slept well. In the morning I boarded the ship. The engineer advised me to be stubborn about landing on Mailu. I did this; I left my position on the captain's bridge, and—*oh shame!*—we were just coming into Mogubo [Point] when I threw up. Hon. De Moleyns came aboard and told me that the missionary had not yet arrived in Mailu. Mailu and the trip from Mogubo were wonderful. I disembarked somewhat annoyed, but happy to be in such a marvelous place. Five minutes after I landed and said hello to the policeman, and after I got my things ashore, the missionary's boat appeared on the horizon. Now I was completely happy. The surroundings of Mailu: mainland overgrown with tamarisks with long trailing needles reminiscent of spruce, with needles of stone pines and silhouettes of larch trees.

Beyond the low-lying plain at Baxter Bay, near Mogubo, we sailed past a region where the mountains tower right out of the sea—it reminds me a little of Madeira. Between the Amazon [Bay] and Mailu, two coral islands with sandy beaches, covered with palm trees, coming up out of the water like a mirage in the desert. Mailu itself is fairly high (at first sight); the hills are covered with grass, treeless, steep, about 150 m. high [500 feet]. At the foot are flat areas covered with palms and other trees. There is a strange tree with broad leaves, the fruit of which is shaped like a Chinese lantern. My traveling companions on the "Wakefield" were the captain, a stocky German with a big belly, brutal, continually abusing and bullying the Papuans; the engineer, a vulgar Scotsman, arrogant, rude; McDean, a squint-eyed, tall, and handsome Englishman who curses the Australians and adores the Papuans, but all in all likable and somewhat more cultured than the average; Alf[red] Greenaway, an elderly good-natured Quaker—I am now really sorry I haven't become better acquainted with him, he would have been of greater help to me than this stupid Saville.* Capt. Small most congenial of them all, with a scattering of artistic interests, well bred—unfortunately seems to be a drunkard. I was fed up with them all, especially the captain and the engineer. De Moleyns, son of a lord, a drunk and a rogue, nice, and certainly a thoroughbred.

Diary of my experiences in Mailu: Friday, 10.16. After

* W. J. V. Saville, a missionary of the London Missionary Society then working in Mailu. His "A Grammar of the Mailu Language, Papua" had been published in *Journal of the Royal Anthropological Institute* in 1912.

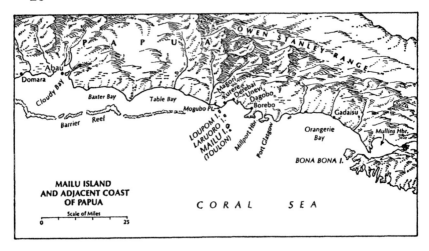

MAILU ISLAND
AND ADJACENT COAST
OF PAPUA

Scale of Miles

0   25

CORAL   SEA

meeting Mrs. S[aville], who greeted me in a rather vague way,
I said hello to S[aville] whom I saw through the rose-colored
glasses of my a priori sentiments. He generously invited me to
spend the night and take my meals with them, and this made him
even more appealing to me. In the afternoon I went to the village
and to the gardens with a policeman; I attended evening service
and despite the comical effect of the Psalms being roared out in
a savage language, I managed to feel well disposed to the farci-
cal humbug of it all. Spent the evening in their company.

Saturday, 10.17. In the morning S. took me on a tour of
the island—to the flagpole, to the village, then to the gardens,
then across the hills to the other side where we were given coconuts, and I watched the making of *toea* (armshells). Then we
rounded the promontory and went along the mission shore.
After dinner I read a little—I had done no work as yet, waiting
for the help S. promised me.

Wasted all day Saturday 17 and Sunday 18 waiting for
Saville, and reading *Vanity Fair* and in my desperation—complete obfuscation, I simply forgot where I was. I had begun to
read V. F. at Zakopane, having borrowed it from Dziewicki

that spring when I spent six days there in May; Staś was in Brittany, I was staying with the Taks. Now the fate of Becky Sharp and Amelia did not awaken my memories of old times. That period was a complete fog to me now. On Monday morning (the 19th) I spoke to S. about the terms of my living there and was extremely annoyed by the crudeness with which he treated the matter. Very much disillusioned regarding his friendliness and disinterestedness and, from that time on, *this*, combined with S.'s casual attitude to my work, has made him loathsome to me. —Oh yes, Sunday evening I went out in a boat to the little steamship, mishandled the outrigger, and fell into the water. It was perhaps a narrower escape than it sounds. Managed to get up onto the capsized boat, and then the launch picked me up. When I got back, being still (inwardly) on good terms with the S.'s, I changed clothes and treated the whole thing as a joke. My watch and some leather things in my pocket were ruined.

On Monday I went to the village and tried to make some investigations, with great difficulty. Ill feelings toward S. On Monday evening a conclave of old men in Mission House. Tuesday evening watched the dances. Extremely impressed. On a dark moonless night, by the light of bonfires, a crowd of savages, some of them wearing feathers and white armlets, all in rhythmic motion.

Wednesday morning I collected material about the dances. It was about that time that I read *Romance*. The subtle spirit of Conrad comes through in some passages; all in all, a novel "more spasmodic than interesting," in the broadest sense.—I still think about and am in love with *T*. It is not a desperate love; the feeling that I had lost creative value, the basic element of the self, as happened with *Z*. It is the magic of her body that still fills me, and the poetry of her presence. The sandy beach at Folkestone and the cold, piercing glow of that evening. Memories of London and Windsor. My recollections of wasted moments—when we were arriving at Paddington or when I lost an opportunity to spend an evening with her by going to the School of Economics—are so many stabs at my heart. All my associations lead in her direction. Moreover, I have moments of general dejection. Themes from walks with Kazia and Wandzia, memories of Paris and elements of France, which took on indescribable charm for me because of some mysterious association with *T.*, perhaps memories of *Z.*, the daytime trip through Normandy and that evening between Paris and Fontainebleau—memories of the last evening with August Z. in Warsaw, the walk with Miss Nussbaum. At last I begin to feel a deep, strong longing for [Mother] in my innermost being.

I have resolved to keep a day-to-day account.

10.29. Yesterday morning got up fairly late; I had engaged Omaga [a Mailu informant and village constable] who waited for me below the veranda. After breakfast I went to the village where Omaga met me near a group of women making pottery. My talk with him was rather unsatisfactory. . . . [In] the middle of the street a woman was making drawings. Papari* joined us; we talked again about the names of the months, which Papari did not know. I was discouraged. After dinner I read the *Golden Legend*, then took a nap. I got up at 4, took a dip in the sea (I tried to swim), had tea; at about 5 I went to the village. Talk with Kavaka about funeral rites; we sat under palm trees at the end of the village. In the evening talked with Saville about the southern coast of England from Ramsgate to Brighton. This got me. Cornwall. Devonshire. Digression on the nationalities and character of the population (natives of Cornwall, Devonshire, the Scots). I was depressed. Read a few pages of Cherbuliez's *Vlad. Bolski†*—a sketch of a spiritually unusual

---

* Papari was the headman of the Banagadubu subclan, a man who could predict weather; Malinowski considered him a friend and gentleman.

† Victor Cherbuliez (1829-1899), *L'aventure de Ladislaus Bolski.*

woman; she reminded me of Zenia. Elated, humming a tune, I walked to the village. Fairly fruitful talk with Kavaka. Watched lovely poetic dances and listened to Suau [an island to the east] music. A small ring of dancers; two dancers facing each other with raised drums. The melody reminded me of Kubain laments. Went back home where I wasted time leafing through *Punch*. Vision of *T.* Occasionally I think of Staś with real friendliness; principally the melody he composed on the way to Ceylon.

10.29. (Written on the 30th in the afternoon.) Was up before 8 in the morning and wrote my diary. Was busy writing when S. brought my mail. Letters from *N.* (5) and a number of letters from Australia. Charming, friendly letters from the Mayos and [Le Sones] gave me real pleasure. Also an extremely nice letter from Mrs. Golding. Staś's letter deeply annoyed me. At the same time I reproached myself for not having behaved in a perfectly unimpeachable way and I felt deep resentment and hatred for his behavior toward me. My feeling for him was almost completely ruined by his letter. I see almost no possibility of reconciliation. I also know that however many faults I have committed, he acted very ruthlessly toward me; all the time having gestures and airs of persecuted greatness and moralizing in accents of deep, mature, objective wisdom. There was not a trace of friendliness in his conduct toward me.—No, objectively, in the scale of rights and wrongs the platter dips down on his side . . . I am terribly dejected and dispirited by the bankruptcy of my most essential friendship. The first reaction of holding myself responsible for everything predominates, and I feel *capitis diminutio*—a worthless man, of diminished value. A friend is not merely an added quantity, he is a factor, he multiplies one's individual value. Too bad—the responsibility for the break lies primarily in his unrelenting pride, in his lack of consideration, his inability to forgive others for anything, though he can forgive himself a great deal.—Then I read *N.*'s letters, which are the only thread linking me with the past, and the *Times*, which Mrs. Mayo sent me. I visited the village depressed. Conference with Kavaka in his house, about burial rites; analysis of the sago spade. In the afternoon I began to read *Bolski* and did not put the book down until 5. Went to the village for half an hour, feeling very dejected by the novel and Staś's letter. In the evening I felt very disturbed; nevertheless I prepared a plan of campaign with S[aville] and went to the village to get Kavaka and Papari. After long parleys I got them out, and I came back home. At last the mystery of the names of the months is being clarified. Went to sleep without reading.

10.30. Got up very late, at 9, and went straight to breakfast. After breakfast I read some issues of *Punch*. Then to the village. With Kavaka things went very badly, he was somehow lazy and unwilling, nor was I in good form. During lunch I talked with S. about ethnological matters. Then I glanced through the newspapers. Took a walk. Talked some more with S. about ethnol. and politics. He is a Liberal—at once I found him more to my liking.

Derebai, [a mainland village], 10.31. Then I wrote my diary, and tried to synthesize my results, reviewing *Notes and Queries.** Preparations for excursion. Supper, during which I tried to lead the conversation around to ethnological subjects. After supper short talk with Velavi. Read some more N & Q and loaded my camera. Then I went to the village; the moonlit night was bright. I felt not too exhausted, and I enjoyed the walk. In the village I gave Kavaka a bit of tobacco. Then, since there was no dance or assembly, I walked to Oroobo by way of the beach. Marvelous. It was the first time I had seen this vegetation in the

* *Notes and Queries on Anthropology*, 4th edn., London, 1912.

moonlight. Too strange and exotic. The exoticism breaks through lightly, through the veil of familiar things. Mood drawn from everydayness. An exoticism strong enough to spoil normal apperception, but too weak to create a new category of mood. Went into the bush. For a moment I was frightened. Had to compose myself. Tried to look into my own heart. "What is my inner life?" No reason to be satisfied with myself. The work I am doing is a kind of opiate rather than a creative expression. I am not trying to link it to deeper sources. To organize it. Reading novels is simply disastrous. Went to bed and thought about other things in an impure way.

10.31. In the morning S. woke me. Got up and dressed just in time for breakfast. Then breakfast, packing, and off. The sea was covered with mist, the land looming behind it. The launch rolled a great deal. My head was foggy. We approached magnificent mountains covered with luxuriant cloak of vegetation. Fjords, valleys, romantic cliffs towering above the sea. A village at the far end of a little bay. Above it were hills covered with a vast wilderness.—I sat on a veranda. Bougainvillaea blazed against a background of greenery, the green sea framed between coconut palms.

(I am finishing this entry at Mailu, 11.2) I took Igua and Velavi and went to the village. Before that I heard S. in some underhanded dealing with a native teacher, and listened to his vituperations against the policeman. My hatred of missionaries increased. The village is badly built. The houses stand in two rather irregular rows, forming a street neither as pretty nor as straight as in Mailu. In the middle stands a taboo sign, a little gate adorned with dry leaves and white seashells on top. I tried to learn something, to collect information—nothing worked. For the first time I was met with laughter. I walked through the village with a cynical fellow, Bonio. Ran into Saville, who was taking pictures. The only decent house, with carved alligators on the ceiling of the veranda, belongs to the policeman. I went back to lunch. Then I dozed in the church—not much of a nap. I went to look at the garden with Igua, Velavi, Bonio and the fellow with *sepuma*. We walked through jungles: gigantic trees with "buttresses," thickets of lianas. The forest is not so dark and wet as the one in Orauro (the mission plantation where I had gone with S.). I asked the names of the trees and their uses. A little banana garden. Here and there you can see the green slopes of the surrounding hills, but otherwise the thickets cover everything. We crossed a muddy little river. A garden on one slope. I stopped to rest when we came to a little burned patch. It was hot and very humid, I felt fairly well. I began to climb up through the overgrown garden and impassable paths. Slowly a vista opened up: a flood of green; a steep ravine overgrown with jungle; a rather narrow view on the sea. I asked about the division of land. It would have been useful to find out about the old system of division and to study today's as a form of adaptation. I was very tired, but my heart was all right and I was not short of breath. . . . The little valley is crowned with a hill from which I had previously seen the village—it is broader and drabber than it seemed. I walked up and enjoyed the view on both sides and on the sea. We went down the other side; marvelous fragrance; lovely view of the cirque—crowned by Derebai-*oro* [Derebai Hill]. My feet went numb, could barely walk. Once we were down, we walked through a fairylike jungle. I was carried across the river. In the village [. . .], I sat by the sea. Had supper; very tired; pretty picture of children burning fires in the moonlight. Slept badly, fleas.

11.1. In the morning went to the village, where I found pigs. I thought about the irrationality of prohibiting pigs and the injunction to concentrate the villages; about the suggestions I'd

like to make to the Governor, about the excursion with Ahuia. I
was tired but not too much. Went by boat to Borebo [village on
a shallow bay west of Millport Harbor]. The mist made it impossible to admire the view. I went to the village, to the *dubu*.
Collected information which here bubbled out as fast as I could
take it in. Went back for dinner. After dinner did not sleep.
Took four pictures. Then I went to the village and collected
material. Very intelligent natives. They hid nothing from me, no
lies. Walked leisurely to (Dagobo) Unevi [both are neighboring
villages]. Ah!—marvelous landscape which I admired: Bright-
colored rocks protruding from the verdure. A deep valley with
fantastic towers. The road to (Dagobo) Unevi was marvelous.
Palm trees, thickets, clumps of mangroves near the sea; little
cliffs on the other side. The village is small and miserable; *not**
built in two rows. (Oh yes, Borebo is very poverty-stricken, but
five *taboo* gates, *dubu* in the middle of the street, and every *aura*
has its own *dubu*.) The little Unevi cirque is magnificent; mounds
terminating in towers and covered with vegetation; between
them a narrow valley, ending in a perpendicular wall, down
which a waterfall plays in the summer. I came back by boat and
said a prayer to the wonders of nature. Felt tired in the
evening, had no desire to go to the village. Dozed through prayers; went to sleep. The whole day has been spent in harmony
with reality, actively, without spells of dejection. The coast covered with tall palm trees, bending like giraffes—makes a lovely
frame for the craggy landscape.

11.2. Got up with a bad headache. Lay in euthanasian concentration on the ship. Loss of subjectivism and deprivation of the
will (blood flowing away from the brain?), living only by the
five senses and the body (through impressions) causes direct
merging with surroundings. Had the feeling that the rattling of

* Underlined in original.

the ship's engine was myself; felt the motions of the ship as my own—it was *I** who was bumping against the waves and cutting through them. Was not seasick. Landed feeling broken; did not lie down at once; had breakfast and looked through the newspapers with illustrations about the war. Looked for something about Poland—there was nothing. Very tired. Right after dinner, went to bed. Slept from 2 to 5. I did not feel too well afterward. I sat by the sea—no fit of dejection. The Staś problem torments me. In fact his conduct toward me was impossible. There was nothing wrong about what I said in Lodge's presence; he was wrong to correct me. His complaints are unjustified, and the way he expresses himself precludes any possibility of reconciliation. *Finis amicitiae.* Zakopane without Staś! Nietzsche breaking with Wagner. I respect his art and admire his intelligence and worship his individuality, but I cannot stand his character.

—Alas, stopped keeping my diary for a few days. Back from an excursion—on Monday—I took a whole day off. On Tuesday the 3rd did not feel too well either. In the morning went to the village and, finding no one, went back home in a rage, intending to look through my notes, but in fact I just read newspapers. The following day (the 4th) I sent Igua to the village to see whether there were any informants. Once again no one was there. Stayed home. *No,** that was Thursday. I don't remember Tuesday. Anyhow, on Thursday I learned that Greenaway had arrived. I went to the village where G. on an *oro'u* with a retinue of natives. We returned together to the mission. In the afternoon we went to the village where I [grumbled at] *laura* and we talked about clothes and other details. Next morning (Friday the 6th) we went to Port Glasgow. Throughout that time I felt rather poorly. I read [*The Count of*] *Monte Cristo* without

---

* Underlined in original.

stopping. On the way to Pt. Glasgow, did not feel too well—I read the novel. We sailed past a little inhabited island, rather like Mailu, then along shores covered with vegetation. I felt too rotten to look and was bogged down in the trashy novel. Even in the fjord, where the sea was calmer, I could not manage to come back to reality. My head was heavy—I was sleepy—kept reading in the boat, waiting for tea. Then I went ashore, landing near the plantation storeroom. Some of the houses in the village had concave roofs, some had walls under the roof, *not** the Mailu type. Tried to get old men together speaking Motu. Out came an old man with a pleasant expression and clear gaze full of calm and wisdom. In the morning, collecting of information proceeded well. I went back, ate on the ship, and read. Around 5, went ashore and sat by the sea in the shade. Collecting information went less well. The old man began to lie about burials. I became enraged, got up and went for a walk. Damp misty heat; sago palms. Gardens; all around, above the trees, wooded slopes and hilltops. A deluge of green. A lovely walk which I could not enjoy. Started uphill—fascinating. Hot. Beautiful *coup d'oeil* on the slopes. Occasional marvelous fragrance; blossoms on some tree. Profound intellectual laziness; I enjoyed things retrospectively, as experiences recorded in memory, rather than immediately, because of my miserable state. Very tired returning. Went back by a slightly different route— felt edgy; I was afraid I had lost my way and was annoyed. Evening under palm trees. Igua, Velavi; we talked about old customs. Velavi opened new horizons to me: about *bobore*, about fights, etc. Slept badly, a pig kept disturbing me. Woke up unrefreshed. Went to the launch and read *Monte Cristo*. Saville and Hunt appeared. I read on. We went to Millport Harbor. Pretty wooded shores, remind me of Clovelly—but what a different atmosphere! Those things you cannot experience here. We en-

* Underlined in original.

tered the marvelous Millport [Harbor]. . . . Then we went
around to another village. Back, we climbed up to Saville's old
house. I felt dreadful and could barely drag myself. Splendid
view. To the east, massive compact wooded shores surround
somewhat curving basin; to the right, higher mountains, hanging over the bay. Strong fresh breeze. On the way back I threw
up. Read in the launch, then in the evening read and finished
Monte Cristo, swearing that never again would I touch a novel.

On Sunday 8th I talked with G[reenaway] in the morning,
then we went to church, then to the village where we studied the
tattooing of the girls. Then back. Haddon; meeting with the
whole gang. After dinner we went to the village together; before
then I showed Haddon my notes. In the village Haddon and his
daughter loafed about; he—[with] boats, she—cat's cradle.
We went back home—phonograph after supper. At night, stars
and barrel organ.—On Monday 9th, Haddon with family went
to the plantation. I went with G[reenaway] to the village. Nap
in the afternoon—I got up late with G. at home. In the evening
I walked to the village. I forbade hymn-singing, annoyed by
Haddon. There were no dances. We went back. They played
billiards. I looked at the stars.—On Tuesday 10th with Haddon
to the village. I talked with G., Puana, and others about burial
rites and exorcisms. We went back home in the boat. In the
afternoon I went with G. to the village, we work on the boat. In
the evening I talked unnecessarily with S. about arranged marriage among the Papuans. Wednesday 11th got up late. Felt
very miserable in the morning. I took injection of arsenic and
iron. Packed. In the afternoon we went to the village in a dinghy.
Fairylike mood of departure and lovely trip with magnificent
yellow sail. Laruoro [a nearby island], photos of Mogubo.
D[ick] D[e Moleyns]—son of a lord—drunk. I was horribly
tired, couldn't do a thing.

Thursday 12. In the morning I talked with Greenaway

about boats, then Dimdim. In the afternoon Dimdim again, then Greenaway; then short walk, supper, and I went to bed.—Passions and moods: hatred for Haddon for annoying me, for conspiring with the missionary. Envy because of the specimens he is obtaining. In general, overpowering numbness. But after finishing *Monte Cristo*, fairly good work.—The day of 11.12 was exceptionally active. In the morning I took a bath. Then I accomplished a great deal, wrote and collected information efficiently.—11.13. After a rather good night's sleep I got up fairly early, wrote my diary, and then went fairly early for information to a little village (Charlie and Maya). Collecting information was rather hard, though not without results. It was very hot. I began to feel miserable. Came back almost in a faint. Took a nap on some cotton bags. Then dinner—ate too much. Slept until 4 1/2. Then I prepared to go to Kurere [a Mailu village on Amazon Bay, near Mogubo Point, a colony of Mailu village]. Before going I talked with Dimdim and became extremely impatient—I closed the notebook. Hon. D.D. has a horrible hangover, for the day before he finished the *whiskey*. Greenaway left in the morning.—In the evening went to Kurere. Not very tired. Walking was easy. The light of the lantern transformed the palm grove into strange, fantastic, vaulted interiors. On the shore, uprooted mangrove stumps. Big dark houses standing in a row. Dances. *Tselo*—the prettiest of the melodies I have heard here. My artistic and scientific curiosity were both gratified. Despite everything there is a great deal of primitive man in this, going back to the age of polished stone. I also thought about the extreme rigidity of habit. These people cling to certain specific forms of dance and melody—a certain rigid combination of buffoonery and poetry. I have the impression that changes occur only slowly and gradually. Doubtless the contact between two cultural spheres must have had a great deal to do with the change in customs.

11.14.14. Evening. I am sitting with Dirty Dick with whom I
have just been talking. Now he is reading some article or short
story in a magazine; I am giving in to moments of dejection.
The fog induced by it is like a mist in the mountains, when it is
driven by the wind, and discloses now one now another patch of
the horizon. Here and there, through the enveloping darkness,
there emerge remote, distant horizons, recollections; they drift
by like images of distant worlds, lying at the foot of the mountain mist.—Today I feel much better. Moments of dimness, of
sleepiness, as if I were in the Reading Room. But all in all, none
of the hopeless exhaustion that paralyzed me yesterday.—Today I had moments when I breathed in freely the beauty of the
scenery here. Today both Charlie and Dimdim went to the island
of Anioro. I decided to go. Under a yellow sail, spreading its
wings, immensely marvelous trip. I felt that one is strong on the
waves—on such a raft—direct contact with the sea. On the
green water—turquoise, only transparent—the violet silhouettes of the mountains, like shadows cast on the screen of the
fog. Behind me, over the trees of the jungle covering the shore,
slopes a lofty pyramid covered with woods. In front of me, a
glittering belt of yellow sand, above it the silhouettes of palm
trees seem to grow up out of the sea. A coral island. The water
laps between the boards of the raft—the sea peeps through the
holes and the spray smashing against the edges of the boat. A
sandbank, and the boys push the boat off. The bottom is visible
—purple weeds in the transparent green. Mailu in the distance
—the mist-covered silhouette of a volcanic rock with a noble
profile. A little village—with a few well-built houses of the Mailu
type and several characterless tumble-down huts. A few trees on
the bare sand—for the rest, little gray houses; dark columns
protrude from the waves of yellow sand. Surrounded with a
fence—in spite of that, pigs walk about as they like among the
houses. Charlie and a few old men sawed stone tools. In my pres-

ence they pounded obsidian—I carved off a side myself. They shaved a boy. I ate a coconut and went to sleep. . . . Fatigue. Then I talked freely about *maduna*, about dances, about the house. Great commotion—two dugouts appeared out at sea. The boys rushed to the boat and rowed with all their strength. All around cries resounded—advice. Dugouts are equipped with outriggers—as if dragging a strange shadow behind them as they glide over the sea. In 'the distance the white breakers smashed against the coral reef. In the west, scarlet spots on the dark clouded sky—strangely gloomy—like a flush on a sickly face, marked by death (like the flush before death on a diseased, agonized face). I sat down—in a position of unstable balance—in the dugout and went to the *lugumi*. The sail was unfurled. We floated toward the land. Dark rainclouds. We had to go northwest as Igua said this was a sign of strengthened *laurabada* (southeaster). Evening with D.D.—

Sketches: (a) Whites. 1. Hon. R. De Moleyns, nicknamed Dirty Dick—son of a Protestant Irish lord. A thoroughbred, noble figure. Drunk as a sponge, so long as there is any whiskey to be had. After sobering up (I was present when he had his last bottle of whiskey) fairly reserved and cultured with strikingly good manners and very decent. Poorly educated, little intellectual culture.—2. Alf[red] Greenaway "Arupe" —from Ramsgate or Margate—working-class background—extremely decent and sympathetic boor; it's "bloody" all the time, and he drops his h's and is married to a native woman and feels miserable in respectable company, particularly feminine. Has not the slightest wish to leave New Guinea. (b) Colored. Dimdim (Owani), modern Orestes—killed his own mother when he ran amok. Nervous, impatient—quite intelligent.—Life with De Moleyns completely uncivilized—unshaven, always wearing pajamas, lives in extraordinary filth—in a house without walls— 3 verandas separated by screens—and he likes it. Much better than life at the Mission House. Better lubrication. Having a crowd of boys to serve you is very pleasant.

Kwatou, 11.29.14. There follows a fairly long mental fogginess. Sunday 11.15 I got up rather early and got busy. Wanted to do some work on my notes. Tried, but simply couldn't. My head did not respond. Around 11, Saville (unpleasant impression). Felt miserable and could not work. Talked with D.D. After dinner I felt quite bad: went to bed. At 5 didn't want to go to the Savilles: I lay on the bunk by the cotton bags and the *bêche-de-mer*. Felt sick, lonely, in despair. Got up, and covered with blanket sat by the sea on a log. Sky milky, murky, as though filled with some dirty fluid—the pink strip of sunset gradually expanding, covering the sea with a moving blanket of rosy metal—enclosing the world for a moment in some strange enchanting spell of imaginary beauty. Waves smashing against the gravel at my feet. A solitary evening. I barely touched a rich supper.—

Monday morning: sea fairly restless. I lay down and saw nothing of the lovely landscape between Mogubo and Mailu. At home I sat and read newspapers; tired, dejected, fear of long disability: my head completely anemic. D.D. left before lunch.— Tuesday the 17th, S. left in the morning. I tried—but not very hard—to look over some notes. Read Kipling, stories. Period of dejection, no hope of working, reminds me of that summer in England. I must have felt very miserable. I almost gave up all idea of going on with my work. I was very content with plan for going south. Tried to drown my despair by reading stories. Most likely, seasickness combined with a bit of a chill at Mogubo is ruining my health.—On Wednesday the 17th [18th], tried to go to the village and work a little, but all that very cautiously and without trusting my strength. In the evening I read Kipling. A fine artist (naturally not if compared with

Conrad) and a very admirable fellow. Through his novels India begins to attract me.—On Thursday felt better and began to
do some gymnastic exercises—those nights I suffered from insomnia, I felt a nervous restlessness in my whole body. Began to
feel incomparably better, particularly one day when I took quinine (Friday?). Then again one day of relapse. Main interests
in life: Kipling, occasionally strong yearning for Mother—
really, if I could keep in communication with Mother I would not
mind anything and my low spirits would have no deep foundation.—All in all, I began to feel less hopeless, although anything
but fine. The last time I took an injection of arsenic was the 18th
inst.—about twelve days ago. Too long an interruption!
Throughout that time I was strongly under spell of *Kim*—a
very interesting novel, gives a great deal of information about
India. During Saville's absence, life with Mrs. Saville not bad
at all. She is much more lively. She talked a few times with me
about ethnological matters, and once even interpreted
[*Yenama*] for me.—Saville arrived on Monday 23d (?)—*yes*.
Departure for Samarai moved ahead. On Monday morning I
went to the village and worked on children's games and child-
rearing with Dagaea [headman of a subclan]. In the afternoon
made a genealogical census of the village. Saville's underhand
dealings with Armit annoy me, as well as the persecution
of people unfriendly to the mission. Mentally I collect arguments against missions and ponder a really effective anti-mission
campaign. The arguments: these people destroy the natives'
joy in life; they destroy their psychological *raison d'être*. And
what they give in return is completely beyond the savages. They
struggle consistently and ruthlessly against everything old and
create new needs, both material and moral. No question but that
they do harm.—I want to discuss this matter with Armit and
Murray. If possible also with the Royal Commission.—Armit
has promised that he will have me "shown round" his dis-

trict. This reassured me and pleased me a great deal: he might have done the same in the neighborhood of Rigo.—Wednesday the 25th, packing. Some sort of nervous disorganization, sentimentalism, agitation. Regrets about the period that is over, and fear as to what will happen next. In my thoughts I am often back at home. Developed and fixed photos. Discovered that *T.* had been developed on *self-toning* paper and made a print. The sight of her sad face—perhaps still in love?—dejected me. I recalled the mood in the black-papered room, that dark afternoon, when the husband found us in the end and she could not go out with me.—A moment of strong deep love—I see in her face the embodiment of the feminine ideal. Once again she is immensely, indescribably close to me. She is once again *my** *T.*— What is she doing now? How far away is she from me? Does she still remember me emotionally?—On Wednesday I did not go to the village, went to bed early, slept poorly.

Thursday, 11.26. [Up] at 5 A.M.—marvelous morning mood. I vow that I'll always get up early.—We leave. For a moment I looked at Mailu—magnificent curving ribs of mountains. Then I lay down and stayed so about 4-5 hours. Didn't miss much anyhow, for there was a thick fog over everything. Seasick but without vomiting; unbearable but no despair. Near Bona Bona [island at east end of Orangerie Bay], I got up and sat on deck with a bad headache. Mist-covered hills, fairly dry and not terribly beautiful. Isulele Bay very pretty as we sailed in. Brings to mind mountains around Lago di Garda—the broad ridge covered with green vegetation. Rich is a friendly, frank, jovial fellow—I think I'll get on with him much better than with Saville. I went up, lunch. Rich received me very affably. S. on the whole unpleasant. After lunch and a long talk about politics, etc., Rich took me downstairs; I read some issues of *Times*— nothing whatever draws me to ethnogr. studies. Around 5 P.M.

* Underlined in original.

I went to the village and I surrendered artistically to the impression of the new *Kulturkreis*. On the whole the village struck me rather unfavorably. The huts—of the old type, with curving roofs—are certainly more interesting and prettier than the houses in Mailu. But there is a certain disorganization, the villages are dispersed; the rowdiness and persistence of the people who laugh and stare and lie discouraged me somewhat. Saw three types of houses—I'll have to find my way in all this.—Evening at the Riches', supper, I went down and read; went to sleep late. In the morning I got up, went to breakfast late, then worked a little with the son of a Samoan. Very tired and numb. Isulele is very hot. After lunch went to bed and slept until 4, then I again worked a little. Evening— Captain Small, billiards, brief clash with Saville. On Saturday 28, at 4, we left. I lay down till 6, then got up. Lovely landscape. The shores of Lake Waldstadt with fronded palm trees at the very bottom. We passed through the Suau canal. I thought how perfect it would be to live here permanently. Fantastic, apparently recently formed volcanic rocks with sharp contours—their ridges and peaks firmly imbedded into ravines and atop pinnacles—slope steeply toward the sea, the dark rocks continuing down into the blue depths. I sat there, watching and humming a tune. My mind blunted by seasickness, I did not feel hedonistic, but my eyes drank in the pleasure of the landscape. Beyond Suau the mountains get lower and go off to the left; in the distance looms a range of high mountains on the other side of Milne Bay. Fairylike effect of the coral reef, peeping up out of the depths. The silhouette of Roge'a slowly emerging in the distance—thrill—a new phase of the Pacific. All this time I sat up on deck.

Arrival in Kwatou. Abel * reminds me of Don Pepe Duque.

* Rev. C. W. Abel, of the London Missionary Society, author of a booklet called *Savage Life in New Guinea* (no date), which Malinowski described as "amusingly written though superficial and often unreliable."

Horribly tired and sleepy. Sat on the veranda and leafed through Chalmers.* Cricket downstairs. Fairly pretty, very sweet children. The whole family, by the way, very like the Rich family, makes a most favorable impression.—Lunch, then to Roge'a. Talk with Dr. Shaw, collector of cockroaches. I made up my mind to stay in Kwatou. Made friends with Saville, who offered to go over some manuscripts. Supper at the Abels'. Talk with Abel about the savages and about Maori. Evening and morning on the water. Before me blue waves—or more accurately shallow, smooth water. In back, the wooded hills of the mainland. To the left, the very tip of Roge'a, little houses amid palm trees. In front of me the little green dome of the island. Everything very pretty. Excellent mood.—This morning lost a pin which I had let *T.* wear at Sandgate. Once again dejection, a feeling that I am still in love with her.

On Sunday 29th I am at home, writing the words above. Feel beginning of fatigue. Around 11, Saville and Ellis came down and talked for a moment. Then around 11:30 I went slowly up, with distinct feeling of weakness. Service with Abel. We sat in the rectangular chapel or lodge that looked like a rotunda. Very distinct stench. The service was long, with hymns repeated several times. I felt tired and distinctly demoralized. After the service Abel introduced me to Johnnie, his best informant.—Then I went down to lunch. After lunch I went in a dinghy to Samarai with Igua, Utata, and Sanyawana. We passed quite near Roge'a. Through the flawlessly transparent water I saw violet and [. . .] stones in a green glow. The palm trees bent over the sea protrude from the hedges of green thicket. Above them steep slopes of not very high hills covered with tall trees and a thick undergrowth. The hills and the all-powerful, lovely jungle a dark green, the

---

* Rev. J. Chalmers, a missionary on the coast of the Gulf of Papua, author of *Pioneer Life and Work in New Guinea* (1895).

transparent water bright green, the sky frozen in perpetually good weather, the sea a deep azure blue. Over it the outlines of countless distant islands; closer to me, I distinguished bays, valleys, peaks. The mountains of the mainland—everything immense, complicated, and yet absolutely harmonious and beautiful.—In front of me, Samarai in the calm languor of a beautiful Sunday afternoon. Waiting. I went to see [C. B.] Higginson [resident magistrate of Samarai], who very politely offered me help, but received me rather curtly. Then I went down and didn't find Dr. Shaw at home; always before he had been very courteous, invited me to come by. On the way down I met Solomon with whom I talked about ethnological plants [*sic*], I encouraged him and promised my co-operation. With him I went to call on Ramsay; very favorable impression and friendly reception.—Then saw Dr. Shaw, who asked me to stay for supper; I was fairly brilliant and felt in excellent form. Went back quite late; the boys were hungry. Rain had begun to pour earlier (that's why I had not gone home for supper). That night the roof began to leak, woke me up; I cut the big toe of my left foot. In the morning I worked with Saville; then he went with me to Samarai. He told me to wait until 12, which annoyed me for the Dr. had asked me to lunch. I arrived in Samarai some minutes after 12. Higginson gave me [an introduction] to the *jail*. Nikoll, an old man with a purple nose, went with me; the prisoners lined up; I picked out a few for the afternoon. Lunch at the Dr.'s was fairly dull: enormous pineapple very juicy, rather sour. With Shaw we went to the hospital; then to the prison. At first I was somehow sluggish; then I felt better. Charlie a very pleasant fellow, not as intelligent as Ahuia. I returned around 6; Saville came at 7.—

Tuesday, December 1. In the morning Saville as usual; I try to be polite and to avoid friction, which is not always easy. For instance, one day—that very Tuesday, I had to go to town in a dinghy. S. offered me the launch but told me to wait for an indefinite time. I told him that in that case I'd take the dinghy; thereupon he replied that he could not give me the dinghy. Throughout these negotiations I kept my temper.—On Tuesday morning I worked an hour or so in the *jail*. Shaw again asked me to lunch; we made a date for Thursday to take a walk to Ebuma. Then I went down to the *jail*. Two boys from Rossel Island—mediocre. At 4 o'clock I went over to see Ramsay and until 6 we reviewed the stone implements. A fellow (Hyland), who promised later to give me some *curios*, turned out to be a nuisance, and nothing came of his offer.—On Tuesday evening, I think, Saville too came, or perhaps I went up, and we talked about Conrad; I took *Youth.*—On Wednesday, *a government whaleboat* came to pick me up. First time I traveled under sail. Immensely delighted with the impersonal, calm, mysterious strength of the wind. Crew consisting of ten men—I felt like a sahib. . . . Late morning at the *jail*—got ready rather late. Lunch, consisting of three bars of chocolate, I ate walking around the island. Lovely view to the southeast, over the open Pacific from a prettily laid out path. At moments, I had the feeling that the sea is lovelier when we view it from civilized surroundings.—Afternoon at the *jail*. Big stir. Two *destroyers* sailed in with lightning speed. I could see the *Union Jack*. Went to Ramsay's—he was out. Went to the shore. Spoke with a sailor. Then supper, very tasty and pleasant. I drank beer and talked against the missionaries. Hig[ginson] agreed with me, while Naylor, a sympathetic, ratlike fellow, defended them.—He took me down to the *whaleboat*. I went by moonlight to Kwatou.

On Thursday, 12.3.14., I was working with Saville when the "Morinder" was announced. I went by *whaleboat*. I found out when the "Morinder" was leaving. In the *jail* I met a policeman who had just come back from *German* N[ew] G[uinea], and six prisoners who had beaten up a missionary. Visit to ship. Brutish German faces. . . . My leave-taking with the Savilles [was] cool. (In the morning I had had very unpleasant dealings with S. about using and paying for the launch.) Talk with the policemen. Natives from German N.G. strong and energetic. I was very late to lunch at the Shaws. There I met Stanley, a government geologist. Very pleasant and friendly, a little *rough*. We agreed that next day we'd work with rocks. Then I went to Ebuma with the Dr. I could not work (a grand woman; the main guard of Kiwai). I proposed a *yachting cruise*. We went to Roge'a, then to Sariba [a neighboring island]. At moments I was discouraged by the heavy seas. We came back. The evening was marvelous. I went back in my big *whaleboat*. Then I went to talk with Ellis and both of us groused about Saville. I am sorry I treated S. so decently. Ellis came down and talked with me about various things.

On Friday morning I went to Samarai in the dinghy [since I had] business with Aumüller, who took me to lunch. Then work with Stanley at Ramsay's; Charlie did not come. I learned a great deal and I liked Stanley. Lunch with Aumüller. Marvelous vast view from the veranda. Talk about Germany, the war—what else? Then again at Ramsay's. Then I met Hyland who gave instructions. In the evening I talked with Leslie* about the *whaler* who was accused of venereal disease. At Samarai I felt *at home, en pays de connaissance*. Went back to Kwatou—I did not feel too strong and went to bed at once without waiting for Ellis to come down. From time to time I found myself in a rage about Saville, and I was angry because I was not told that Ruby was going to Mailu.

On Saturday I went to Samarai in the dinghy, fairly early. Along a short street baking in dazzling sunshine, covered with powdery white sand, I walked in the shade of a gigantic fig tree,

* Proprietor of a hotel in Samarai.

from the church and *Rectory* to Stanley's house. He saw me from a distance and came out to meet me. At the same time I engaged Charlie and two prisoners. We made a discovery concerning the obsidian ax and the classification of axes into utilitarian and ceremonial. Actually interested in what I was doing. At noon I wanted to lunch at Leslie's Hotel, but I ran into a drunkard who wanted me to have lunch with him and I had to think up an excuse. Sat on a bench by the sea and munched chocolate and biscuits. In the afternoon went back to Stanley's; Hyland worked with us—then the Orakaivans came and identified the obsidian ax. In the evening I dropped by the doctor's for a moment; then, with Igua, we rowed to Kwatou.

Sunday. Barely time to pack, I took the doctor's boat, for the first time I steered. It was slow going, for I did not hold us in the wind. The Dr. met me at the *quay.* We went via Roge'a, then by way of Sariba, then another *tack* to the right and we entered the little bay. This time the sea managed to dispirit me —light spell of sickness. The boys of Dobu* are very handsome and likable—they sang, and Igua was in a good mood. We inspected the house, I robbed a tomb, I lost and found my *fountain pen.* Trip back went faster. Supper at the Dr.'s. Annoyed and furious because I had no dinghy. I suspected the *boys* of a conspiracy instigated by Saville. Scolded Arysa, who seemed submissive and obedient. This calmed me. Igua packed and I read.

On Monday, 12.7, said good-by to the Ellises and to the old spinster, called Miss Darby, whom I dislike because I associate her with Saville. Fine weather—the sea drenched in sunlight. We said good-by to the region of Samarai. Went back to Kwatou (that scoundrel Hyland lied to me, he did not leave any parcel on B.P.). Generally speaking, I disliked the whole trip and the boys. Tiabubu refused to discuss astrology with me, which put

* Natives from Dobu, an island in the D'Entrecasteaux group.

me in a really bad mood. I sat out on deck and looked at the landscape—I had almost forgotten it by now. Did not look at the pretty stretch that is reminiscent of Castel dell' Uovo [Naples]. Lovely landscape [. . .] at Suau: to the right a steep range of high mountains in the background. To the left a number of islands. Suau looks very pretty. On land I met a group of people who spoke English: Biga and Banarina [an ex-policeman]. Then went to the lagoon. Pretty view and very narrow entrance, almost a circular lake; flat shore covered with tall trees, in the background high mountains, beautifully silhouetted. On the shore I sat on a cannibal *gahana* and talked with Imtuaga, master carver; in excellent spirits. We returned in a night scintillating with stars; I talked with the boys about the stars; they were rowing.—Then Biga and Banarina came to me and talked; I was very sleepy.

Next day trip to Nauabu. Behind me, the flat and, from this side, uninteresting Straits of Suau. For a moment a view opens on the lagoon; then broad and shallow bays with craggy, volcanic peaks and knife-edge crests. Farm Bay looks shallow and uninteresting. As we entered it, it grew gradually prettier. In the background a mountain with a few peaks. Palm trees lining the shore.

Mailu, 12.19.14. Today I feel much better—why? Could it be that arsenic and iron take so long to work? I have finally arrived in Mailu, and I really do not know, or rather I do not see clearly, what I am to do. Period of suspense. I came to a deserted place with the feeling that soon I'll have to finish, but in the meantime I must begin a new existence.

I shall complete the systematic account of events, in the order they happened. Arriving in Nauabu I was a little tired from the rolling seas, though I was not actually seasick. When I go ashore I always feel a little subdued. At Nauabu I was surrounded, enveloped in the splendor of subequatorial vegetation, spread out with majestic simplicity in almost geometric order: the semicircle of the bay, the two pyramids of the mountains, the line of the western shore running straight down to the sea. Here and there little houses among the palm trees. Boo broke an oar just offshore.—Amid regularly planted short coconut trees was the house of the *native teacher*. A scrawny emaciated Samoan woman treated me to a coconut; the table was covered with a cloth, there were flowers on the table, and garlands of flowers around the room.—I walked out, a crowd of people, a few *boys* spoke pidgin English. I went to [*Rialu*], Samudu came out to meet me. Not a single *gahana* left (all destroyed by missionaries!); not a single tombstone. [I found a] house built in the Misima "*turtleback*" style. I crawled inside. It seemed to be merely a place for storing things—"*yam house.*" I acquired the carved "*prow*" of a war boat. Samudu, a tall, good-natured, serviceable fellow, spoke English and Motu fairly well. We went near the boat of Dagoisia (Charlie) from Loupom [an island near Mailu]. Then, inspection of the houses, [which the natives were] getting ready for a feast. Magnificent houses, beautifully decorated, with effigies of totemic animals in front.— At a corner of one of the huts I saw *bagi*, etc.—*Sobo*, which is taboo—at first I thought this was connected with the need to make "*pigs plentiful*," a kind of Intichiuma.* But it turns out the purpose is only to attract the pigs to the *so'i*.—At all events, an important discovery—the only form of religious ceremonial.—I had no camera, put off taking pictures. After lunch to sleep—got up tired. Samudu did not come; I went out in the boat and bathed.—I went out in the evening, but there were no dances. I was quite tired. For the first time I heard the protracted, piercing sound of a sea shell being blown—*kibi*—and with it a monstrous squealing of pigs and roar of men. In the

---

* An Australian magic ceremony to increase the clan's totemic species.

silence of the night it gave the impression of some mysterious atrocity being perpetrated and threw a sudden light—a somber light—on forgotten cannibal ceremonies.—I came back very tired.

12.9. After breakfast I bought a mat for Igua, tipped the Samoan woman, and we parted on friendly terms. We were off —I don't remember the landscape—the high mountain over Farm Bay shifted, covering Suau. Isudau [Isuisu?] did not look festive. A narrow strip of sand, on both sides mangrove thickets, with a strong stench of rotting seaweed. Before the village, the *teacher's* house, where I "stop" with the whole "*kit.*" Went to the village. Many people were sitting under the trees, near the boat, on verandas. Many pigs. The people wore holiday clothes; a few had bones in the nose—women only. A few persons with *bagi* and *samarupa* on their necks, holding ebony sticks. Those in mourning recently painted—they shine like chimney sweeps. I exchanged greetings with the "*boss*"—the *tanawagana*. I returned and walked out a few times to see how they were carrying the pigs. In the afternoon went again and talked with Tom and Banari, two ex-policemen. I took a *snapshot* of a *pig* being brought in, strolled about and bought a few curios. Thursday morning took a walk in my pajamas, inspected the boat. An *amuiuwa* from Amona, magnificently carved. As I walked among the people, almost no notice was taken of me.— Quarrel about pigs with the sergeant—I think it was the first day in the afternoon or evening that I made the acquaintance of Sixpence and Janus, who later became my friends. On Thursday afternoon I again walked about and observed things. On Friday, 12.11, in the morning I observed the interesting ceremony of payment, with *Sinesaramonamona;* then I went to sit with the pigs in the house of the *tanawagana;* very bored by what went on. In the afternoon, went again, hoping there would be a ceremonial slaughtering of the pigs. Actually it seems there is no such thing.—Around 4 o'clock I went to Isulele in a dinghy. Marvelous afternoon, filled with all kinds of light. Before me, a gigantic green wall saturated with the gold of the sun gliding along and squeezing into the green vegetation, blazing brightly on the chalk cliffs. The sea was smooth; open all around, deep blue. The calm of a fine afternoon; festive mood. I felt as though I were on a vacation, as free as air. Rich received me kindly and hospitably—without formalities. I went for a walk along the foot of the hill. There was a fairylike view on the mountainside, now filled with the rosy light of sunset, and on the bay. Overcome by sadness, I bellowed out themes from *Tristan and Isolde*. "Homesickness." I summoned up various figures from the past, T. S., Zenia. I thought of Mother—Mother is the only person I care for really and am truly worried about. Well, also about life, the future.—Went back to the Riches'. Supper. Trip back. Utata and Velavi; they carried me through a mangrove swamp.

On Saturday, 12.12, I got ready in the morning (woke up very late) and went to the village. It was quite empty. Rich came. He gave tobacco and received pigs. The two of us examined the *fish trap*. Mrs. Rich took pictures.—I went back with them in the dinghy. . . . Then, in the afternoon, talk about *so'i*, with Laure as interpreter. With Velavi I took a boat trip around the island. I was in an excellent mood as I went down at night amid the thicket of luxuriant mangroves—watery glades, among the climbing trees on the stony little island. Then supper; Bastard was late. They played billiards. I listened to a terrible phonograph which engrossed me (*"Unter dem Doppeladler"* [Under the Double Eagle] and trashy waltzes). Slept. Next day breakfast at the Riches', who very hospitably invited me to stay on a while. Said individual good-bys to the children. Gave 1/- to the Samoan, who in return gave me a fan.

The sea beyond Fife Bay (I observed little islands with

graveyards) was less calm than on Monday and Wednesday. We passed one deep bay. The *boys* did not know where to go. We asked somebody in a little boat. Silosilo to the right. A circular bay without indentations, with a narrow entrance. I had the impression of a mountain lake [. . .]. We turned left, found out where Silosilo was: at the bottom of the only hollow, under a high pyramid exclusively dominating the whole landscape. Garlands of dry leaves thrown into the sea from two tall mangrove trees, as in Nauabu, like arms stretched out to welcome holiday visitors.—A new house, or rather a *dubu*, and emaciated, dirty figures. The *tanawagana*. To the left a second *dubu*, where a true mummy is reigning, *Kanikania*. I met Sixpence, whom I persuaded to organize a *damorea*. There were women with feathers on their heads. Then the first pig arrived, and the women went out to meet it and danced. I enjoyed the spectacle, the sound of drums and the decorations.—After lunch and after a nap (at the *dubu?*) I went to the shore. *Damorea*. Took down the song and the figures. The girls were not painted. Sixpence sang too, and the other boys—which is not *en règle*. As it grew dark, I went to the *dubu*, where I decided to spend the night. Very bad night.

Sunday, 12.13, I awoke feeling as if just taken down from a cross—just wasn't functioning. Rain, cloudy—a Roman bath *à la lettre*. [I rowed to the mainland] ; took a walk amid the sago palms: antediluvian forest: [like] ruins of an Egyptian temple: gigantic, or rather colossal, trunks covered with geometric husks, mossy, enclasped in a tangle of various kinds of bindweed and climbing plants, with short stubby arms of leaves—strength, obtuseness, geometric monstrosity. A sago *swamp* gives an impression that cannot be compared with anything else. And a terrible stifling heat always goes with it. I visited a few huts in the jungle, and entered an abandoned house. Came back; started to read Conrad. Talk with Tiabubu and Sixpence—momentary excitement. Then I was again overcome by sluggishness—hardly had the strength of will to finish the Conrad stories. Needless to say a terrible melancholy, gray like the sky all around, swirling around the edges of my inner horizon. I tore my eyes from the book and I could hardly believe that here I was among neolithic savages, and that I was sitting here peacefully while terrible things were going on *back there* [Europe]. At moments I had an impulse to pray for Mother. Passivity and the feeling that somewhere, far beyond the reach of any possibility of doing something, horrible things are taking place, unbearable. Monstrous, terrible, inexorable necessity takes on the form of something personal. Incurable human optimism gives it kind, gentle aspects. Subjective fluctuations—with the leitmotiv of eternally victorious hope—are objectivized as a kind, just divinity, exceptionally sensitive to the moral aspect of the subject's behavior. Conscience—the specific function that ascribes to ourselves all the evil that has occurred—becomes the voice of God. Truly, there is a great deal to my theory of faith. The apologists ignored this aspect, giving all their energies to combating the most dangerous enemy of religion—pure rationalism. The enemies of religion resorted to purely intellectual tactics, tried to demonstrate the absurdity of faith, because this is the only way to undermine faith. Consideration of the emotional basis of faith neither destroys religion nor adds any value to it. It derives solely from trying to understand the essence of the psychology of faith.

Sunday afternoon I could not do a thing. Came back with James (Tetete) rather early—he helped me find a big house at Kalokalo. I cannot say that the moments spent in that house were pleasant. The stench, smoke, noise of people, dogs, and pigs—the fever I must have had during those days, all this greatly irritated me. The three nights I slept there were not good; throughout that time I felt exhausted. On Monday morning, after drinking cocoa ashore, I went with Velavi in the boat. Don't remember very well what I did. Generally there is less animation in the morning. The fun begins in the afternoon. There are always a few processions with pigs.—On Monday afternoon—*damorea?* On Tuesday—? On Wednesday the pigs were finally moved to the *tanawagana.* Quarrel—almost a brawl —about pulling down a coconut palm. The *raua* dance. Very impressive, when a gang of fellows who looked really savage broke into the midst of the obviously frightened and nervous crowd. I am not surprised that such things formerly led to fights. Before that I had a useful talk with Carpenter who gave me a number of valuable explanations.—On the whole, these few days which might have been extremely fruitful—I really could have obtained a multitude of important things—were greatly spoiled by my lack of strength. In the daytime the heat was such that I sweltered on the platform where I lay. The greater part of Monday I sat on the platform doing almost nothing. On Tuesday afternoon I went with Sixpence to his tiny village where I took the last three pictures of the day, then back to the beach where I ran into a procession marching straight toward me, with the *tanawagana* at the head; they offered me a pig. I tried to give it back but that was impossible. That day (Tuesday) they began to dance the *damorea,* but I was so fed up with the pig and so monstrously tired that I went back to the *dubu* and went to bed. I heard furious roars. Tiabubu said that perhaps the *bushmen* had come and were pulling down the huts and destroying the palm trees. A number of cries that sounded like "*Hurrah!*" and the replies to them, "*Wipp!*" Next day I observed the same thing and ascertained that this was when one of the mangrove trunks that stood on the shoal was toppled over with the help of a long beam from the platform, with a pig tied to it.

On Tuesday morning I came over to the left, behind the

creek, and saw sago being cooked, stirred with a kind of oar. On Wednesday morning I brought *kuku* to the *tanawagana*, who then coaxed more out of me, taking me to Kanikani. Wednesday afternoon was the most intensive day: the culminating point of the *raua*. Throughout that time, unfortunately, I felt rather miserable. Fever or the frightful heat was destroying me. On Thursday morning we went to Dahuni. Beyond Silosilo, an open bay; to the left (west) an enormous cliff overhanging the end of a narrow strip: on it, Gadogadoa. A few ships from Mailu— the farther west we went, the more *crab-claw* sails appeared. We sailed around another shallow bay, we passed right near the cliff, and entered the Bona Bona bay. The island Bona Bona Rua reminds me of the foothills of the Carpathians with its many arms—Obidowa beyond Nowy Targ. Here and there clearings—patches of badly irrigated earth, overgrown with grass —but they strangely remind me of the coombs somewhere on the slopes of Kopinica, near the old road to Morskie Oko.—To the right the gateway to Mullins Harbor, Gubanoga. To the north, flat shores and a luxuriant belt of thick, impenetrable vegetation, running right along the milky blue sea; here and there palms, like bright geometrically parallel lines, etched with some sharp tool on the belt of green. To the right, broad bays and mountains covered rich vegetation. We entered from Dahuni Bay. Very tired. Looked with pleasure at the pictures in a three-year-old copy of the *Graphic*. Went to sleep. In the afternoon, walk. In the 2nd *dubu* visitors were sitting— 2 Mailu and 2 Borowa'i [an inland tribe in the Mullins Harbor area]—eating taro from large wooden plates. The Borowa'i types were extraordinary: entirely Australian faces, smooth hair, monkey noses, wildly frightened expression.—Still unable to work, I came back and went out in a boat with Igua, Boo, and Utata. We met the Mailu *lugumi*, to which I attached myself for a moment. Marvelous view of the yellow sail on a

background of darkening blue sky; the low shores of Mullins
Harbor loomed in the distance. On our return we had hard work
with the oars. In the evening I bought a few objects—the beginning of a "new type museum": household objects.

The next morning (Friday, 12.18) was a bright, clear day
—Mullins Harbor not clear in the distance, for there was a
storm there. Orangerie Bay could be seen perfectly. Difficulties
with the *boys*, who were getting rebellious. We progressed along
the flat green shore—a number of hills behind the plain—in mist
and clouds. Gadaisiu; the plantation seemingly dead, gloomy.
Lunch with Meredith. Talk about the Grahams; about the sea-
sons in this region of New Guinea.—In the dinghy to the village; the village miserable, hardly anyone there; the tall houses
built à la Suau, though some are particularly miserable. We
sailed away; from behind the mountains a white fog crept steadily down on us, as if blown by some violent wind on the other
side. Apparently the strong monsoon from the other side runs
here into the south wind which cuts across it. Fairylike view of a
number of hills with auras of white fog, mysteriously creeping
up out of the deep valleys. Baibara. Clash with Arysa; rage. I
walked along a winding path between thick vines tangled around
a young palm grove; Mrs. Catt and Catt; garrulous; I looked
through the illustrated papers; I felt that I wouldn't learn
much from him about native agriculture. We went for a walk on
the beach; he was effusive about the plantation, I was full of
admiration. He showed me his old house and told me a story
about a snake—how many times has he showed someone around
and told the same story? On the beach discussion of missionaries
—slight friction; I lost all feeling for him. We returned; supper; discussion with Mrs. Catt, who is very pleasant. Went
to bed very late. Slept badly.

Not too well in the morning. . . . Daba came in, and we
went in a boat to the graveyard. Platform, bundles with bones,

whitened skulls on the rocks. One had a nose attached—very impressive. I asked about burial customs. Meanwhile the boys were yelling and blowing the horn. I was furious with them. We said good-by to Catt.—The coast is rocky, covered with stunted vegetation. The entrance to the lagoon where the cemetery is lies between two rocks. . . . Farther on the hills are higher and an extremely intense green. Unfortunately the day was very foggy; you could not see very far back. We reached Port Glasgow, which looks fairylike—a fjord flanked by two sphinxlike pylons, surrounded by high hills, with the shadows of the gigantic mountains of the Main Range [Owen Stanley Range] in the back. I disembarked—at once I felt rotten—and returned to the boat. *Stop* near Euraoro. A sandy and rocky little island with a dozen rather miserable houses.—We reached Mailu. I suddenly felt empty: the future was a question mark. Only a short while ago I was planning my activities in Mailu—description and photos of economic activities, in the garden and at home, an attempt to collect examples of all technical objects, etc.—At Mailu I waited for the *launch* and *dawdled*. I did not feel too bad; apparently I had my sea legs. Wrote my diary. Around 6 went to the village, distributed tobacco and ordered a model of an *oro'u.*

Oh yes: the little mission house tidied up to receive me made a pleasant impression and mitigated my anger against the Savilles. Around 7 o'clock I went back home and learned that the "Elevala" had arrived. I took out the dinghy. Talk with Murray and Grimshaw. Supper with H[is] E[xcellency] and talk. I was on the same footing with them as before; free friendly conversation, and it was I who gave it color, without feeling obtrusive.—Read 4 letters—one from Mrs. Mayo (kind and friendly); one from A.G. [Alfred Greenaway], successful regarding the 200£, a bit short, but apparently well disposed; and two letters from *N.*, the first fairly dry and short, peeved by my silence. The second cordial, in reply to my letters from Cairns and Pt. [Moresby] and the photos—my only contact with a world that is friendly to me. Though I must admit that the people I meet here are on the whole very well disposed and seem hospitable, so that I have a feeling that I am among friends. I don't feel too cut off. Even people met "on the way"—the Riches, Catts, Meredith—are human, are "acquaintances." In Samarai the Shaws, the Higginsons, the Ramsays, Stanley treated me with great kindness. . . . Igua went to the ship. This morning with tears in his voice told me that his *"uncle"* Tanmaku had just died—he burst into tears.

Today I sat home all day, writing my diary, dressing my finger, preparing for taking photos—this was Sunday the 20th. In the afternoon I had a very invigorating bathe in the sea, swam, and lay in the sun. I felt strong, healthy, and free. The good weather and the comparative coolness of Mailu also helped to cheer me up. Around 5, walked to the village and met Velavi. Ordered a stone for grinding sago and a model of a boat, for 10 sticks of tobacco.—Back home—my finger hurt badly. Sat reading Gautier; Velavi, Boo, and Utata acted as my "court." The night was very bad; I awoke with a headache— my finger was very sore all night; apparently I infected it again bathing.

Yesterday, Monday 21st, all day at home. Morning and afternoon, Puana; we talked about fishing.—Occasionally in the afternoon—violent fit of dejection; my loneliness weighs upon me. Amused myself with Gautier's short stories, but I felt their hollowness. Like an invisible nightmare, Mother, the war in Europe weigh upon me. I think of Mother. Occasionally I long for Tośka, often look at her *photo.* Sometimes I can't believe that that marvelous woman—Work goes rather badly.

12.22. Tuesday. Puana came in the morning and offered to take me to Kurere.* Once again I sat on the float and glided through space, amid the wonderful spectacle of the surrounding islands and mountains. We arrived at about 4 o'clock and were installed in the missionary's house. My foot hurts, I can't wear my shoe. Here and there in the village I met someone I knew, and we talked. We go outside the village—at a distance on the left, a dancing procession was moving along the shore. All one could hear was the fairly complicated rhythm of drums and the song. I saw the procession at closer quarters. In front two men were carrying small mango trees; from them hung garlands of some kind of leaf, the other ends of which were held up by two men in the rear. These were followed by two "headmen" smeared with soot and painted. Then came a crowd of people singing and dancing, some with, some without drums. The song was fairly melodious. The dance: jumping up on one leg, then on the other, raising the knees high. At moments they danced doubled over, turning their backs to the mango trees, surrounding them as if in worship of them.—Near the entrance to the village they were met by women wearing ornaments, with diadems of white cockatoo feathers on their heads; they danced in the same way as when the pigs are brought, i.e., they skipped from one foot to the other, although they don't seem to raise their knees as high as the men. Everyone was acting with great gravity; clearly, this was a celebration, but there was nothing esoteric about it. Moreover, the majority of the "company" were actors. After the "entrance" of the women, large *ebas* were spread; everyone sat down—the leading actors in the first row—and went on singing while eating betel nuts. The song was once again melodious; I have the impression that the same melody is used

---

* An *oilobo* feast was to be held there. This feast was always held around the end of the year and inaugurated a period of fasting in preparation for the main feast of the native year, approximately two months later.

for all incantations. After the betel nuts were eaten, the mango
trees were cut up; later, wrapped in *eba*, they serve as a *charm*
for the pigs. Then I went back to the missionary's house and
had some conferences with the savages. Night—very tired—I
slept poorly—toothache. There was dancing in the village. . . .

On Thursday morning we went to Mogubo Point. As there was
almost no wind, we decided to stay over. Camp[b]ell Cowley
fairly decently dressed, quite energetic. He made a good impression on me. Lunch. Then we talked. I read Dumas. [. . .]
I sat alone on the beach and thought about home, Mother, my
last Christmas Eve. That night we chatted. C. C. told stories
about Africa; about elephant hunts—he is a son of Sir Alfred C., whom I remember well from Brisbane. I rather like him;
a typical Australian: open, frank, expansive (he told me about
his matrimonial intentions), rough. Neither of us had a good
word to say for Saville. Friday (Christmas Day) and Saturday
I spent reading Dumas without interruption. Saturday afternoon Puana arrived, and I saw Dimdim. Then by moonlight we
went back to Mailu. Sunday 27 and Monday 28 I kept on reading Dumas. Tuesday 29, Wednesday 30, Thursday 31. Sick.
Fever. And a violent toothache.

Friday, 1.16.14 [*sic*—the actual date was 1.15.15]. From the 1st
(Friday) to the 7th (Thursday) I worked not badly. Pikana,*
Puana, and Dagaea came to see me, and I talked with them.
Puana turned out to be fairly intelligent and more open. With
Papari they gave me some interesting data, and I felt that I
deepened my knowledge of *gora* (i.e., taboo) and kinship prob-
lems, etc. Some day or other I made an excursion with Puana,
Boo, and some other man to the top of the hill—I had literally

* Pikana, a middle-aged Mailu informant, shared a house with Omaga
and his family; Malinowski considered him greedy and sophisticated.

to be pulled up. Waking up in the morning (woke up fairly late, around 9), I yelled for cocoa. As a rule Puana would be already sitting near the house, then he would come up and talk with me. Pikana came once or twice in the afternoon. The village was full, almost everyone was home. Dances every night—now in full dress, with feathers, body paint, etc. Frightful heat—at times I felt wretched. Around Tuesday the 5th the wind changed to a northwester—once again mood of trade winds—considerably colder, weather and sky fine, sea blue, light mist on the horizon. You feel more lively at once. . . . After the wind changed to NW I moved the bed . . . so as to get the air. Sat by the window and looked at the palms and the agave plants (two flowering right under the window), the papayas, and a strange little tree with violet blossoms, smelling like refined benzoin, and blossoms that look molded in wax. Through the trees I see a bit of the sea.—After lunch and in the evening I read Cooper's *Pathfinder*, which I thought was pleasant, but it did not seem imbued with the frenzied poetry I had read into it in my youth, in Polish. Unfortunately, with the east wind, absolutely everybody left Mailu. I wanted to go with them, but I bargained, and they wouldn't take what I offered to pay, and this infuriated me—against the two policemen and the majority of the inhabitants—and completely discouraged me as well. Moreover there was *absolutely* nobody. Thursday I began to read *Bragelonne* [*The Vicomte de Bragelonne*, by Alexandre Dumas (père)], and I read it literally without interruption, until Wednesday or Tuesday night. Dumas, say what you will, has a certain fascination. In the end he held me in his grip, though he doubtless has enormous shortcomings. . . . And the reconstruction of the past is carried out disgracefully. Aramis comes out a perfect ass, makes no sense at all. I would start reading the moment I got up, I didn't stop while I was eating, and I kept on till midnight. Only at sunset did I drag myself from my couch, and went for a short walk along the seashore. My head was humming, my eyes and brain were [. . .]—and yet I read, read, and kept on reading without letup as though I were reading myself to death. Resolved that after finishing this trash I wouldn't touch another book in N[ew] G[uinea].

Tuesday 13, I stopped—or rather finished. Wednesday I slept late. Then I went to the village in the morning and took a few pictures. I didn't find anyone to work with there, so I went back and began to read the letters from M. Even before my period of intoxication with Dumas I had begun to read and arrange N.'s letters. Now I continue reading them. At moments I feel like writing the story of my life. Entire periods already seem so remote, alien. Boarding school; Slebodzinski—Glowczynski and Gorski, Bukovina with Wasserberg—Chwastek and the preparations for the doctorate—these things seem almost to have nothing to do with me.—Wednesday I had temperature, Thursday, too—rather weak, 36. 9[C.] but I still was exhausted. Tuesday or Wednesday night I took quinine, Wednesday morning arsenic too. Fairly unpleasant nights—sleepless, with that typical headache you get after quinine. Yesterday (Thursday) began again to take notes. For the time being I confined myself to working with Igua. In the afternoon I leafed through Shakespeare and had a headache. In the morning I looked through Norman Angell and Renan. In the afternoon I took a nap and at 5, feeling like death, dragged myself to the village. They were decorating a house for the *maduna,* hanging bananas all around it. I came back in the dark and once again frightened a little boy whom I call Monkey; he utters strange sounds when frightened; I persuaded him to come a stretch of the way with me, bribing him with tobacco, then I would suddenly disappear in the bushes, and he would begin to squeal. In the evening I was quite *kaput;* I did not read anything. I had moments of wild longings to hear music and at times it seemed to me I was actually hearing it. Yesterday, for instance, the 9th Symphony.—I am still in love with T., and I miss her. I find her body ideally beautiful and sacred, but I realize that psychically we had nothing in common, not like with Z., for instance. But I am no longer in love erotically with Z. If I could choose one of them as a companion at present, purely impulsively, I would without hesitation choose T. A great part in this is played by the marvelous photos I have taken along.

Saturday, 1.17.14 [*sic*]. After a sleepless night, despite the bromide, and after drinking a lot of tea, I feel not badly at all; though the heart is not too strong. We'll see what comes next! Yesterday morning I worked with Igua and Velavi on native foods. Velavi is very chaotic. Then athletic wrestling with Velavi. Then lunch (papaya); then I read Rivers and looked through Hill Vachell. The sky clouded over; in the morning the boys call "*Sail o!*" The "Wakefield" arrives and a whole flotilla of *oro'us*. In the afternoon, around 3, my temperature went up to 36.9, almost 37. This had been going on for several days—also headache and mental fogginess. Reading Rivers, and ethnological theory in general, is invaluable, gives me an entirely different impulse to work and enables me to profit from my observations in an entirely different way.—I am still obsessed by thought of some ethnological government post in N.G. I suspect that Haddon favors Layard * for this job.—Around 4, demoralized by fever, headache and rain, *sin embargo* nevertheless went to the village. The mountains were dark sapphire; bluish white cumulus clouds amid dark leaden shadows; the sea shimmers emerald against these bleak colors. It was sultry and oppressive. *Lugumis*, covered over by little huts [i.e., made into houseboats], stood near the *ogobada* [*ogobada'amua?*]. Unusually low tide. A large number of people were collecting *frutti di mare*

* J. Layard, an anthropologist, author of *Stone Men of Malekula* (1942).

[small shellfish]. Sat and watched women make *ramis* and weave baskets. The rain became more intense. I sat on a porch; first at Vavine's, then inspected a porch filled with little girls; "there is fire in the stove" and they were cooking some food. I walked in the street, and on returning sat on the porch. Tired. Night fell. The houses in transparent gloomy shadows; little streams of water trickling down the middle of the street. Longed for music, for *Tristan and Isolde*. I went back home and read Rivers, then Hill. For a long time I couldn't fall asleep. Erotic thoughts. . . . But I believe my monogamous instincts are stronger and stronger. I think about *one* woman. I miss only *T*.—no one else. My mind makes me eliminate *T*.—she is but a provisional substitute for the *only one*. Lewdness is beginning to be something alien to me. I only recall with a shudder the night of 9.10 at Olcza; memories of Windsor, of Meck[lenburgh] St.—I think of the little room with the door locked at [Chilt] Farm. I am certainly still in love with her. . . .

Sunday. 1.18.14 [*sic*]. After doing my exercises I collected myself (rather slowly) and went to the village in a bad mood, for they are asking an exorbitant price to rent an *oro'u*—20 sticks of tobacco. Full tide, very high—*new moon*. I went with the intention of taking pictures of types. In village, pre-holiday activities: cooking of sago, peeling of coconuts. I photographed this—losing control several times, cursing and raging. Then telephoto pictures. At about 12:30 went back home. Read Rivers a while, ate lunch, made prints of my photos. At about 4, took my camera to the village. Took two pictures of the general view—2 of an *oro'u* and 5 of dancers. Later I watched a *bara*. I could tell that I had a fever again; I felt tired, and my head swirled. I went back; it began to rain. At home I read Hill—afraid to overstrain my eyes, and at 9:30 went to bed. Slept well—I did not drink tea, and this was a good thing.—Problems of the

Rivers type occur to me. Until now I have not paid enough attention to them. Yesterday was a clear transparent day, the view extended as far as Bona Bona and Gadogadoa. Main Range in clouds. Sea like a plaque of greenish metal. Now that the Mailu people have come back, I am less impatient with the governor. On the other hand, this rain decidedly depressing. This morning when I got up and saw that it was pouring, I had a wild desire to just sail away from here! Performed some light gymnastic exercises. Once again I am continually thinking about poetry, and I should like to write some poems, but I don't know what about!

Monday, 1.19.15 [*sic*]. Yesterday before noon, Pikana came. With great effort—for he was sleepy, kept yawning, and I had a headache and felt poorly—I wormed out of him material relating to kinship. Then at 12:30 I was so exhausted that I went to bed. After lunch (no appetite), headache. I took injections of arsenic and iron. Began to read Rivers, but had to stop. I took up poems of L. Hope [Laurence Hope, pen name of Adela F. C. Nicolson]. Around 4 got off my bed with great effort—headache and frightful sluggishness—and went to the village with Igua. Took Omaga, Koupa, and sitting in the *Urumodu* we discussed legal relationships. Around 6:30, again exhausted. At home drank *brandy & soda;* headache; bromide, massage, and to bed. Fell asleep [. . .]. At night a strong gust of wind woke me up. Toward morning I dreamed about my ideals—about Zenia, *T., N.,* all of them in one room and they sleep separated by *corrugated iron* partitions. This takes place somewhere between Zakopane* and New Guinea. Feeling of wasted happiness, lost treasures. I stood with a piece of cardboard in my hand to cover up the last window!—The weather has changed. The sky

* A resort town in the Carpathians, about sixty-five miles south of Cracow.

was overcast from morning on, but no rain in the evening. Downpours toward morning. These days I am not seized by longing, But the poems moved me to tears yesterday. Decidedly they are first-class.

Tuesday, 1.20.15 [*sic*]. Yesterday I slept very late. Got up around 10. The day before I had engaged Omaga, Koupa, and a few others. They didn't come. Sent Igua to the village—he came back empty-handed. Again I fell into a rage. Looked over my notes; rearranged them. Discovered that a little map I made from the top of the hill is missing. I felt decidedly better (arsenic Sunday), although I was excited and *irritable*. In the afternoon glanced through CGS [Seligman] and Rivers, and made preparations to go to the village; Pikana arrived. I wanted to work with him on *bara*; I used pawns (patterns) for this purpose. He didn't catch on and made a *muddle*; I got angry and shouted—the situation was tense. Both of us went to the village at 5. They performed some dances.—Rain began to fall. I took shelter under the roof of Omaga's house. Marvelous sunset. The whole world drenched in brick color—one could *hear* and *feel* that color in the air. Here and there the sky peeped through, eerily blue. On the mountains, little white clouds—the kind we see in Poland during a storm—here and there it was as though woods were ablaze on the slopes. I stood by myself on the shore, near the *lugumi;* near one of the huts a little girl stood gazing at me. Light withdrew slowly—what did I think about? About the cause of the little white clouds; about the pictorial opportunities for Staś; I was not homesick, I didn't think about Poland. When I feel fairly well physically, when I have something to do, when I am not demoralized, I do not experience a *constant* state of nostalgia.—After supper I read [Prescott's] *Conquest of Mexico*. Went to bed about 11 and for a long time couldn't fall asleep. I thought about "woman," as usual under such

circumstances. About *T.* I recalled dates from last winter.
Tuesday, date of the last lecture. 3.17, and the trip to Windsor,
3.18—to Windsor and back. In the evening, *"parliamentary
dinner."* Thusday, Mother's name day, K. and Kasia came to
see us. Saturday: concert at Alexandra Palace. Bach (?) with
K. & K.—Then Sunday 22nd, arbitration court (?) Debr. *vs*
Prusz. We met on Primrose Hill; at the very end, on the path
parallel to Adelaide Rd. Then we took buses home (Gray's Inn
Rd.). I recall the moment when we reached St. Pancras. I asked
her whether she liked this place—"No—[. . .] with visits to
the Gardiners* (?) when I was in a hurry to make the train!"
That was the last time. Then on Wednesday we were supposed
to meet—a physical obstacle! Then on Friday, expedition to
Earls Court Skating. On Saturday, 3.28, Ninth Symphony—
very bad, growling, contemptuous mood. She controlling herself,
I enraged. Then Sunday; longing, and dull regret and anger. On
Monday she came in a violet dress with fur collar, the front in
black and white checks. I sat at the piano singing *"Uber allen
Gipfeln."*† Talk with Mother *en trois;* I made stupid, malicious allusions to her work, her assistance to her husband.
Walked her back to the door—we snarled at each other; I reminded her of her Wednesday promise. Wednesday morning
strong upsurge of love; I telephoned—answer negative. I im-
plored her; meeting in the little garden; negative; no re-
proaches. Seeing her coldness I also shut myself up in
indifference. Yesterday night it occurred to me that if I had
dragged her to my house, enticed her, persuaded her, begged—
and *raped* her, everything would have been fine. And so that
April 1 was a day of bitter disappointment. Last night I again
had a strong attack of monogamy, with aversion to impure

* This is probably a reference to Dr. Alan Henderson Gardiner, a well-
known archaeologist and Egyptologist, who was a friend of Malinowski's.

† "Wandrers Nachtlied," a famous poem by Goethe, set to music by several composers, notably Schubert.

thoughts and lusts. Is this because of loneliness and an actual purification of the soul or just tropical madness?

Wednesday, 1.21.15 [sic]. Yesterday I got up early, at 6. (Throughout the period of my weakness and later, I got up between 9 and 10!) Washed to wake myself up (I very rarely washed in the morning, altogether bathed only two or three times). The pure fresh morning air had a tonic effect on me; as usual, sorry that I do not always get up at daybreak. Went to the village hoping to photograph a few stages of the *bara.* I handed out half-*sticks* of tobacco, then watched a few dances; then took pictures—but results very poor. Not enough light for snapshots; and they would not pose long enough for time exposures.—At moments I was furious at them, particularly because after I gave them their portions of tobacco they all went away. On the whole my feelings toward the natives are decidedly tending to "*Exterminate the brutes.*" In many instances I have acted unfairly and stupidly—about the trip to Domara, for example. I should have given 2£ and they would have done it. As a result I certainly missed one of my best opportunities.— After taking the pictures [. . .] I had breakfast; then again to the village. As I walked, I half made up my mind to go to Mogubo. Stayed at Koupa's and sent Igua to reconnoiter. He reported that Pikana would go. I went home, and we left. Once again a lovely feeling of freedom and happiness on the translucid open sea. I talked with Pikana about heredity—but it didn't go too well. . . . On the way from Laruoro to Mogubo, I sat in front—before me wooded slopes, extending far inland, opened to the left where Magori stands isolated above the velvet plain of Bairebo River amid low hills. I could see the high mountains of the Main Range.—Today a canopy of lowering cumulus clouds over them, from which a rain pours. To the right, the sea and clear sky—a view as far as Bona Bona. Very faint wind.

We talked with Igua about gardens. Interesting, should be developed! Not until Mogubo did I feel tired from the rocking of the waves. Cowley was not at home. I looked through the magazines which he had brought. [Later] talked with him about the war, about the events at Pt. Moresby (Fries killed some fellow with his revolver); about Armit and his pro-missionary policy. Then I asked him to reserve me passage on the "Wakefield." As a whole, my talk with him left not too pleasant impression.— We started back; strong wind and waves. Near Laruoro we sailed inside a reef. They turned the sail round; I was scared; quite considerable *breakers* pounding all around the reef; the sail was full of holes, and we had to get through the *breakers.* Otherwise calm, fine weather. Igua reassured me; the first time we did not get through properly—we had to turn back. The second time everything went well. On the way to Mailu we were splashed a great deal—I was drenched. At Mailu, bargaining with Pikana—I gave him nothing in addition, except for six sticks of tobacco. I was again angry at the natives. In the evening I read *Conquest of Mexico.* Fell asleep quickly. Strange dreams. In one I dreamed that I was re-experiencing the chemical discoveries made by [Dr. Felbaum] and Gumplowicz, and that I was reading their works or rather studying them from a book. I was in the corner of a laboratory. A table, instruments, and [Dr. Felbaum] sitting there. He made six inventions; he studied chemistry: I saw an open book before me and I read his studies. Then Gumplowicz; he had some problems of his own.— In dreams, the immense rapidity of experiences consists in the synthetic apprehension of complexes. Characteristically, we have a feeling of sensory experiences: we see, we hear (?), we touch (?), we smell (?).

Thursday, 1.22.15 [*sic*]. Yesterday I got up late—at 9. After breakfasting and writing my diary, went to the village at 10.

First I went into an *Urumodu* house and watched them eat, and
ate too. But I saw that the atmosphere was unsuitable for discussing theoretical problems. Sent for Velavi and his father—
they did not come. Then for Omaga. I scolded him, then gave him
a half-stick of tobacco, and we went to get "an old man." We ran
into Keneni. It went very well. At 1 o'clock I went back home.
Then lunch—I had a slight headache, felt sleepy. I read *Mexico*,
and lay down, resting, humming a tune. At 4 Omaga and Keneni
came. I sat with them on the ground on a mat and discussed
things; it went well enough. Then back to the village with Omaga.
Marvelous view of the *mainland*. Our shore was in deep
shadow, and the air was somehow imbued with the shadow. I
looked—the shore near Borebo was bright green, the color of a
leaf just flowering in spring. Above it, a wall of white clouds,
beyond it the sea, an intense, polished, tense blue (something
that lies in wait, where you feel life, as in the eyes of a living
person—such is the character of the color of the sea here on
some occasions)—the effect is wonderful. I wonder where that
color comes from? Is that contrast between light and shadow, that
absence of darkness, related to the swiftness with which the sun
sets in the tropics? Or is it the strong zodiacal light, the glow
given off by the sun, that illumined the other shore with yellow
light? . . . At home, headache; I hummed Zenia's songs—gypsy
and Ukrainian tunes. Went to the mission and gave presents.
The boys and girls behaved in a silly or perhaps hostile manner.
I went back and looked at the stars. I changed the plates [in my
camera] and walked along the shore; at moments felt a nervous
dread. The stars sparkled; the view of the sky did not fill me
with mood of ∞ [infinity], but rejoiced my soul as a "decora-
tion of the tropical nights."—For a long time I could not fall
asleep. I dreamed of traveling—I'd marry *T*.—but not erotic
dream. I also thought about the possibility of staying with E.

E. in some palace surrounded by a park.—In the evening I
felt rather rotten, but not weak.

Friday, 1.23.15 [sic]. I am "covering the ground" of my territory more and more concretely. Without doubt, if I could stay
here for several more months—or years—I would get to know
these people far better. But for a superficial short stay I have
done as much as can be done. I am quite satisfied with what I have
done under the poor circumstances.—The arsenic works perfectly.
Tonight I made an experiment. I took 10 *grains* of quinine and
toward morning I felt quite terrible. Apparently quinine is not
good and doesn't help me at all—could it have a bad effect on
the red blood corpuscles? I wonder whether arsenic is a specific
against malaria? If so, what is its value in Alpine countries?

Yesterday I walked to the village at 7. Photos of the
lugumi—from behind the *boathouse*. I discovered this was the
proper place for taking photos of Mailu (village). Then I went
back, took Omaga and went to Keneni's—Pikana joined us. I
ignored him, turned my back to him. He began to talk of his own
accord—and he was exceptionally good. We talked about gardens, about *"Bittarbeit"* [voluntary exchange of garden work]
etc. . . . After breakfast I took a pile of tobacco and went to
the village and photographed the *lugumi*, then . . . went to
buy stuff. Usually I overpay tremendously, I think, but I bargain till I am ready to drop. After lunch lay down and read
Mexico. Two fellows brought me *oba'ua*—little axes made of
shells. I went to the village around 4, bought two bamboo sticks
with feathers; then I sat by the sea with Keneni and his family.
Dini, Kavaki's brother, came. Keneni [their uncle] and Dini
went home with me and gave me descriptions of the specimens.
After supper, terrible thirst—drank some soda water—then,
very tired—changed plates; I walked down to the sea; the stars
were shining and there was a crescent moon in the west. I sat

withdrawn, not thinking much, but without homesickness; felt a dull pleasure in soullessly letting myself dissolve in the landscape. I fell asleep with difficulty, dreaming about the possibilities of research in New Guinea.

Saturday, 1.24.15 [*sic*]. Yesterday, Friday, I felt quite rotten. In the afternoon and evening I suffered from characteristic lack of energy, which makes even trifles—like repacking plates, putting things tidy, etc.—appear a monstrous cross on the Golgotha of life. Yesterday at noon I took arsenic + iron, and today since midday I have been feeling better. Yesterday morning I got up as usual. Photos: making of boats; the street; 4 women. Most of the photos poor. Omaga [brought] letter from Cowley. Around 10 Omaga and Keneni came. Talk about taboo and its connection with magic practices. After lunch I waited for Pikana; happy he didn't come, and read *Mexico*. Very tired. With a very great effort (today, now, in the afternoon, I do not feel sleepy in the least, and I am impatient to go out, to get dressed, etc.—whatever the price, this is the result of arsenic: it is worthy of gratitude and an altar) I went out after having collected the medicines I wanted to give Keneni's son (he has an abscess on the leg) in exchange for bird-of-paradise feathers. He did not come out of his hiding place. Went to Dini's where I discussed baskets. Came back fairly early, monstrously tired; sat behind a little rock at the *ogobada* and watched the sunset. Very weak. Stuffed myself too much at supper. Then I had an inspiration—I wrote a poem [. . .]. Igua massaged me and told stories in *delightful* Motu, about murders of white men, as well as his fears about what he would do if I died in that way! I fell asleep feeling very poorly. My heart a bit restless. This morning I did not feel well at all. I could barely drag myself to the village—characteristic dullness and sleepiness. I tried to obtain stones from Aba'u. . . . Before noon Omaga came and told me about his black-magic secrets. After lunch, read *Mexico*— right now (4 P.M.) I feel fairly well and am about to go to the village. Today at noon I gave myself a shampoo, bathed, and performed a basic evacuation—all this did me good.

Wednesday, February 3. [Aboard the] "Puliuli"—I am about to arrive in Kapakapa. Continuation of interrupted diary. End of Saturday 1.23 (I was one day ahead of myself): Went to the village, ceremonial dances in progress—took a series of snapshots. Then to the seashore where women were performing some strange ritual over a sick woman.—I went back—in the evening?—For some days I looked at the stars often and a long time.—On Sunday 24 I got up a little later, put off going to the village. Around 7, "*Sail 'o*"—the *Governor;* I got ready in a hurry and went in a dugout (horribly scared that I'd arrive drenched) to the "Elevala," where I was greeted with a distinct blunt, cold reserve. I gradually invited myself aboard ship —got my things, said good-by to the whole crowd of savages and the blubberers of the mission. At first I sat with the Governor, then went astern—happy feeling to be getting away, a sense of freedom—as if I were starting a vacation. . . . At lunch table very little talk. Read Jacobs' novelettes. In the morning I climbed up the mast for a moment. Delightful feeling of freedom mixed with fear and depression, for I lost my "nerve." In the afternoon I climbed up a second time. Around 4 or 5, I was there again, we were near an alluvial belt covered with vegetation, beyond Domara, when we ran against a coral formation; I could see bottom from the mast and I felt us scraping against the stone. I rushed down; rescue operation. Despair: I thought about the possibility of losing my things, my materials. I felt sympathy for the Gov. and young Murray,* and

* Leonard Murray, nephew and private secretary to Judge J. H. P. Murray.

terrible disappointment with the ship itself. I now understood clearly what this must mean to the captain. The ship wriggled and twisted into a position on the bottom, exactly like someone [with a bellyache]. Afterward—and now on the "Puliuli"—I have a hysterical fear of this hideous contact with the bottom. I helped pull the cable—joy when we finally got free again. Rest of the evening: supper, talk with H[is] E[xcellency] and Murray. Grimshaw had a fever. Fairly pleasant chap.—I also read an idiotic novel in which I found one or two excellent phrases.

Monday the 25th, slept badly. Got up very early. Climbed up on the mast. Sunrise. Observed the clouds laying siege to the whole horizon. As the sun rose they dissolved. They are apparently produced at the edge of the activity of the sun's rays. They are terribly compact, low cumulus clouds. At last the sun broke through. Breakfast; H. E. gave the impression that he was in a bad humor. In the morning I read, talked with Igua, chatted with Murray and developed views to which he paid no attention, rather treated them lightly. Near Hulaa we met O'Malley; Grimshaw gave me a lesson in navigational theory.—After Hulaa it began to be sultry. Heavy clouds hung over the shore, black or rather dark sapphire with a steely glint. I again went up the mast. From a distance we saw the smoke of a Dutch steamer; we sailed outside a reef. Entrance [to Port Moresby harbor] near the *wreck* of the "Merry England." A downpour covered everything. Then we arrived; the sun shone through the rain, everything in marvelous rainbow colors. Night fell quickly. I went to see Mrs. Ashton but the house was deserted. . . . Drank a few beers and went to sleep. Monstrous roars during the night. Next day a whole gang of drunks; a character with glasses, reminiscent of Prof. Los and Bernie Cybulski; a tall brunet who was late for a trial, etc.—I shared a room with a pleasant Finn, a sailor. The fat captain is quite congenial and not a drunkard; he showed me maps of western N.G.

Tuesday the 26th, in the morning I got up tired and edgy. Igua was late, and I had the labor of repacking. I was deeply moved by letters from Poland. Halinka wrote about Mother, Staś about [Strzelec]. At noon I went to Champion's; spoke a long time with Bell. Telephoned Dr. Strong* and made an appointment with him for the evening. (I am finishing this entry on 2.4 at Rigo, under a mosquito net, to the music of *laughing jackasses* and crickets.) In the afternoon I rummaged in the B[urns] P[help] store, then went to the village with Igua. Visited Ahuia's wives. I went (in a strongly blunted mental state) to Elevala; sat in the village and read Halinka's letter—at moments everything around me vanished. In a boat we went near the *lakatois* from Hulaa—strange picture of home life on the water; they offered me a fish. A. was not yet home. I walked back; was late at Strong's. . . . Conversation about many things; S. impressed me little with his knowledge. For instance, he didn't know that *merchi* is not a Motu word for dish. His theory about the real Papuan soul did not seem to me extraordinary. His views concerning the *vada* are inadequate; also concerning the nature of magic. I drank beer and got passionate on the subject of missionaries.

Wednesday the 27th, in the morning I had a slight headache; hangover after two glasses of beer. Did some packing. At 4 went to the village with Igua and my friends on the *govt. whaleboat.* . . . In the evening went to Dr. Simpson's; he was not at home. Then to the Duboises'. Dubois very likable and intelligent. . . .

Friday the 29th, morning with Ahuia. Then to Herbert's. . . . With Miss Herbert and the nurse, who reminds me a little of Hel. Czerw. I flirted with her a little. Talk about the

* Dr. W. Mersh Strong, mentioned frequently by Seligman, whose main work was with the tribes of Roro-speaking peoples in the interior of New Guinea.

war; I tried to prove my superiority by cheap pessimism. Evening at Dr. Simpson's. Glass of sherry; talk about the war. Supper; talk about Australia. Then music. I talked a lot and got rather worked up; stirred by *Rosenkavalier*, "Preislied" [Prize Song], and "Marche Militaire." Drank a great deal of beer. I was drunk when I left for home.

Saturday the 30th, morning, Ahuia. Igua no longer comes. Said good-by to the Governor; a little disappointed because he did not take me along. . . . In the evening I went to see Dirty Dick then to the hospital with someone and his wife, then to Dr. Buchanan's where [a bridge game was in full swing]. Two enormous glasses of icy beer—pure bliss! Drunk again when I left for home.

Sunday the 31st, read N. Machiavelli, went to the village. *Gurha, taubada.* Plan for excursion to Hanahati, hunting. Afternoon, read Machiavelli, wrote letters; under the influence of a certain spiritual elevation, took a walk; thought about love, about *T.* I wanted to visit the Duboises and then the Ashtons; they were not home. Went back, talked with McCrann and Greenaway.

Monday, 2.1. Morning with Ahuia. Around 12 or 11 went to see Stamford Smith—rather I first went to Kendrick's, then to S. S.'s, who promised me a ship. Then, in the afternoon I went to see Champion, with whom I talked about the promise of the Australian government to keep me in N.G.—I see clearly that whatever I get out of this later, I will be supported by the government. I was very glad about it, and on account of it did nothing all afternoon. Did *not* go to the village; wrote a few letters, read Machiavelli. In the evening I was excited and nervous, took a walk by the sea; then dropped in on the Ashtons where we played the gramophone. Then again I walked by the sea, and went to see Dirty Dick.—Throughout that period I read Machiavelli. Many statements impressed me extraordinarily; moreover, he is very like me in many respects. An Englishman with an entirely European mentality and European problems. Description of attitude toward Isabel, love permeated and interwoven with intellectual understanding—I was violently reminded of Z. Margaret with her eternal passivity, all affirmation, anticipation, and "second sight," utter inability to say no or question anything or anybody. That's an image of the emptiness I felt, except with *T*. Reading of this book takes me away from *T*., brings me closer to memories of Z. In spite of that I feel *T*. with all my strength, all my body. Today (2.5) I again dreamed of her.

Tuesday, 2.2. Morning (and day before) I had no news about the "Puliuli." At 10, Ahuia, Koiari. A. asked for 15/- which I promised him. Letter from S. S. that we are going. Teleph.—went to the bank, to the M[ission] G[overnment], to report about my delay; then Champion, who promised me to send ship in case of need. From 1 o'clock (drank 2 glasses of *shandy*, headache) to 3 I got ready in McCrann's hotel, with an effort. Got together my things from B[urns] P[help], from home, and went on board. They raised the blue flag, I was on "my ship"— strong feeling that the ship is for my exclusive benefit, and I watched them maneuvering. The bliss of traveling under sail. We turned back to pick up two parcels for English.* Sailed toward a little island before we turned back (*about ship*).—Sat and watched and was happy. As soon as I went down to the little cabin, my head began to turn; on top I felt all right. The shores are now entirely green, splendid. Night fell near Taurama; after that we sailed on in moonlight, coxswain tense; I must confess that I was a little scared about reefs, unpleasant feeling we

---

* A. C. English, a colonial official at Rigo, where Malinowski planned to gather data with Ahuia's help on the Sinaugholo tribe, a people who lived in close contact with the Mailu.

might scrape the bottom again. That night I slept badly. In the middle of the night I was awakened by the scraping of the boom against the mast. Went up on deck. The moon was shining; the coxswain stood motionless, his face an animalized Buddha's, staring straight ahead of him. We sailed in close to the land, parallel with it; the wind had shifted to *NW* but was very weak.—In the morning (Wednesday, 2.3) we sailed along low emerald-colored shores; behind them rose a *tableland*. The wind was stronger, we approached quickly, going past Tavai. I wrote my diary and collected my things. A boat with a policeman and an interpreter came toward us. We went ashore; inspected the *dubus*, partly in ruins, with magnificently carved columns. English arrived on a bicycle. The conversation irritating—I made proposals to normalize his collections, but he received them rather coldly. I waited while he rummaged in his store. . . .Very hot, sun beating down on us. Glad to be walking, good *exercise*. The road was lined with coconut trees, frangipani, mimosas, cold as ice with cinnabar blossoms, lovely odors mixed with monstrous stench. Here and there were hedges and arbors, as in English parks; cultivation. We saw the mission, then English's house; the hill of the government station. A nice old man, Stanley; lunch. Then he took me up the hill to the M.G. house. I was very tired, went to sleep. About English: we talked against missionaries; he made a number of fairly reasonable remarks; generally speaking, he made a sympathetic impression on me. Then supper with Stanley, talk about the war. Mosquitoes ferocious. I was beside myself. The fleas, too, disgusting. I slept well enough.

Thursday 4. I felt rotten. All morning I dozed and read obscure stories. . . .

Friday 5. In the morning I felt pretty rotten; weak, lazy, and tendency to sleep, *Bob Hunter's sleeping sickness.* (During the night, toward morning, I dreamed about Mother. Large room at 153 Marsz[alkowska St.], at the Szpotanskis', furnished with large beds, cupboards, etc. Mother was strangely dependent on Szpot. and Lach. *She scores small advantages.* We talked about some trip to North America.) I got up and fumbled a great deal writing diary—through an opening in the veranda I could look out on green meadows and hillsides—it was like a valley in Central Europe in spring. Around ten I went down, after a bath, via Stanley; we picked coconuts; we followed a pretty path lined with bushes, white flowers smelling like Z.'s perfume, big shady trees, to the Gomore village *dubu*. Beautiful big houses with double verandas, two or three "stories" high. We sat in the policeman's house near the *dubu*, and men from another village came to see us. We talked about *taboo feast.* . . . With Diko I walked through the village, and then to English's. . . . Sweated horribly and felt heart fatigue. But I worked not badly both in village and at English's. Came back under a marvelously colored sky. Peace, I felt relatively better—much better than before, and I felt *joie de vivre tropicale*, something like being drunk on strong wine, at once oppressive and stimulating—broadens horizons and paralyzes you utterly. Met Ahuia and Inara gathering coconuts in the woods in front of the station. We walked together, I talked with Inara, a blond man with light skin and highly arrogant manner. Prognathous, he reminds me of M.S. and M.O. from Zwierzyniec [a district in Cracow]. For him too I felt symp. . . . Sat there despite horrid stench of smoking coconut shells—talked with Ahuia. Went to bed around 9. Slept not badly.

Saturday 6. Today I feel, I think, a little better. Got up late, at 7:30. After breakfast, discussion with men from Kuarimodubu, who came here with a policeman; a strong *NW* wind drove us from the front to the back of the platform. At moments I felt

tired, particularly after lunch; directly afterward I read a little
book about Java. At that moment I was highly *irritable* and
unstable. On the whole, these people [the Sinaugholo] are very
sympathetic, incomparably pleasanter than the Mailu people
and easier to get on with. They tell everything without embarrassment and speak good Motu. There is no question but that—
especially with Ahuia's assistance—I could collect more material
here in a month than at Mailu in six months.—Yesterday I
worked well and strenuously for about 5 hours and I accomplished a great deal. Around 4:30 I went to see English; I met
him as he was leaving in a four-wheeler. Apparently he took
offense at my being late. I was annoyed, angry, and felt like
taking offense myself and "showing him my ass." I recalled
Strong's saying, *"he must be humored"* and with a certain contempt I told myself it wasn't worth it. In spite of that, as I took
a walk, I imagined what we should say to each other, etc., and at
moments I worked up a real rage. Went back home, then out
again, to Kuarimodubu, and then I sat for a while in a lovely
place—it reminded me of what we saw near Brisbane; we heard
the sound of liquid pouring from enormous decanters (laughing
jackass), but the mosquitoes kept spoiling the *Stimmung*
[mood]. In the evening I sat with Ahuia, discussing white
people, particularly officials, and we talked about sexual matters
among the natives. A. says that Koiari committed incest. At
night furious *guba*—I wondered how we'd get back to Port?

Sunday 7. Morning as usual; I got up at 7. Breakfast, diary,
work with Ahuia and the others. I learned that the "Puliuli"
was here. Around 4 went to see English—sent Ahuia to Gaba-
Gaba. English received me coldly; with the help of his wife he
was numbering *clubs*—I suggested making a catalogue for him.
In the end he became very amiable, making plans for the future,
helping me, etc. A typical character (like me)—he won't do

82

anything disinterestedly, he recognizes and appreciates people only to the extent he needs them at the moment. Wonderful violet cloudlets in the pale sea-green sky; red sunset, under it glows the narrow belt of the sea. A shallow little valley, covered with vegetation; I like the scene from his veranda—typical plantation atmosphere. Went back home, at moments fear of *gaigai*. Stopped by at Stanley's; he talked, I nodded affirmatively while leafing through an article on the history of the war. It began to rain, Ahuia came back. I read some stupid publication—*Papuan Times*. At night I dreamed of a mistress with a white body. All in all, I feel fine here: in the shadow of government protection; in my relations with the friendly Rigo people; in the lovely surroundings; in my good health.

Monday, 2.8. Got up around 7. In the morning crowds of women; people out to gather *coconuts*. My usual informants came. They were joined later by Maganimero* whom I disliked at once for a certain missionary casualness. The discussion was brisk. Maganimero was spontaneous, particularly when telling old legends. After lunch we talked about magic. M. and the other *boys* seemed to be afraid or embarrassed. Ahuia is invaluable as a helper. At about 4, I rushed over to English's, where I quickly and efficiently finished cataloguing his collections. Supper at English's. Before supper I walked on the veranda and had moments of concentration and spiritual elevation, interrupted by violent surges of sexual instinct for native girls, for English's servants. I dissolved in the landscape. The little valley is surrounded by low hills, behind which loom distant peaks as far as Main Range. Around the house, tall trees with white trunks and shining leaves. Through them one can see the plantation and the wooded hillsides. Open horizon on the

---

* Maganimero, a native of Rigo district whom Malinowski reported an exceptionally clever man.

west. The sky ablaze above the narrow bit of sea—and black silhouettes of low circular hills. Literary conceptions; in the beauty of a landscape I rediscover woman's beauty or I look for it. A marvelous woman as a symbol of the beauty of nature. Subtle emotional hesitations; search for truth. Struggle for liberation from fetters of sensual pleasure in feeling of beauty.— Came back in the dark, with Diko. Strong liking for him. Talk about *sihari*. *"Gagaia namo, usi ranu ia lao, namo herea."* He shows me what [gestures] they make to a *kekeni* when they want to *gagai*—how *sihari* sits* at Motu and Rigo. . . . I went with him to the kitchen. A snake lay on the veranda. We sat on the stairs in the kitchen. . . . I asked him whether they knew about homosex. here. He said no, *"kara dika."* For this reason, *"lau hereva henia lasi. Dohore ita lao mahuta"* [I say no more. After a while we turn in].

Tuesday, 2.9.15. Got up fairly late—Ahuia went to Gaba-Gaba. Maganimero and other friends came. I felt completely [broken]. With Ahuia we [looked for] tobacco (after breakfast); then inspection of the whole crowd from Ikoro, a nearby village, speaking a dialect different from Sinaugholo. Their noses a little like those of Benin [a West African culture] bronze figures, and hair curly but not fuzzy. A. says that such straight hair can be found in this region—at Hulaa, Babau, Kerepunu, and inland, but not very deep inland. They also have fine beads made of white [fiber or shell] wound circularly and worn on the backs of their heads, from ear to ear. I talked with Maganimero—rather slowly because of fatigue and continual interruptions. Lunch at the Stanleys'. Then packing (A. packed, I dozed or read). Then the *kekenis* came and we sent them to get baskets. End of talk;

* In his Mailu study, Malinowski reported, "Among the Motu the right conventional attitude whilst courting was for the boy to sit on the knees of his mistress."

at moments I was furious because of their narrowmindedness or rather because they didn't understand me. I said good-by (mentally) to the pleasing, extremely pretty house at Rigo.—The horizon is solid vegetation. It reminds me of some views at Ceylon—though the others are prettier, more sculptured. However, regarding the over-all character of the vegetation, the landscape might have been anywhere (England, etc.) : Emerald meadows in the midst of thick woods, surrounded by thick woods. . . . Excited, but also feeling strong and healthy, I walked to the village. I don't know whether this is the effect of arsenic, or the fine climate of Rigo, but I feel exceptionally well. (The last time I took an injection of arsenic was on the 1st or 2nd. I should note the dates so as to find the best system.) We picked lemons and I was bitten by ants. (The mosquitoes were monstrous throughout our stay at Rigo. Particularly toward the evening, or when just a few got inside the mosquito net.) As I walked quickly to the village, . . . from a distance I recognized the melodies of *bara* or, more accurately, *koalu*. The dance was rather poor; on the slanting, clayey ground, with deep puddles left by the rain, they could have neither *Schwung* [swing] nor breadth. They sloshed through it; the *loa* had neither the wildness nor the springiness of the Mailus'. Three or four *kekenis* were circling around the boys. The artistic effect during the day—*nil*; at night, by the blazing light of the torches, the charm is always the same; here enhanced by the wide street, in which the trees and the *eva* pillars create mysterious shadows. I sat on the high porch of the policeman's house as Maganimero explained the songs and E. the meaning of the dances. Every dance, it would seem, has its own *badina*, only the Mailu did not know. *Koalu* originates in Kerepunu, now fashionable in the entire *beau monde* of N.G. A prostitute or divorcee from *gunika* (*gunika haine*) attracted my attention—*gagaia ura!* Diko and I went from the village to Gaba-Gaba. Again I felt healthy and

strong; a little fed up with the savages, eager to renew contact
with nature. I am beginning to concentrate *and* to relax! Plans
for the future. . . . As I walked I threw enormous shadows on
the palms and mimosas by the road; the smell of the jungle
creates a characteristic mood—the subtle, exquisite fragrance
of the green *keroro* flower, lewd swelling of the burgeoning, fer-
tilized vegetation; frangipani—a smell as heavy as incense, with
elegant, sharply drawn profile—a tree with an elegant silhouette,
its green bouquet with blossoms carved in alabaster, smiling with
golden pollen. Rotting trees, occasionally smelling like dirty
socks or menstruation, occasionally intoxicating like a barrel of
wine "in fermentation." I am trying to sketch a synthesis: the
open, joyous, bright mood of the sea—the emerald water over
the reef, the blueness of the sky with tiny clouds like snowflakes.
The atmosphere in the jungle is sultry, and saturated with a
specific smell which penetrates and drenches you like music. The
line of the mountains and over-all character of the island is
fairly *commonplace*. Before reaching Gaba-Gaba we encountered
kekeni and went with them. I sat by the dark sea; the outline of
the village barely visible, flattened by the darkness. We sailed in
the midst of thick pilings, a sort of stockade that surrounds the
whole house, filled with the bliss of direct contact with the *"lake-
dwellings* culture." The genuineness of the mood—in this Venice
of the Pacific—the sound of the water splashing against the
pilings. . . . I talked with the policeman about the customs of
Kapakapa. The Lombi resemble the Sinaugholo. Their friendly
attitude to the mainland may have been precisely the result of
their excellent defense against attack from that quarter.

Wednesday 10. Slept well—cold night with moon. Got up at 5.
Ahuia packed. I crossed over a few platforms. We were on our
way. The "Puliuli" waited until the sails were up. Farewells.
Mirigini fades away—rustle of fluttering sails (I finished writing

this Thursday afternoon, on Tom McCrann's veranda). In the morning I felt well. Around 11 came a furious *guba*—the sun beat down pitilessly, the wind blew without interruption—before long I had a splitting headache, at moments I almost felt like throwing up. But particularly at the beginning and for a long time during the *guba* I got intense enjoyment out of the trip. I was stretched out on pillows on top of the cabin, moving to the other side at each *about ship*. I ate breakfast. Very strong wind, deck was drenched, my seat splashed. I moved to the back, to the aerial w.c., on which I sat wrapped in the coxswain's cloak. Beyond Kapakapa there extends a series of rather thickly wooded green hills with the meadows of *lalang* (*rei kurukuru*) —the region is similar to that right around the Rigo station, only this seen from a distance, without sharp outlines, is less pretty. Five miles past Gaba, plantation [. . .]. Then there extend the same hills culminating in one considerably higher one, covered with grass, behind which lies Gaile. All this time we could see quite far inland, a chaos of chains ever higher, mixing, and disappearing into Main Range far in the distance. We moved slowly closer to the slopes of a high *tableland*, the shape of which we saw from very far away. A very high wall, some 1500 m. [about 5000 feet], covered with vegetation, furrowed with shallow troughs—reminiscent of the green slopes in the Drohawa valley. This wall obviously conceals everything behind it and dominates the landscape. Under it a number of low hills. We tacked constantly, shipping a good deal of water which sloshed around the floorboards all over the deck. Tacking again we reached Gaile, then on again. I began to feel rotten and I don't recall much, at all events I had at moments the hedonistic feeling that I was having *"the time of my life."* We reached Tupuseleia—right behind a little round hill Barakau lies hidden; we tacked again for a few miles; at 3:30 we dropped anchor; I sat dejected on the deck. Tupuseleia is built like Gaba-

Gaba over the water; houses covered with thatch, running in a continuous surface from roof to bottom. They look like a lot of haystacks set over the blue lagoon. Freshly covered (with *kuru-kuru* grass) they are golden like wheat (rye) straw, others washed by rain have the gray color of old haystacks. At low tide, the houses stick up high on their pilings. Small openings, with a high gutter, and something like strange snouts looking out from the furry wrapping; this complete lack of an open "inside" creates a strange *stimmung* [impression] of desertion, lifeless-ness—something of the melancholy of the Venetian lagoon—a mood of exile or imprisonment. In the dark openings bronze bodies appear, the whites of the eyes gleam in the shadow of the rooms, from time to time firm breasts stick out—*maire* (cres-cent-shaped pearly shells). Seen from inside the village, from the street or rather the canal, there is more life. The verandas are crowded with people; many gondolas, squealing children and dogs. . . . I made up my mind to spend the night in the village. In extreme exhaustion, I went to sleep. Then . . . I sailed in a large boat ("*double canoe*") with the policeman and another savage. . . . I was frightfully tired and had a fit of "pointo-phobia" (nervous aversion for pointed objects—"stichopho-bia?"). At a late supper, I talked with Ahuia about *vadas*, about *belagas*, about the fact that the *vada* was formerly a public figure, that he dressed differently, and so on. We discussed the initiation of the *vada;* we also talked about *babalan*, about methods of cure, etc., about when Ahuia would go to the *dogeta* and when to the *babalan.*—I got a good night's sleep. Evening in a "*lake dwelling*": screaming children, barking dogs, urina-ting from a height of 4 m. [13 feet]. In the morning, a very high tide—the haystacks stood not on high pillars but directly upon the sea, dipping their long thatch beards in the water. In the morning Tupuseleia is lovely. Above the village are gentle hills, with here and there a fantastically sprawling tree; these solitary big trees looked rather spidery. To the west—which is now directly illumined by the sun—lie little islands and hills of the bay ending in Taurama. Above the village is the slightly inclined wall of the tableland with the sharp profiles of the ravines. The previous evening marvelous play of lights: saturation with deep yellow color characteristic of this season.

Thursday, 2.11. On "Puliuli," pillows comfortably arranged. I lay astern, shifting with each " 'bout ship," and talked with Ahuia about Papuan "science": about the names for reefs, clouds, winds. We talked of the sun and the moon, about the causes of things; and also about the *koiaras*. We passed by Taurama; I evacuated straight into the sea from a privy above the water. Beyond Taurama, Puri; then Vabukori and Kila-Kila on a hill. I do not feel so rotten. We passed Manubada; then we sailed straight to Ele[vala]. I went forward—yachting is a marvelous sport! Ate a light lunch; the boys got me ashore [at Port Moresby].—McCrann's hotel; I got dressed (I was a bit tired). Went to see Champion—O'Malley and Champion—both very pleasant. Back at the hotel I wrote and dined; it began to pour; went to see Mrs. . . . —talk about [Priddlam]; she was terribly vulgar, *beyond endurance.* Then to the Duboises'; lot of people, talked French with Dubois. Back to hotel, discussion with McCrann. Learning about the unpleasant position of the "government" because of the Oelrichs affair, I was greatly upset.

Dikoyas [a village on the north shore of Woodlark (or Murua) Island]; Monday, 2.22.15. I am in a tent of palm leaves pieced together over a shaky floor made of sticks. The open side faces the village about 60 m. [about 200 feet] away, below me, as on the palm of my hand. Low huts directly on the ground—they look as if the earth had suddenly been opened by some mysterious tide and half swallowed them up. After landing in this village, I took a marvelous walk through the tall [luxuriant] jungle, à la Kandy—I felt fine again, in my element. . . . My health has not been too good the last few days. Exhaustion, lack of strength, and characteristic nervousness: acrophobia, aversion for protruding objects.—I stayed at the port from Thursday to Tuesday. I did almost nothing with Ahuia. Planned an expedition with him to Koiari, for Saturday. But having learned that the "Monudu" (late because of the wreck of the "Marsina") might arrive Monday, did not go to see Ahuia. On Saturday afternoon I talked with Stamford Smith who is unbearable and interminable on politics; he constantly uses the conditional mood (future) and always talks in the first person and has no modesty whatever. Saturday night I spent at Dr. Simpson's with gramophone, but fatigue and [effects of drink] (on Friday I went to dinner at the Duboises'; sherry and 3 glasses of icy beer) prevented me from taking real pleasure in music. All day Sunday I felt especially rotten. Read Kipling's stories, far weaker than the ones I read at Mailu. Sunday evening spent 2 hrs at Strong's who had asked me to supper.—Then Champion, with whom throughout that time I [got on well]. Oh yes, on Saturday (or was it Friday?) morning I went to the museum with Brammell * and had with him a "conspiratorial gossip" about the state of the local colony.—Monday morning packed and repacked at Burns Phelp's; got back only with tremendous effort and labor. In the afternoon wanted to write letters, but Champion sent me letters to translate from Giulanetti's relatives. Then went with him to the hill where he lives. [H. A.] Symons [resident magistrate of Woodlark Island] came—introduction. Evening at Strong's; conversation about various things other than ethnology. Tuesday morning got ready in a hurry; ran to Mrs. Ashton's, to the bank, to Dubois's; moved my things to the ship.

* B. W. Brammell, resident magistrate, Central Division.

The trip: 1st day (Tuesday) I worked. I read Seligman; I outlined an article on Motu and Sinaugholo. Lunch—furious at Brammell. Talk with Symons. In the afternoon again worked a little but without excessive enthusiasm. The shores of N.G. wrapped in mist, in the rain. In the afternoon we passed Hulaa, Kerepunu. In the morning (in the evening and afternoon I read a borrowed Kipling) at about 7, mountains of the bay in the rain. I conjectured that we were near Millport Harbor. Went back to the stories—apparently my health was not too good. After breakfast (no, *before** breakfast) we could see Suau. I saw the pyramidal mountain at the entrance of Farm Bay. Walls of rain shut out the view of the mountain and then shift and reveal it again—the damp velvety sheen of the vegetation, the marvelously deep shadows, the freshness of the stones darkened by the rain, the outline of the mountains through the curtains of rain, like shadows of reality projected on the screen of appearances. —The passage through Suau spoiled by the rain; but even so, it seems really wonderful. I did not see the inside of the lagoon.— The rain subsided. Suau in the sunshine. I sat with a book (Kipling) and looked at Modewa Bay and the pretty Bucklin promontory on which, I think, I saw cows grazing! Roge'a emerged as a pyramidal silhouette. We reached Samarai. I was strongly under the influence of Neptune: headache and general weakness. Strong wind; the doctor's boat did not come out at once to meet us. I said hello to him. Then Newton† with whom I talked a long time. Went ashore. Lunch with the doctor and his wife. Mrs. Shaw this time impressed me far more strongly—a marvelous woman, an aesthetic phenomenon. In the afternoon went down via post office, Higginson, to the rectory. Talk about general matters. Newton gave me a book. Walk around the is-

---

* Underlined in original.

† Rev. Henry Newton, assistant to the Bishop of New Guinea, mentioned by both Seligman and Malinowski.

land. Went to see the doctor and his wife. Went back to the ship
with them. Dinner—great enthusiasm for Mrs. Shaw—almost in
love with her. Then we sat and were joined by some miserable
cockney who once tricked Shaw out of some money. I went
ashore early. Then, around 9, to the rectory; talk with Newton
about politics; perfect night spent in the bishop's room. The
morning mail, Higginson, I read Kipling. Said good-by to
Shaw, Newton, etc. Tooth's pretty daughter (oh yes, morning
at the hospital).

Trip to Murua [Woodlark Island]: At 1 o'clock lunch. I
was out on deck, as we passed through the China Straits. The
uncreative demon of escape from reality prompted me to sit on
deck with a book (Kipling, *Plain Tales*) in hand. What was
going on around was marvelous! Sea perfectly smooth, two
abysses of blueness on either side. To the right the indentations
of Sariba, islands, islets, covered with tall trees. To the left, the
shadows of distant mountains—the shores of Milne Bay.
Farther, the shores move away on either side; to the left only
the high wall of East Cape, covered with clouds, forming the
threatening point of the horizon; to the right pale shapes loom
up out of the eternity of blueness, slowly turning into volcanic
rocks, sharp, pyramid-shaped, or else into flat coral islands:
phantom forests floating in melting blue space. One after the
other comes into being and passes away. The space darkens—
brick-colored spots on the clouds—to the east, a flat sheet of
coral covered with gigantic trees over yellow sand in the cold
blueness—strangely reminds me of the islets in the Vistula. Dinner. I read a little, went to bed early—marvelous sky. Slept late
—Murua already in view—landscape not too pretty. Mangrove
lagoon—on the south the Suloga mountains; before us a low hill
—Kulumadau. Long wait before going ashore. Trip in a motor
boat; *creek* with high trees all around; boathouse, policemen in
it. Back to the ship; I went with Symons in the *whaleboat*. Had

to clamber up without assistance. I was horribly tired, hideous stifling heat. Never before in N.G. have I felt so low. . . . I was completely demoralized. Went to see "Dr." Taaffe. Then to M.G. *office*. Symons not too friendly. Then Charpentier, who received me as a Rev. Father. Conversation about the natives, but chiefly about politics. Around 6 went to dinner, and met McCliesh. Then again to Charpentier's; a drunken Englishman; two little Jews; I drank beer and got tight. Charp. talked about the natives, but I absolutely forget what. Then to bed. Slept well enough, but felt awful—sticky with sweat, disgusted with my own sluggishness. Went to see Charp.; talked about technology. . . . Went home; was utterly exhausted. Read Kipling. Suddenly a policeman appeared at the head of a group of boys. I was so tired that I could hardly walk a few steps. Nevertheless I got ready; via Charp.—who tried to persuade me that government help is harmful—I went with the boys. Occasionally I leaned on [Moreton] and another *boy*. Then stop in the woods. The boys carried my things. Marvelous, enormous wilderness. . . . Like *Lady Horton's drive* in Kandy. The candelabra of ferns on the trees; the enormous trunks of the gigantic trees; utterly unchecked *undergrowth*. Dark, gloomy, strange. I calmly leaned on two boys and walked along looking at everything. After some time we entered a dry jungle. I was madly happy to be alone again with N.G. boys. Particularly when I sat alone in a hut, gazing out at the village through the betel [palms]. Once again the disheveled figures of the boys, once again sitting a few steps away from me. That evening, despite my exhaustion I talked with Aus about [. . .]. Went to the village and called on an old man.

Sunday morning, scientific meeting. Then dinner; then I read Shaw in bed, headache. . . . On Monday (pouring rain all night, roof leaked over the bed) pouring rain; sat in the *kaha* and again conferred with [Moreton] and the old man. Then, after lunch, I read again, and had a headache. Marvelous walk to Spimat along the seashore. Arsenic and caffein [woke me up]. In company of Ameneu I went from [. . .] to W. . . . Then the vast jungle against the brash of coral. The path, covered with the tangled roots of gigantic trees, led downward—an inconceivably wonderful park. Farther on we slipped over [enormous] roots, damp rocks, and half-decayed trees—until through the branches we saw the blue glow of the sea and the dull rumble of the breaking waves—reduced to indistinct noise by the echoes of the trees and the hillside. I recalled Ventnor. Enormous trees covered with bindweed, ivy, *creepers;* made my way down to the sea through a round dell. The sea and the sky were dark. Hard white sand beach. The bay is small, shallow, inclosed by two short low arms of land—two walls of thick vegetation. The beach covered with woods and palms. Clumps of coconut leaves and other trees hang over the sand like stray rejects from the thick green mass behind. Marvelous mood. Ameneu was almost hoarse with joy; I too. We inspected Aus's *waga.* Then return. Occasionally tired, but not very. In the evening I ate fried sausages and a pumpkin, and talked with Aus about spirits and *rabu.*—Today (Tuesday, 2.23.15) Mewad' woke me up very early.

March 1. Aboard the "Marsina," as we are nearing Cairns. My head a little congested, nonetheless I feel relatively well and energetic. The most important thing now is not to waste my stay in Australia but use it carefully in the most productive way. I must write an article about Mailu—maybe a few others in addition, but Mailu first and foremost. I must check the museums insofar as possible. So there won't be time for nonsense! I must give a detailed account to Mr. Atlee Hunt and try to impress him. For the last few days I have not felt very bad, but I have not been strong enough to get really to work. Read Newton a little—talked with Lyons. The fact that I am not flirting with Miss Craig and Mrs. Nevitt is not to my credit. I especially intended to pursue the latter, but I was vexed by the fact (1) that she did not go beyond Cairns and (2) that she is boundlessly stupid and does not really attract me. But I must get the order of the events straight. On Tuesday 23, I worked at home in the morning, not too productively. Waus [apparently an alternate spelling of Aus] had a friend to whom he gave *bagi* and with whom he talked.* In the morning I discussed dreaded spirits and funeral rites. Suddenly decided to stay over another day. In the afternoon I went to the *creek* where they draw water. I walked among fern trees—lace umbrellas. A river flows through a tunnel of dense vegetation. I went down in the midst of fernlike leaves. The *creek* covered with moldering tree trunks, the murky greenish water skips over stones; the gently [sloping] banks are covered with vegetation—here and there the *creek* squeezes through a steep-walled ravine [of which] I saw only tiny sections. I climbed up—some kind of resin stinking of iodine and nitrate stuck to my neck and burned me horribly. I walked on, to a deserted garden—again a stretch of the creek— bend, two arms, I entered deep dark tunnels. A little tired when I got back (I visited the sick Ameneu). On the second day (Wednesday 24) I got up early, made ready, and went to the village [. . .] to Kulumadau. Newad and another boy carried me while a group of others carried my things. Got there in the

---

* This was evidently the first indication Malinowski had of the *kula*, the complex exchange of gifts throughout the region, which became the subject of *Argonauts of the Western Pacific*. In that book he writes (p. 477): "Early in 1915, in the village of Dikoyas, I heard conch shells blown, there was a general commotion in the village, and I saw the presentation of a large *bagi-do'u*. I, of course, inquired about the meaning of the custom, and was told that this is one of the exchanges of presents made when visiting friends. At the time I had no inkling that I had been a witness of a detailed manifestation of what I subsequently found out was *kula*."

nick of time. Rain. Went down. Ride in a boat—sheepish joy
that I was under way. Ship—lunch—finally hoisted anchor. I
sat astern and looked out over Suloga Bay—lovely view. Mountains covered with thick vegetation, blue sea with green ribbons
here and there of shallower water over the coral. At first we
moved in a western direction. To the north, low mangrove lagoon, to the south the mountains of Suloga—this is the only
place where stone objects were produced in the old days.—Particularly the coral banks on both sides of the smooth channel we
were following, green, surrounded by a strip of white breakers. I
felt fine. Then the sea got rougher. I worked out a program with
Brammell to add to the museum collections. Brammell and I
chatted about a number of things—fairly interesting; in the
main I get on well with him.

In the evening I was gripped by amorous desire for Mrs. N.
Went down and looked for her—I found her with the Balls in
their cabin. Next day (Thursday 25) woke up at 6, after bad
night—we were sailing through China Straits—the pink body of
the naked earth steeped in the dawn light showed through the
tropical forest; the sea was porcelain blue. Magnificent view of
the [basin] of Samarai. Roge'a, shaped like a Tibetan hat;
magnificent belt of hills on *mainland*. I went ashore with Shaw,
had breakfast, got a parcel for Biddy and a letter for Anderson.
Walked around the island with Ball. Lovely view. Sea at its
Sunday best, the shore perfectly elegant, surf breaking, de-
positing a silvery foam at the foot of the gently tilting palms. I
longed to write a letter to *N.*, and composed one mentally—
(3.3.15) to tell her the quintessence of my experiences here. At
moments I feel strong sympathy and friendship for her. But my
erotic feelings are reserved exclusively for *T.*—Ran into Newton
and went with him to the *Rectory*—there very pleasant chat with
him and Mrs. Newton. Went to see Higginson. H. had malaria.

After a talk with him, I returned and told him about the sergeant and that I took the liberty of asking for coconuts. I asked Dr. Shaw to lunch and went to get the Newtons who politely accepted my invitation.—The lunch was not too amusing; we sat around talking afterwards. Went back with them to *Rectory*, and I got a present: the carved prow of a *canoe*. Departure of the ship—feminine company—Miss Craig. I sat astern—the Samarai basin passed by in full sunlight; very beautiful—golden verdure of the woods, the sea dark sapphire. Behind Roge'a, a number of cliffs hanging right over the open sea. Night fell before Suau. We sailed past on the seaward side. Chatted with Brammell, then with Burrows, a man from Samarai, very pleasant and amusing. I discussed with him possible expeditions and eventual collaboration, program for collecting ethnological data.

Friday 26. Sailing along the coast of N.G.: Morning misty. Table Point. Finished writing out instructions and gave them to Brammell and Burrows. I gazed across at Hulaa. A few unsuccessful *attempts* in the direction of Miss Craig. I became a rather good-natured friend of Mrs. Nevitt's. Fairly long talk with Burrows. Evening, arrival in P[ort] M[oresby]. I stood on the bridge and watched us sail through the *passage* in the reef. Then, lowering of the anchor; the calm, smooth water of the port. The Duboises. Went to bed late, after drinking beer.

Saturday 27. Slept badly because of the mosquitoes and the net. Trouble with papers at Port. I got out my things from the *hold* and took them ashore. McCrann, Mrs. Ashton, Champion, Ahuia, H. E. [Murray]—once again I was very tired and did not feel in form. Departure. I sat in the back and looked at the port, the wall of mountains above Tupuseleia—a lovely view, *after all*. Touch of seasickness. Turned in. Evening—

Sunday 28. Morning—? Read a little of [Newton]. In the

evening I thought about Staś and began a letter to him. At moments I was very exalted; I have been in N.G., I have accomplished a good deal. I have prospects of far better work—fairly certain plans. And *so**—it's not as hopeless as I thought when I arrived here. Moreover I don't feel a bit worse than when I came. I am a better sailor and I walk much better—the distances no longer terrify me.—Gazing at the sea I have a strong feeling of happiness. True, it's not all over yet; but in the light of old fears and uncertainties I have decidedly won a victory.

Monday, 3.1. Magnificent approach to Cairns. From the morning on, view of mist-covered shores. We pass right near the reef against which waves are breaking. Mountains more and more distinct—rosy above the green sea. Some show scars of recent rock-falls. To the left, high mountains with magnificent domed peaks, like cathedral spires. To the right, a long chain of beautiful mountains. The town in a hollow between mountains, a flat spit or tongue. Simply intoxicated with the view. Reminds me a little of Palermo. The mountains covered with lush vegetation. This time I ignore the mangroves which had so enchanted me at first. The doctor very courteous. Military control. Walk along the shore. I feel incomparably stronger than in September when I walked along here. Back to the ship—if it had not delayed sailing, I should have missed it. Departure; instead of watching I drank liqueur with the Balls. Then I read Newton (I am keeping my promise about novels). Then, in the afternoon, I worked with Lyons, but actually spent most of the time talking against Haddon and L. M. S. In the evening I drank beer (3 glasses). As a result, on Tuesday (3.2) I had a hangover or fever—sluggishness, anemia of the brain, no energy. In the morning I worked on my MS.—But in the end felt rotten. In the afternoon I read a novel (by Jacobs) and out on deck gazed at

* Underlined in original.

the marvelous *Whitsunday passage*. In the evening, read the novel (not bad, by the way) until [it produced the desired effect] and I went to bed at 10 after taking 10 *grains* of quinine.

Wednesday (3.3) not much better. Still anemia of the brain associated with characteristic congestion between the brain and the optical nerve. In the morning worked with Lyons. In the afternoon . . . I read some more N[ewton], at odd moments planned my stay in Australia; at other moments thought about my article on Mailu. In the evening I talked with the men, went to bed before 10. Rotten night, fleas biting; ship rocking and tossing.

Thursday, 3.4. Today I feel fairly low. Slightly seasick. Should like to make a synthesis of this voyage. Actually the marvelous sights filled me with a noncreative delight. As I gazed, everything echoed inside me, as when listening to music. Moreover I was full of plans for the future.—The sea is blue, absorbing everything, fused with the sky. At moments, the pink silhouettes of the mountains appear through the mist, like phantoms of reality in the flood of blue, like the unfinished ideas of some youthful creative force. You can just make out the shapes of the islands scattered here and there—as though headed for some unknown destination, mysterious in their isolation, beautiful with the beauty of perfection—self-sufficient.

Here and there flat coral islands, like enormous rafts gliding over the smooth water. Occasionally these forms take on life, passing for a moment into the realm of [crude] reality. A pale silhouette suddenly turns into a rocky island. Gigantic trees rise right out of the sea, set on an alluvial platform. Slopes covered with green thickets, here and there a tall tree towering above it. At places bits of white or pink stone stick out of the vegetation.

August 1, 1915—after a five-month interruption. Omarakana.*
What a pity I stopped keeping my diary for so long!—Today
is an important day. Yesterday and today I have clearly realized an idea that had long been dimly present, wandering
through the welter of wishes, dreams, and uncertainties—it has
now clearly emerged—I am thinking seriously of marrying
N. In spite of that, I am very uncertain. But I want to
see her and try. Beginning tomorrow—no, today—I'll start
another diary, and I must fill the empty blank pages of these
last five months. If in the end I marry N., March and April
1915 will be the most important months in my emotional life.
Evelyn Innes left a strong impression on me—Conrad's novel an
incomparably stronger one.

* This is the only entry from Malinowski's second field-work expedition,
which he spent in the Trobriand Islands, May 1915–May 1916.

PART TWO

᠕᠕᠕ 1917–1918 ᠕᠕᠕

.

A DIARY IN THE STRICT SENSE OF THE TERM

Day by day without exception I shall record the events of my life in chronological order.—Every day an account of the preceding day: a mirror of the events, a moral evaluation, location of the mainsprings of my life, a plan for the next day.

/\\.\\/\\

The over-all plan depends above all on my state of health. At present, if I am strong enough, I must devote myself to my work, to being faithful to my fiancée, and to the goal of adding depth to my life as well as my work.

/\\/\\/\\

Sunday, Oct. 28, 1917, on the Tropic of Capricorn.

Review of last few weeks:*

In September I went to Sydney, to catch the "Marsina," [for Port Moresby]. The last evening was spent with Elsie† in my room. On Thursday packing; Paul, Hedy,‡ and Lila.§ We lunched together; Elsie there. Came back. Lila went home. I went with Elsie. At the station we drank tea and talked about the separation of Teppern and Ann Delprat. Mim, good-bys.

* The second diary includes a section at the back of the book which Malinowski refers to as a "retrospective diary." The first entry, written after his arrival in New Guinea for his third expedition and dealing with the period just before his departure, is actually the only one that deals with past events. Since it gives some picture of Malinowski's circle in Melbourne, including names and occasions that are frequently mentioned in the second diary, the entry has been inserted before the beginning of the diary proper.

The remainder of the "retrospective diary" consists mainly of notes on sociological theory and outlines for possible articles. Most of this has been omitted.

† Elsie R. Masson, daughter of Sir David Orme Masson, professor of chemistry at the University of Melbourne. At the time she was a nurse in Melbourne Hospital. She and Malinowski were married in 1919; she died in 1935.

‡ Paul and Hedy were Mr. and Mrs. Paul Khuner of Vienna, lifelong friends of Malinowski who were in Melbourne during this period.

§ Lila or Leila Peck (Malinowski uses both spellings). There are also references to Mimi Peck, apparently a sister.

Trip [to Sydney]. I told the fellows where I was going. Felt fairly well and was glad at the thought I would soon be in the wide open spaces again. . . . Sydney: vexed on learning that the ship was full. B[urns] P[help]; Charlie Hedley. *Military.* Aversion for the city of Sydney.

Return (aborigines, half-caste & co.). Paul at the station. Lunch at Café Français; Elsie: *"many happy returns"; concert,* the two Misses Peck; Brahms; evening at the Pecks. Sunday at the Khuners' (Judge Higgins); evening with Mim & Elsie, whom I walked back to the city.

I settle down in Melb. as if I had to live there for a lifetime. I stayed in the house, and the first Thursday zlotko [literally, "gold," a term of endearment for Elsie] came to see me in the evening. Usually I spent the evening from 4 to 8 with her. Very much attached to her, I like her company very much. Nor can I bear the Dostoevskian reactions I used to have—some sort of hidden aversion or hostility, mixed with a strong attachment and interest. I was then (before going to Adelaide) very unhappy, and a few times I had "to run away from myself." My hypothesis is that my feelings for her are based on intellectual and personal attraction, without much lust.

During this period between my return and my setting out again, I worked fairly well, chiefly on social economics. I read *Shares & Stocks* and the textbook of economics written by Ely. —I was greatly annoyed by a meeting with Spencer,* and by a visit to Atlee Hunt. I met Sp. on Wednesday, went to see him on Thursday and I wrote a letter to Hunt on Thursday. Elsie saw this letter on Sunday (I spent the night with the Khuners); then on Tuesday, Hunt again. Next Thursday, E. & M. at the Khuners'. The third week, on Saturday morning I learned that

---

* Sir Walter Baldwin Spencer, a noted British ethnologist who with F. J. Gillen had published several important monographs on the Australian aborigines. He had encouraged Malinowski in his early work.

I would be leaving on the 19th. I felt rotten. Walk with Mim
and Bron. [Broniowski]. Evening at the Khuners'.

On Monday, E. came to the Kh.; I felt simply rotten; slept,
then she and Paul came to see me; we talked; I read O. Henry;
Paul read excerpts from Walter Pater. Elsie woke, got up. Talk
on the grass. I walked her to the hospital. Next morning,
zlotko came to see me, *on her own accord.* Wednesday—? On
Thursday we met in the afternoon. Zlotko came to my place that
morning, then I went to lunch with Mim (passing the hospital,
M. said that we must be quiet so as not awaken E.!)

In the afternoon, around 4, we made up our minds to go to
Pt. Melbourne. Sat up in front. New surroundings gave us
feeling of new existence. [Elsie] was hungry; we drank tea in
company of some young *marines.* We went to the shore; marvelous sunset; we made plans for a trip together in *clipper-packets*
to South America (one of the rare occasions when we assume
that we are engaged). Golden tones over the sea, complicated
clouds, silhouettes of ships misty in the distance. We walked
along the beach to St. Kilda. Night fell. Train back to the city.
Last supper at the Café de Paris. We went back to Pt. Melbourne for a parasol. In 128 only a short while.—She went to
Chanonry, I to the Khuners.

Next day Hedy and I went to 128 and packed; Paul made
various purchases. (I packed hurriedly, so as to be on time to
meet Elsie.) . . . In the afternoon . . . with Elsie to Military, where I waited a long time for a redheaded girl to make
out my *permit.** Then to Atlee Hunt, who was apparently in
good humor (a raise in salary?). I met Elsie in the park, we
went together to the Botanical Gardens (the day before I had
bought her a parasol); that day we bought lace at Mis-

---

* As an Austrian national during World War I, Malinowski was technically an enemy alien in British territories.

sionary House. In the park, tea and walk around the pond, wis-
teria along the river; I caught the evening train, she bought a
kimono for Marian. At the Khuners I had several drinks and
offended Mim with my cynicism. Broniowski at the last moment;
we went back home, we walked [her] to Chanonry, talking.

Saturday. E. R. M. came; we were together for the last
time. We packed (she in a red kimono). I went to the pharmacy,
Buckhurst, lunch (bad news by telephone); I went to 128,
E. R. M. in nightgown, got dressed quickly; I telephoned Molly;
we left; we calmed down; return; my beloved very dejected, I
too was upset. P[aul] & H[edy]; good-by to household; drive *à
quatre* to Melb. Hosp. I was calm, bent on winding everything
up. Trouble with the sending of parcels. . . .

Sydney deserted and sad. Victoria. Coffee Palace hot and
dirty. I sat and wrote; overcome by depression. I went to the
port, I wrote to Elsie and Kh. I still was not too sentimental. At
night I returned and went to bed around 10. Monday: B. P.,
Bank; station; Milit.; B. P. again; Hedley at lunch. . . . In
the evening I stopped at the Mitchell Library. Wrote to
E. R. M. for the second time. Went to bed. Tuesday morning
boarded ship; purchases; lunch with Broniowski frère.

Departure: backs of the business houses—last glimpse of
civilization. Women on the bridge. Worried by the present uncertainty of sea trips. In the middle of Sydney harbor I felt
suddenly alone and I longed for E. R. M. In the evening I made
friends with the second mate, we talked about N.G. . . . and
about the last voyage. N.G. attracted me again; I was happy at
the idea of going there.

Wednesday uneventful—I made friends with a navy officer,
read, wrote a little. I was slightly seasick. Thursday: around 4
P.M. we sailed into Moreton Bay. Peaceful trip. I did not look
around enough, I talked too much. I looked at the river in moon-

light, and recalled the British Assoc., Staś, Mackaren, and Miss Dickinson. Gloom of deserted wharves; enormous gray transports. Message from the Mayos; drive; telegram to E. R. M.

At the Mayos, heroic intervention in discussion of religion. Then we talked about politics and his activity among workers. I slept little and badly. In the morning, short talk; I wrote E. R. M. We left, they got off near Queens Bridge. I took a tram and bought raspberry juice; the ship; we sailed at about 1 P.M.; large number of cuttlefish in the river. . . .

Trip to Cairns (Friday-Tuesday): letters to Frazer, to Gardiner; played bridge with some fellows; I felt fine but not creative. Cairns: I reported to two men; first breath of the tropics. Tuesday-Thursday to Pt. Moresby: seasick, I ate nothing and vomited from time to time; headache but no feeling of hopeless despair; I felt rotten, but "not beyond endurance."

At Port Moresby, went to see Strong; the pig did not ask me to stay in his house. I invited myself to his porch, where I pitched my own "tent." Terrible heat; mornings and evenings on his porch and in his house. I wrote letters; longed for a glass of brandy in the evening. Strong did not conceal his irritation at my staying with him. Generally speaking, unpleasant and unintelligent. [Boag] much more amiable, but also warped. Thoughts about the emptiness of these two men, their attitude toward the war, toward women, their purpose in life. They have a tremendous amount of material available, and they do nothing about it; they mess up normal life, and take no advantage of extraordinary opportunities.

Samarai. 11.10.17. Yesterday I got up around 6:30 (the night before I had gone to bed early). I read my diary (a piece I had written previously), and a short story by O. Henry. Moments of violent longing for E. R. M. I recalled her physical presence— her direct emotional impact: how she meets me on the Library staircase, how she comes to visit me early in the morning and wakes me up, etc.—Around 12 I went out, walked around the island. It was muddy underfoot—a rainy day, chilly, the wind blowing from the mountains (are they covered with snow?). Had lunch, talked with Solomon; afternoon nap, awakened by a cry "Kayona" [name of a ship]—I confused it with "Itaka." I go to the bank, B[urns] P[help], & B.N.G. (Mr. Wilkes, who talked with me about Thomas and gave me a few photographs and asked me to visit him some evening). Then the hospital. Mentally I caressed the "matron," who seems an attractive dish. Teddy [Auerbach] told about the gold mines, shares, and claims in his amusing jargon. Once again I walked around the island (met two fellows from Mailu); supper, conversation with Solomon and Capt. Hope, who advanced paradox that *all business is gambling,* whereupon I defined Socialism as the elimination of *gambling* from *business.* Repulsive fellows with tropical slothfulness and [brazenness]. In the evening I went to the hospital. Teddy [Auerbach] told stories about *"holding court."* . . . All through this I was subconsciously waiting to be introduced to the nurse. At 9, I left with some fellow. I sat around until 10:30, making up to Mrs. . . . , who is not stupid, though quite uncultured. I fondled her and undressed her in my mind, and I calculated how long it would take me to get her to bed. Before then I had lecherous thoughts about. . . . In short, I betrayed [Elsie] in my mind. The moral aspect: I give myself a plus for not reading novels, and for concentrating better; a minus for mentally making love to the matron and for return of lecherous thoughts about. . . . Also a disastrous tendency to "preach" and to argue in my mind with all the rascals who keep pestering me here, especially Murray. This preaching takes on the form of ironical remarks in the preface to Magnum Opus, in my speech at the Royal Society after Murray's lecture, in remarks addressed to his brother. I also wrangle with Strong,

B. P., Campbell, etc., and irritate them.—On the other hand, I know how ridiculous it is, and I resolve to stop doing it.

This morning I am waiting in vain for the "Itaka." I realize that if I manage to master my momentary moral disorder, really to isolate myself, to start keeping the diary with real determination, my stay here will not be a waste of time.—And so, for the future: E. R. M. is my fiancée, and more, she alone, no one else, exists for me; I must not read novels, unless I am sick or in a state of deep depression; I must foresee and forestall either of these conditions. The purpose of my stay here is ethnological work, which ought to absorb my attention, to the exclusion of all else. I must not think of "revenge" or "punishments," I must not take Spencer, Murray, or any other pigs seriously.

11.11.17. Sunday. Yesterday: in the morning I wrote a little, "thought" a little, and wasted time. About 11 o'clock I went to B. P.—one box missing. Then to B.N.G., I bought shoes, juice. Ted A. was "ill-mannered" toward me, which annoyed me. I kept my temper; went back home, wrote letter to Brammell. Lunch; I showed Ted and the Captain my pamphlets; had a nap; wrote letters to Leila and to the [Tax Office]; I went to Spiller's; the Captain was there, vituperating against the inhabitants of Samarai. Then walked alone around the island; slightly tired, liverish. I ran now and then; in the evening ate little, felt fine. Went to see Hinton; a young cockney, handsome with an open face, tells dirty jokes wittily, and "is interested in music"—he sings and composes parodies of sentimental songs!

I walked around the island a second time. Venus was out above Roge'a. I tried to concentrate on the past and to sum up last year. I formulated my primordial feeling for E. R. M., my deep faith in her, my belief that she has treasures to give and the miraculous power to absolve sins. Hence my confessions, this is why I tell her my "deepest" experiences. Desire for heroic, dramatic experiences, so I can tell her about them. Then I thought about her intensely and burned with passionate love for her. *Meeresleuchten* [phosphorescence]: mysteriously, lazily, a cold green glint appears on the waves and vanishes again. Back home I wrote Elsie.—Morally I am doing well. I repress lecherous thoughts about L. by recalling the fundamental difference between my attitude toward L. and toward E. R. M.—Wave of strong feeling for Paul and Jadwiga [Polish version of the name Hedy].—I have almost stopped thinking about "the persecution": I can face everything that comes quite calmly and readily. Resolution: Today, write down for myself my recollections of Melbourne.

Monday, 11.12.17. Yesterday, after writing the diary, I took a short walk. The day was clear, there was a cool breeze, but the sun was very hot. I felt very well, I needed exercise, I ran part of the way. After breakfast I wanted to start the retrospect diary. I dawdled a bit, I glanced through Sydney *Mail*, the illustrations. I got back my writings from the "Captain" and passed them on to Hinton. The Capt. said that the natives here were not interesting, an ungrateful lot.—Then, with interruptions and digressions, I wrote the retrospect in outline style. At about 12:30, gymnastics: I felt up to it. Terrible heat. After lunch I read Swinobury [Polish pun on Swinburne—"gray pig"]. I lay down, but didn't sleep; I was chasing away lecherous thoughts. I got up at 3. With Ted, waited for "Itaka"; it was too hot even for Ted. I was so exhausted I couldn't do a thing. Wrote letters: to the Mayos, to Bor[. . .], and to Elsie. I went to bathe; to Spiller's where we talked about wrecked ships and about black fever. Then walked around the island: many people; boys eating *coconuts* and playing the flute. The half-civilized native found in Samarai is to me something a priori repulsive and uninteresting; I don't feel the slightest urge to work on them. I thought about Elsie and recalled the phases of our last times together, associated with the Socialists. Dinner and talk with the Captain on the veranda about English politics. His excited passionate invective against Asquith, and his personal acquaintance with Smuts, Botha, etc. etc. His defense of conservatism. I nodded in agreement, then went into an anti-German tirade (actually this was stupid of me). Conversation with the three daughters of the hotel. Their excursion to the *mainland*, their orchids, and their ideas: the lady who paints all the flowers, etc. etc. In the evening I patted the waitress's liver [*sic*] . . . instead of writing a few lines to Elsie. I fell asleep easily and quickly.

Moral: Most important of all is to eliminate states of relaxation or inner emptiness, when inner resources are insufficient. Like yesterday afternoon when I didn't know what to do with myself, or in the evening when I wasted time taking the line of least resistance, subconscious lewdness (chatting with women). I should clearly and distinctly feel *myself*, apart from the present conditions of my life, which in themselves mean nothing to me. Metaphysically speaking, the tendency to disperse oneself, to chatter, to make conquests, marks the degeneration of the creative tendency to reflect reality in one's own soul. One should not permit such a degeneration. How would I define Samarai for Elsie and her book? The contradiction between the picturesque landscape, the poetic quality of the island set on the ocean, and the wretchedness of life here.

Tuesday, 11.13. Yesterday: I walked around the island and wrote my diary on a bench. Slightly tired; pressure in my eyes and head (quinine?). At home, I wrote the Melbourne Retrospect. At 10:30 went to B. P. and asked Burton to look for Staś's lost box. Tea (*"morning tea"*) at Henderson's, orchids and ferns. Mrs. Smith—poor thing—spoke to me about Pt. Darwin and about Elsie—I had mentioned her name. Then back home, read *folk tales* in Seligman, dozed before lunch; took a nap after lunch; at 3:30 shower bath, and I read again. I had no strength to finish diary. At 4:30 or 5 got up and took walk around the island. After lunch, passionate longing for E. "If I could get up and walk to her, I'd start at once." Same longing in the afternoon. Around 4:30 when I finished reading Seligs, metaphysical longing, imprisonment in existence symbolized by the island. To get up, to walk around, to look for what is hidden around the corner—all this is merely to run away from oneself, to exchange one prison for another.

In the evening I talked with Ted, made up my mind to wait for the "Itaka," so as to get boys in Dobu. I went to the hospital with him. Hartley, a pleasant fellow, told us about Nelson who worked his way out of poverty and has been waiting in vain for his wife, meeting every ship as it comes in. I walked around the island; the stars were ablaze, the sea was phosphorescent. Went back home—all that time had been thinking of Elsie; I wrote to her.—Emotionally, my love for her—strong, deep, all-pervasive—is the main element of my life. I think of her as my future wife. I feel a deep passion—based on spiritual attachment. Her body is like a sacrament of love. I should like to tell her that we are engaged, that I want the whole thing made public. But my experience with N. S., to whom I proposed too impulsively and prematurely, inclines me to go slowly.—I am still calm and composed. The heat doesn't tire me excessively. I look upon my temporary imprisonment on Samarai as inevitable and desirable, provided I use this time to collect myself and prepare for ethnological work. I have got rid of my distracting mental lechery and my impulses to superficial flirtation, for instance, my desire to get acquainted with the attractive women here (particularly the matrons); in short, I am trying to overcome the metaphysical regret of *"Vsiekh nye pereyebiosh!"* [Russian; literally: "You'll never fuck them all."] Thoughts: writing of retrospective diary suggests many reflections: a diary is a "history" of events which are entirely accessible to the observer, and yet writing a diary requires profound knowledge and thorough training; change from theoretical point of view; experience in writing leads to entirely different results even if the observer remains the same—let alone if there are different observers! Consequently, we cannot speak of objectively existing facts: theory creates facts. Consequently there is no such thing as "history" as an independent science. History is observation of facts in keeping with a certain theory; an application of this theory to the facts as time gives birth to them.—The life that lies behind me is opalescent, a shimmer of many colors. Some things strike and attract me. Others are dead. My love for E., which for a time was a fairly inert element, is now alive with color. My intellectual interests (scientific work; sociological projects; discussions with Paul) have lost some of their intensity. Ambitions, urge to be active and to give more precise expression to my ideas, are even grayer in retrospect.

Wednesday, 11.14. Yesterday morning I worked fairly well on my diary, I wrote intensively and steadily. E. R. M. still with me. I don't read novels, I am reading Swinburne. I have her letters and telegrams almost by heart, and I keep looking at photos of her. Took a nap in the afternoon, read Seligman; shower; went for a walk. I felt strong enough to climb a hill, all the time thinking of Elsie. After dinner, sat and talked with Truthful James and Mrs. Young about coconut plantations and about rubber. Then to Leslie's Hotel, where I met a young fellow with whom I took a walk around the island. We drank *ginger ale;* then I went to Hinton's and looked at his tortoise shells. Then back home; wrote letter to E. R. M.

Today: I got up at 6:30, and "*sail-o!*" At 7:30 the "Makumbo" was at the wharf. I took a walk on the shady side of the island. Wrote a letter to E. R. M. and N. S., looked over the other letters, added things, sealed them. Sent letter to E. R. M. by registered mail. Went aboard ship. Captain Hillman treated me to *claret and soda*. Discussion with Commander Burrows on German "administration." He praised their systematic, *efficient* hospitals and their concern for the well-being of the natives. I denounced them and praised *laissez faire*. He lashed into Sacré Coeur in German New Guinea and praised the Marist Mission. —Then back to town; *ginger ale* with Ted and Capt. Hillman. Then returned to ship, gave parcel to McCrann and wrote letter to the Khuners. Conversation with Higginson and the Commander about natural phenomena, etc. Then lunch; we talked about ethnography. We looked at a German map of German Guinea. He told me about his experiences, about the diversity of the natives on the various islands, about the German colonists, and above all about Dolly Parkinson, her mother and aunts. At 3:30 went back home, chatted with Ramsay. Then again to the ship; conversation with Dr. Harse and the commander about German administration, Russia, and the war.

Thursday, 11.15. Yesterday: at 5 I took a walk around the island, felt a need for *exercise;* wrote my diary on a bench. Was a bit excited and unable to concentrate after visit to the ship. I went to the promontory and gazed at the sea. E. R. M. still with me. (But I have completely forgotten what I thought about during that walk!) Oh yes—among other things I am interested in nature. The evening before: the poisonous verdigris of Sariba lies in the sea, the color of blazing or phosphorescent magenta with here and there pools of cold blue reflecting pink clouds and the electric green or Saxe-blue sky.—Last night: sea and sky of a calm, intense blue, the hills shimmering with deep purples and

intense cobalt of copper ore, and above them two or three banks
of clouds blazing with intense oranges, ochers, and pinks.—I'd
like to have her here. Back home I listened to "My boy, fulfill
my dreams" on the phonograph, and I was overcome with
longing for the whirlpool of life. Too bad that E. R. M. does not
dance in my style. *Adage:* "Those who dance well together,
won't live in harmony." I met Mrs. Henderson, Baldie, and Annie. Conversation—I tried to be interesting. Women again!—
After supper, talk with Captain Hope, who goes out of his way
to show me his kind *favors.* Then I drew sketches for combs.
Tortoise-shell mania. Took a walk around the island with young
fellow who arrived here with me and stays at B. P. We
complained about the inhospitableness of Samarai, and he
told me his story.—Conversation with the hotel women. I went
to bed, thinking of Elsie. Dream: at the corner of M.H., am
waiting for tram going to Brighton [a suburb of Melbourne]. I
look and listen—is it coming? I catch it at the corner. I am
sorry that I am alone and that E. R. M. is not there. I think of
the day when I will be back at Melb. and she'll meet me at the
station, and we'll ride again up front.

Thoughts: this morning: theory of conscious national action. *A responsible collective action of a state.* Theory of
what I told Elsie during our 1st conversation, that it is
*meaningless** to speak of "England," "Germany" as countries
that "wanted" something, "miscalculated," etc. Write down
this theory for E. R. M.!

Plan for organizing strictly scientific discussions at R. A.
Inst. Elimination *of the hybrid, semipopular meetings without
any discussion, neither popularizing science, nor giving any
definite results.* Needed: definitive formulation of basic prob-

---

* Underlined in original.

lems, and working together; everybody, or at least the representative men, taking part in the discussion.

Friday, 11.16. Yesterday: in the morning worked on the retrosp[ective] diary. Miss H. U., at 11 tea; talk about a missionary at Tule Island who has children, was thrown out and excommunicated; he got married; the natives made plantations for him; he got really wealthy; re-admitted to the Church. (Father [. . .]) Mrs. Gofton told me about a planter who got drunk and abducted a 14-year-old native girl, and kept her two years against her will; he bought her lots of things, a gramophone, a car, etc. Then she became attached to him. He went south, married a white woman; the black one got mad at him, went to his house, took the car away, etc. The white woman learned about it, left him, and went south.—Then I went to see Higginson, gave him my reprints, we talked awhile; he got things from Custom [shed]. Conversation with Burton about the terrible heat wave in W. Australia and about his *secluded mode of living* in Samarai. A tall broad-shouldered fellow with a distinguished face and good manners. After lunch I looked over checkbook and Elsie's letters, and drew up a chronology of our meetings.—Around 4 I loaded my camera, got ready to take pictures of Eli and the Smiths. . . . In the evening I went to see Hinton; tortoise shell; then I called on Wilkes who showed me countless photos and gave me nothing to drink! . . . Fit of undifferentiated sensuality which I resolve to overcome. I thought of E. R. M., but violence of longing blunted. Almost resigned myself to staying in Samarai. After all I'm not exactly wasting my time here!

Saturday, 11.17. I never let myself think of my trip to the Trobr [iand Islands], pretend the possibility is out of the question. Yesterday Retrosp. Diary about E. R. M. in the morning. In-

118

tense re-experiencing of that autumn when I met her. At 11 I went to look at photos which I had put out to dry, and drank morning tea with the women. Before that I had run after Everett and ordered the launch for the afternoon. I talked with Mrs. Mahoney and a certain Osborne from Rossel Island. Their unwillingness to give any information whatever was amusing. I suppose it's just laziness and a kind of void?—I had a drink with Everett; he spoke about kula* and maintained that Misima was not in the kula, but only Panayati and Panapompom; Tubetube and Wari; also Roge'a [. . .]. After lunch I set out; feel-

* The kula, an elaborate system of exchanges between tribesmen of eastern New Guinea and neighboring archipelagoes, became the subject of Malinowski's *Argonauts of the Western Pacific* (1922). The kula itself was a complex and highly regulated exchange of gifts between recognized partners in different villages. The principal gifts were of two kinds: armshells (*mwali*) made from conus shell and worn by men as bracelets for the upper arm, and necklaces (*soulava*) for women made of strings of spondylus shells. In general, these articles had no value outside their significance in the kula, but the possession of a fine *mwali* or *soulava*, each with its own name and history and traditional associations, enhanced the prestige of the owner and his village. The articles were not kept permanently, but sooner or later were given in exchange for articles of comparable importance.

Kula expeditions were made more or less regularly between specific communities (Sinaketa and Dobu, for example) by fleets of sailing canoes (*wagas*), which often covered great distances. There were also some inland *kulas*. Members of a visiting expedition exchanged only with their own recognized partners in the host village, and recognized "trade routes" were followed. For example, a man from Omarakana might obtain a pair of armshells on an expedition to Kitava Island (east of Kiriwina) and then, when an inland *kula* came from Sinaketa to Omarakana, give them to his Sinaketan partner in exchange for a necklace. The Sinaketan in his turn would exchange the armshells when the *kula* from Dobu arrived in Sinaketa. However, there was no direct exchange between the men of Omarakana and the Dobuans.

The life of the tribes of this area was closely bound up in the institution of the *kula*, and it affected to some degree almost all the activities of the participating communities. Malinowski's description of the *kula* and its ramifications became one of the important milestones in ethnography.

Apparently he was not aware of its importance at the beginning of this expedition, although he had become interested in it during his 1915-16 stay in the Trobriands.

ing of "ownership" and "knocking about" in motorboats. Marvelous view. Tropical thicket, deep shadows, blazing hibiscus blossoms. I sat in front of a *native house,* where a *so'i* was being prepared. Feeling of disorientation, which I always have in a new, unfamiliar place among natives. External things (gardens, structure of the house, preparations for *so'i;* overgrown stretches in the village, layout of the villages)—all this stimulates me, but I feel impotent—the pointlessness of the visit unless I can stay some time. The landscape, the conditions of my life here—do not encourage research. In Samarai I simply can't do a thing. What is the deepest essence of my investigations? To discover what are his [the native's] main passions, the motives for his conduct, his aims. (Why does a *boy "sign on"?* Is every *boy,* after some time, ready to *"sign off"?*) His essential, deepest way of thinking. At this point we are confronted with our own problems: What is essential in ourselves? We are back with Adolf Bastian:* *Universalgedanke, Volksgedanke* [universal ideas, folk ideas], etc. . . .

At night in bed, . . . I thought that E. R. M. is the only person I really love physically. Moral: I am beginning to "settle down" in Samarai: tortoise shell; the women; the walk; the view from my window—all this steeped in thoughts of E. R. M. is normally enough for me. But occasionally I long for her, I'd like to see her, to tell her how I love her; how much time I wasted with her on half-love.—A few days ago I was in despair at the thought that I might never see her again. Yesterday on the other hand I tried to recall my apathy and even antipathy a few weeks before leaving for Adelaide.—I am unable to concentrate. I write too little of my diary, I talk too much, and I am not

* Adolf Bastian (1826-1905), German ethnologist, interested in native psychology, who developed the concept of "folk-ideas," which he believed underlay the similarities in customs he had observed in his wide travels.

myself. Yesterday after returning from Sariba I wanted to read a novel. At such moments I feel a sharp though superficial longing for E. R. M. If she were here, would I be happy?

I must collect myself, go back to writing the diary, I must deepen myself. My health is good. Time to collect my strength and be myself. Overcome insignificant failures and petty material losses, etc., and *be** yourself!

Sunday, 11.18. Yesterday: In the morning Ginger came, I talked to him, bargained with him; *sign on.* I got photographic paper; went back, wrote diary; at B.N.G. bought cigarettes and *jelly.* Then wrote retrospective diary. E. R. M. After lunch I cut my hair; read a stupid magazine (which at every step made me think of E. R. M.). Then again wrote; signal that "Itaka" is coming; went up the hill with Ted; worked on the comb; supper; conversation with Mrs. Gofton; sat and thought of E. R. M. Walk around the island; at moments I felt calm and happy; at other moments desperate longing for E. R. M. and "life." I thought about my destiny; if I had not come back, she would certainly have found someone else; I thought about Charles and about the fact that my *attitude* toward him and her past is really decent. I sat on a bench for a while; stars; I thought about objective reality: the stars, the sea, the enormous emptiness of the universe in which man is lost; the moments when you merge with objective reality, when the drama of the universe ceases to be a *stage* and becomes a *performance*—these are the moments of true nirvana. Then I thought again that I might never see her again, and I was seized with despair. I whispered her name into the darkness; I wished I could tell her I wanted her to be my wife; I thought about how we would announce this to the elder Massons, if they were willing to see me on this condi-

* Underlined in original.

tion, I could not hold any grudge against them. I wrote her a very passionate letter.

Resolution: calmly, without clenching your teeth, write the retr. diary, as a preliminary work. The essence of it is a look into the past, a deeper conception of life (during my walk last night I tried to develop this idea). But for this purpose you must write diary, and recall the facts in a somewhat formal way.

You must absolutely eliminate sensual thoughts; only my love for E. R. M. exists. (Last night I thought of L. P., etc., and I realized clearly that on the one hand I write sincere passionate letters to Rose, and at the same time am thinking of dirty things à la Casanova. Reading my letter to E. R. M., she would never suspect me.—When I realize this, my lecherousness vanishes of itself.)

Monday, 11.19. Yesterday: Rain in the morning, rest of day sky overcast; so far I have not felt the heat. At moments I forget that I am in the tropics, I feel subjectively so well. For all that, am considerably less energetic. After breakfast (I had a slight headache, with pressure behind the eyeballs), I lay down for a while. Then retrosp. E. R. M. At 10:20 at a moment of relaxation I took a magazine, and against my better instincts, I read it with revulsion until 11:20. Having lost my bearings, I went for a walk to collect myself. I thought that I ought to write E. R. M. more objective letters, telling her about my doubts (when I try to recall her physical shortcomings and when I remember and analyze my momentary antipathy for her); I should also describe my emotional low tides when I am relatively indifferent and my moral lapses when I make up to other women or have lecherous thoughts.—During the walk I felt perfectly well physically; I need to move about (in the morning I did plenty of exercises). I went up the hill, then down again. I sat on a bench. Osborne came by. We talked about Rossel Island. I liked him better than the first time, he attracted me. Details which seem very interesting to me. I *"bragged"* about linguistic talents, etc. We walked on Yela Gili. After lunch I slept until 3. *Shower bath* (somewhat sluggish; headache worse). Then talk with the boys and Osborne about Yela Gili. I went home, around the island; sunset; I wrote a few lines to E. R. M. In the evening, card game; talk about politics. I am amused by the violence with which these men talk against Bruce* and Murray; I also like the *bad language* used by Ted when Annie is lying on the other side of the partition (we talked of *poles*).

Moral: Reading of magazine was a disastrous lapse. I am strong enough physically to overcome my lack of concentration and control states of mind I don't approve of. Also, high time for me to get rid of my inertia, my taking the line of least resistance. Yesterday I did three most unfortunate things: I read stupid trash; I was listless sitting with the fellows; and I drank with them. Also overly sensual attitude toward Mrs. Gofton and Baldie. I shower them with compliments and behave in a way that hints at the crudest desire on my part.

Resolution. You must not let yourself go under, taking the line of least resistance. You have spoiled enough of the most beautiful love of your life. Now you must concentrate on it. Eliminate potential lechery from my intercourse with women, stop treating them like *special pals*. Nothing will come of it anyway—in fact it would be disastrous for you if something did. Stop chasing skirts. If she behaved this way, it would be a disaster for me.

Addenda: Yesterday during my afternoon walk, I analyzed the causes of my Dostoevskian state. The main cause was probably this, that by yielding to me, by contracting a personal relation with me, she lost the charm of absolute loyalty, as well as

---

* W. C. Bruce, commandant of armed native constabulary.

the charm of something inaccessible and objective. . . . I also thought about N. S. and felt remorse. Still, it is clear to me that my relations with her would have been impossible. For nothing, for no one would I have exchanged E. R. M.

Tuesday, 11.20.17. Yesterday evening and today I have been in a state of excitement, caused by my success in making combs. I have an artistic intoxication, it's a little like writing verse.— Also, I am trying to impress Smith and everybody I see here. Moreover, I am *chummy* with the women, played cards for the second time, and I am decidedly under the sub-spell of Mrs. Gofton, who is undoubtedly in the style of Marnie Masson. I think of her "soul." Decidedly she was "a woman" with me for about two hours. It will apparently be a long and laborious process, curing myself of this weakness!

Yesterday: morning clear but cold; exercises; I shaved. Then I saw Higgins[on] *; he is ready for an excursion to [Sariba]. He put it off till Tuesday. I went back home intending to write retrosp. diary, and to work on tortoise shell only a little while. I started at 9 and was at it until 1, when I saw Smith who gave me some excellent advice. In the afternoon I worked again and wrote a letter to E. R. M. downstairs, while Ginger was cleaning. At 5 I went to see Smith, and we planned to launch a new Papuan style.—In the evening I made new designs; then Smith; then card game with the women. I paid compliments to Mrs. Gofton, succumbing to her undoubted charm. Then we talked, eating crabs (she ignored the allusion when Ted said, *professional barmaid style*) ; I went to bed after talking to Ted. Under the mosquito net I thought of new designs.

Wednesday 21. Generally speaking, I am quite *at home* in Samarai. I don't feel the slightest desire to leave, although I'll be

* Resident magistrate of Samarai.

very happy when I do. When I go alone to the *wharf* on a
moonlit night, I enjoy the tropical mood, the sea with ships on
it, plans for working tortoise shell, my idea concerning the retrosp. diary.—In the last few days have almost never longed for
E. R. M. I feel fine and strong, fellows like Ted, the Capt., etc.,
amuse me and I like them. I like Mrs. Young's family, and I feel
at home in the hotel here. They give me morning tea and afternoon tea. Mrs. G. tells me stories about her hotel, etc. I play
cards with them. Nevertheless I know that E. R. M. is the only
human being who really understands me and at the same time
loves me unselfishly. When I see the humorous aspect of the situation or when I formulate deeper thoughts about my diary, she
is virtually with me in my subconscious mind.

Yesterday: Got up fairly late; wrote diary without concentrating. After breakfast, unwillingness to go to Sariba (inertia!). I ran into Harrison* and made plans for going to Dobu
with him. Then I went to see Higginson and took measures to
be able to get away, leaving things for Ted. George Harris[on]
said that they can take me. *Au fond* I was content. After lunch I
lay down and spent almost the entire afternoon creating a new
design for a comb for Elsie. Afternoon tea. Mr. Osborne. At 5,
walk around the island. I tried to collect myself, to shake off
intoxication with my artistic success. I thought about (?). I
realized that E. R. M. is my best friend. At supper I ate papayas and *pineapple,* and Ted talked about *kula,* saying that
Panayati and Panapompom had not been in *kula.* After supper
I finished and copied my drawing. I went to see Smith. Osborne
read aloud a chapter from [Bulwer-]Lytton's *Zanoni.* (Osborne: first impression, small, wiry, looks at you with suspi-
cion, bloodshot eyes, you are sure he was drunk the night before.
De facto, a theosophist; every day stands motionless watch-

* A trader in the region.

ing the rising sun; vegetarian; believes that natives possess mystical knowledge.) Then Smith cut a comb for me. I was proud of my masterpiece. At 10 went back, sat with Mrs. Baldie, and watched billiards. Capt. Storch. I went down to the *wharf.* In my room Ted and Capt. H. discussed the ingratitude of the natives.

Moral: I am in a period of good health and inability to concentrate. The heat does not bother me at all.

Thursday 22. Yesterday: got up rather late. In the morning wasted some time on tortoise shell; wrote diary carelessly. At 10 looked for tortoise shell and tools. Morning tea with the females; at 11 bought tortoise shell from Bunting at a bargain price. He spoke to me about the *kula.* Then I wrote my retrosp. diary. In the afternoon I dozed in the *parlor bar.* It was hot, the bar was empty; *cane chairs.* Undifferentiated *joie de vivre:* purified reality, possibility of breathing freely the good air of life. Already in the morning tendency to resist pottering with tortoise shell. In the afternoon wrote retrosp., but interrupted at 4 to [look at] combs. While writing, longed for E. At 5, walk around the island. The Governor arrived and Len Murray played tennis. I was vexed for a moment, then I drew myself up and took a walk to calm down. Walked around the island a second time; marvelous richly colored sunset. Roge'a: dark greens and blues framed in gold. Then many pinks and purples. Sariba a blazing magenta; *fringe* of palms with pink trunks rising out of the blue sea.—During that walk I rested intellectually, perceiving colors and forms like music, without formulating them or transforming them. E. R. M. all the time present as co-spectator. For a few stretches I ran, feeling athletic. After supper, drawn by music, I went in and danced. Tired on a full stomach. Once again I took a walk around the island. The basic problems of the technique of living. The moon and Venus over Roge'a. "The presence of certain persons opens up the essence of the universe; the presence of others closes it." People like Elsie, whose presence fills a landscape with a deep silence; others fill it with meaningless noise or, at best, with a sticky sentimental [pompousness]. (Aumüller— I understood why he could love Samarai.) Then I tried to be alone with nature, to erase sticky, meaningless thoughts. . . . I sat on a bench near the *powder magazine* and tried to attain to "the silence of the soul." I was hindered by a mental argument with Higginson: what I would say if he urged me to go to Makambo (Verrebely [. . .] three months). Political discussions in connection with this. I walked around the island twice. I thought about E. R. M., violent pain and regrets about N. S. I reflected that now I, too, have that *joy of small things*, just as she, poor girl, used to. I regret horribly having lost her, but I know it couldn't have been otherwise. I formulated this matter for Elsie. N. S. = C. E. M. or Ernest P. K. How would she feel? And would she wish to be here with me, *an humble outsider?* I had previously wanted to write her about my lapses, tell her that I was still keeping a diary. That I'd like her to write me, and to realize the problems of the importance of life, of self-criticism. This morning in the bath I caught myself thinking sporadically (new legislation concerning condoms in Australia) and I told myself that the chief defect of the English was lack of "stratification" in their lives—*their life flows in a single current. One thing comes and goes and is replaced by another and there you are!* They lack reflection, continuous systematization. Awaken E. R. M. to these problems.

Friday 23. A month ago I embarked in Sydney. Around Monday-Tuesday I was super-energized, and I stopped taking quinine. Last night a certain sluggishness, sleepiness, today, too;

moreover I have a slight sore throat. Today I feel that heaviness in the head and body—the *tropical increase in specific gravity* so characteristic of my former state in the tropics. In any case, I took arsenic again this morning, calomel in the evening, and inhalations for my throat. Last night I probably caught cold because I felt the breeze even under my mosquito net and I slept naked.

Yesterday: Got up at 6. Mr. Bernier arrived; I moved to a little room next door to Capt. Hope's. Intensive gymnastics. Breakfast, diary. At 9, saw Bunting. I began to explain to him what I wanted; unpleasant feeling that I was banalizing and desecrating my work. Then I began a conversation about *kula* with his *boy*. *Kula* in Dobu, Tubetube, Panaete. Characteristically divergent information; however, in the light of my previous knowledge, it is quite usable. At 11 o'clock I went to tea; I checked [work on] the comb. Later I worked on the comb myself in the monstrous heat. At 12:45 took a rest before lunch. After lunch, canoe from Nua'ata; two fellows dragged it to the beach; they measured it with Ginger; I examined the inside; a female with carunculate breasts and elephantiasis. I was seized with apathy in the middle of work. I did things superficially and not intensively. I went back around 4. (In the morning I had received stamps from Pt. Moresby and I took care of Ted's combs.) Occasionally I thought of writing to E. R. M. But the combs and the chatting took up my time. Walk. H[is] E[xcellency] Murray greeted me amiably. I told him the story of my illness. I spoke a little too fast, and arrogantly. I was not myself. I had no *dignity*. Too chummy. He didn't mention my work or anything serious, except for my health. Leonard had read my work, praised it politely. His tone very amiable, almost flattering about my work. I spoke to him about my health, about friends in Melbourne, and fed him compliments about Australians. Then we went back together, I told him about *kula*, he mentioned examples of *hiri** and other forms of trade. I spoke of the importance of economic functions.—Before then he had mentioned Capt. Barton's† article. He also said that if I went to the Trobriands, they might pay me a visit there. To all these advances I answered politely, cordially, as though "nothing had happened." I was *elated;* at all events this eliminates unpleasant personal tension and gives me a measure of confidence that if I apply for an extension of the permit, I'll be granted it.—I was [overstimulated] and conducted imaginary dialogues with Leon[ard] M[urray] about the importance of my work. But I promptly tried to control this euphoria and I reminded myself that the older M. has a smile for everybody, even for those he trips up. Leon. M. is probably more decent, but it isn't worth while cultivating him. I tried to control myself and to remember that I worked with immortality in view and that paying attention to this crew simply banalizes my work. In the evening I walked and talked with Ted. Slept not badly but probably caught cold again—*ut supra.*

Today: I got up at 6:30; felt poorly. I did not exercise very hard, for I was sluggish. Took a short walk and wrote my diary sitting on a bench. After breakfast talk with M. Bernier, a Frenchman, about mathematical schooling, about his friend Malinowski in Paris. He is from New Caledonia, has traveled a great deal, a scoffer, sympathetic and civilized. Charged me 15/- for a bag of betel nuts. At 9 I went to see Higginson; preparations for the trip. At 10:30 I went in a tiny boat to

---

* The *hiri* were trade expeditions between the Motu around Port Moresby and tribes of the Papuan Gulf. The Motu set out in their canoes (*lakatoi*) with cargoes of pottery and shell ornaments, which they traded with the Papuans for sago and the heavy dugouts used in constructing their canoes.

† F. R. Barton, C.M.G., a contributor to C. G. Seligman's *The Melanesians of British New Guinea;* his description of the *hiri* is cited in *Argonauts of the Western Pacific.*

Bow. Marvelous sea, rippled, right there flush with the boat; all around, a wreath of hills. The current and the wind were favorable. I had a nervous panic which I tried to control. In my mind I prepared myself for work in Roge'a. A gathering of natives waiting for [Toreha]. We sailed in the direction of Kwatou. Saw a couple of boats. I made drawings of the ornaments. Scientific and artistic interests (tortoise-shell mania) combined. The dimensions of the large boat. Rain. I sat and talked. Slight fatigue, apathy with regard to my work. The thanklessness of such sporadic work. Characterlessness of those villages. I should take a few pictures of these lousy villages, for my descriptive work about New Guinea.—I sat in a "missionarized" house and talked with a group of fellows. Return. I felt fine; cold, damp day; sky and sea gray; the mountains blue, hung with mists. Elewara came back from Miss Grimshaw's (?). Conversation in the *jail* yard with Mr. Headon. He promised me a better boat the next day and permission to talk with the prisoners. I got the combs for Ted (15/-!) and received advice about my own comb. After supper talk with Aumüller about Verrebely. I expressed my feeling and justified the conduct of the authorities. Then I talked awhile with Hinton, Davis, and Annie; I made arrangements with Ted about the betel nuts and sat down to write a letter to E. R. M., but I was too tired, and am writing diary *instead*. Now to bed.

Sunday 25. Yesterday I did not make an entry (*very bad!*). But this may be justified by the fact that on Friday I recorded Friday's events. Now I must give an account of yesterday's events.

Yesterday: Saturday 24, I felt well getting up but soon after pretty rotten. I did not do my exercises, went for a walk, and wrote a letter to E. R. M. sitting on a bench with a view of Roge'a. Higginson passed by. Mosquitoes were bothering me. I was not too well emotionally. I thought of my plans for the day

—finishing the *wagas* in Roge'a; comparative studies of canoes; but I felt that my ideas were getting muddled. I also thought that I should take a deeper view of things when writing diary. . . . Principle: along with external events, record feelings and instinctual manifestations; moreover, have a clear idea of the metaphysical nature of existence. Of course training myself to keep a diary affects my way of living.—After breakfast I got ready. Went with Charlie, his little son, 2 prisoners, [Davis], and Ginger. It was windy, we sailed fast; I tried to talk a bit with Charlie, at the same time enjoying the experience of sailing. Restless gray and blue sea—*there is a touch of lavish nonchalance about the dark blues and grays of a choppy sea.* Green hills. Roge'a enveloped in soft, deep-green vegetation sloping steeply toward the plain covered with sago, coconut, and betel palms, among which little gray houses are set. We sailed *à contre* across from Kwatou; I photographed a small boat and then the *waga;* then I went to the house where I had been the day before. Talked with Charlie about *kula* and about trade between the islands. Then ate lunch, took measurements of the *waga*, photographed it; the rain was coming closer and I cursed Ginger who had walked out without permission. I went to the east side; inspected the *waga*. Panayati and its artistic character. Return; the *boys* rowed; Ginger made sympathetic impression.—Came back very tired; wrote letter to E. R. M.; dinner.—I felt *distinctly feverish.* I chatted with Mrs. Gofton, I showed her the combs. Mr. & Mrs. Catt. Saville. I went to see Smith, who gave me lessons in bending the combs, then I discussed designs with him. Then I went back and got ready to turn in, indifferent, tired, *feverish*, almost without emotional tonus. (But the thought that letters would come from the south cheered me up.)—Ted came and got me to go downstairs; we drank *ginger ale* and took a walk on the *wharf*. We planned a trip to Simsim, etc. Also to Iwa, Gawa, etc. Went to bed late; at moments attacks of lecherousness, but I repelled them. I thought about my designs but little about E. R. M.

Monday 26. Yesterday I had what is usually called *an attack of feverishness, a touch of fever.* Physical and mental sluggishness. Yesterday, for instance, I felt no desire and was not strong enough to take a walk, not even around the island. Nor have I the energy to get to work, not even to write letters to E. R. M. or look over my ethnographic notes. Moreover, I am extremely *irritable* and the yells of the boys and other noises get horribly on my nerves. The moral tonus is also considerably lower. Emotional bluntness—I think of E. R. M. less intensely than usual. Resistance to lecherous thoughts weaker. Clarity of metaphysical conception of the world completely dimmed: I cannot endure being with myself, my thoughts pull me down to the surface of the world. I am unable to control things or to be creative in relation to the world. Tendency to read *rubbish;* I leaf through a magazine. I seek out the company of various people.

Yesterday's events. Got up at 6:30, not having slept enough *obviously.* I shaved, planning to work on my material, to write to E. R. M., diary. Before and after breakfast, diary. Not too intensively. Capt. Hope interrupted this. (Conversation about the prohibition on sending money from England, his anti-English and anti-Australian tirades.) Then I decided to walk around the island and write to E. R. M., but I felt *feverish* and went to see Smith. He spoke of sending my designs to his brother; I was taken aback at the thought that I made the designs, gave him the idea, and he would exploit it commercially. But I got over it. I went back home; after lunch sat down and made some drawings. The *launch* left without me. I made it clear that I was vexed, although I myself made up my mind that I'd rather stay, do my drawings, and write. A sunny day to the west. Dark-blue clouds. Annie and Mrs. W. stayed at home.

Although only a few minutes before I had "genuine" and "deep" feelings for E. R. M., I couldn't keep my paws off the girls. Then, moral hangover. I could not write to E. R. M. in this state. I read the magazine. Saville came with Ramsay. After dinner (somewhat acidulously we talked about Ted's *launch*). Then I sat on the veranda, went to the *wharf*, sent off Ginger to Sariba, gazed at the marvelous blue-black sea, glowing on one side with a bronze fire. I talked with the men; one, McCrow, with a fairly cultivated voice, speaks with the accent of a *clergyman* but swears like a trooper. He told about a wild brawl between two fellows on the "Southern Cross";* then he talked about Werner and how he was murdered; about *recruiting trips* between Cape Nelson and Banyara. We talked about religion; all of these fellows are atheists, don't believe in God, criticize the Bible from a rationalistic point of view, and generally speaking have a sound *outlook*. The day before we had discussed religion with Ted Auerbach, who quoted [Joseph] McCabe [well-known British rationalist] and [Robert G.] Ingersoll [American agnostic lecturer and writer].—Why are some popularizers successful and others are not?—Then conversation in a group. . . . I went upstairs, sat on the veranda. Lecherous thoughts. I tried to chase them away: "To submerge myself in the deeper, metaphysical stream of life, where you are not swept by undercurrents or tossed about by the waves. There these things don't exist. There I am myself, I possess myself, and I am free." Unfortunately, this motto—powerful in itself—is not enough. I have lecherous thoughts. . . . I think about the technique of gradual deflowering . . . need not be the brutal act that Maupassant makes it.—I think of E. R. M. when I indulge in lewd excesses of the imagination and adulterous lusts—what would be my feelings if she—? . . . Tired; *feverish* I go to bed, I sleep lightly and badly.—I wake up often. This morning I got up with

* There was a Catholic mission vessel of that name.

fogginess in head characteristic of quinine: damp, sticky, gray day. Banks of flat horizontal clouds over the *mainland*.—This morning I decide to exert all my strength to master *feverishness*. Not to read novels, not to be idle. To realize what I have to do and to do it; to get things ready and finish them; to write the *indispensable* letters, to cut one or two combs in addition to those already made.

Tuesday 27. Today is last day of my captivity in Samarai. I must be very energetic, move my things, draw up a baggage list, finish a few letters, etc. I am not too sluggish, but I wouldn't mind flopping down and reading novels. I often think of E. R. M. but without absolute devotion. I still look upon her as my future wife, but I am trying to persuade myself that she is really the most suitable person. In my thoughts I go back to Tośka and I recall scenes from 16 Fitzroy St. and 6 Mecklenburgh St., and I tell myself that she was an incomparable mistress. . . . Today at daybreak I dreamed of T. R. Big hotel, automobiles, I looked for her in various rooms; she was charming in a black blouse with a flowered pattern and very attractive. She didn't want me and escaped the net of my wooing. I was very much in love with her in my dream. This still *persists*.

Yesterday's events: In the morning I wrote my diary. After breakfast I tried to get myself organized; I made a list of things to do; I decided to review my sporadic ethnological notes and write a letter to E. R. M. But I was not too well physically; I finished a few drawings; at 11:30 when I was trying to write, [interrupted] by *morning tea*, and I met Saville. I had been planning to write him, but I suddenly recognized his back. I said hello to him; obvious embarrassment and exaggerated politeness on both sides. We went to their house ([. . .] Mrs. Mahoney). There we talked about my booklet on Mailu; I depreciated it, he praised it, not too sincerely. Then explana-

tions: I talked about my health, about my persecution mania, etc., and told him that I had perhaps been less amiable than I could have been. They tried to gloss it over, but I think we parted on friendly terms. I promised to give him a copy of my booklet. After lunch, tired; I read novels for a while, napped. Got up at 3, went to see Higginson, Smith; I packed the combs for E. R. M. Came back tired. I walked around the island; thought about—? After tea called on Saville, Smith— they were out. I wrote a letter to P. & H. [Paul and Hedy]. Very tired, my head simply would not function.—What was characteristic with the Savilles was my *générosité* in depreciating my work and criticizing my own conduct. He was less broadminded, but he assured me that he could not have helped me more than he had.—In short, the entire day intellectually rather empty. I toyed with the parcel for E. R. M. I thought of Saville, I want to show him Frazer's* letter.

Wednesday 28. Yesterday my health improved. Felt better, particularly in the afternoon. Light headache—I got rid of it by doing some exercises. Then toward evening, considerably better. At night violent sweating (?). I won't drink much today and will continue my diet.

Yesterday's events: In the morning I took care of current business (Higginson, Aumüller); then Mrs. Mahoney and Saville. Showed photos to Mrs. M., who was interested and promised to help me as best she can. Saville praised my photos, I praised his, a little shamelessly. But he certainly has good *canoes*. After lunch, short nap. Ted told me about lading. I loaded my things from Customs. With Ginger, Bonegai. Ted distributed *calico* aboard ship. Then I moved things from B. P. Burton and *shipping note*. I extracted my (?) *camp oven*. I found the linen I had thought was lost and, probably, the table legs. Ubi'ubi [a

---

* Sir James Frazer, author of *The Golden Bough*, a classic study of magic and religion. He wrote the preface to *Argonauts of the Western Pacific*.

native cook he had taken on his first trip to the Trobriands].
Visit to Kwatou with the Savilles, and plans with Saville for
developing work on Mailu. I was again delighted to sail for
Dobu; also, the *absurdity of it.* Before lunch I read Pemberton
and did gymnastics. After supper (Solomon appeared) went to
see Smith; *false alarm "Sail 'o!"* We drew; he certainly makes
progress, and was seized with creative frenzy. Came back sleepy
and tired. Lech. thoughts about L. . . . I fell asleep in spite of
drunken shouts. Ted and Hope discussed the existence of God
and *"worship the alligator."*

This morning I feel decidedly better, heart a bit tired. Fine
cool morning, northwest wind. Yesterday during the afternoon I
tried to understand my *Stimmung* and to analyze *in flagrante*
my psychological state during my *feverishness;* naturally,
emptiness and sluggishness, weak grasp of reality; shallow
associations or absence of thoughts; total absence of metaphysical states.

Thursday, 11.29. Today, I think, I'll feel quite well, as far as
health is concerned; apparently my body needs a steady supply
of arsenic! Cool morning, west wind, fine weather. The ship
is waiting, I heard it letting off steam this morning. It cannot be
seen from our veranda because of a tree. I went to the *Chinese
wharf* and saw the "Marsina," gray, enormous; my cabin of 30
months ago, associations with N. S. Ted changed time of our
departure to tonight at 12.

Yesterday's events. I copied my notes taken on the *gahana.*
At 10, Smith. Then chatted with Mrs. Gofton, whom I treated to
a drink. At 11, Saville; we looked over the passage about
bara'u. He was fairly decent this time, told me some quite interesting details. At 1, lunch. Then heat, sluggishness; I lay down
for a while. At 3 took *measuring glass* to Graham. I watched a
half-caste girl named Mary bathing. Chatted about Campbell

with Billy Priest. I went to the lower veranda, made some drawings. Went to see Smith: irritated by failure, complaints about "the stupidity of the English" who have no proper tools or fret saws. After dinner chatted with Mrs. Gofton, who discusses anything very emotionally but whom I like as a *"glorified Marnie Masson."* At 7:30 went to see Saville. *Heckles me about "filthy rags."* Showed me his notes. He takes this as a personal offense. We talked about the war; he said tactlessly, *"I wonder that you haven't been interned."* I replied fairly sharply. She, as usual, more decent, less tactless.—I went back in a state of slight irritation. I realized that S. is a boor who must get on my nerves the moment he steps out of his shell, and that I am incapable of treating him as a means *pure and simple.* In his capacity as an accessory, he is associated with my tropical impressions and illusions, he inspires in me a certain friendliness. As a personality he is repulsive and contemptible: *a petty greengrocer blown up by his own sense of importance into a caricature of a petty sovereign.* I thought of E. R. M. and her atmosphere so naturally harmonizing with mine, like the Promised Land to me. —Pouring rain, cold northwest wind sweeps the veranda. I slept well.

Monday, 12.3. Sinaketa [village on Boyowa Island, in the Trobriands]. George's* veranda. To the left a few palms, bananas and papayas. Native house, sago roof, walls of mangrove sticks. A few dilapidated pieces of furniture, *litter of sapi-sapi.* At least 200 dogs and cats. This morning aroused by noise of asthmatic dog and chatting natives.

Events of the past few days:

Thursday, 11.29. Arrival of ship. After breakfast wrote to E. R. M., with some difficulty; trying to transcribe diary for her.

* George Auerbach, a trader in the Trobriands, a friend who helped Malinowski in various ways. Ted Auerbach was evidently a relative.

Difficulty in describing my erotic lapses. Went to see a few times
whether mail arrived. Around 11 received letters: Paul; the
telephone irritated me; distressed because E. R. M. sick; (Mim
W. letter somewhat casual). E. R. M.—I read quickly, without
concentration. N. S.—difficult problem as to what to write.
Not offended by the *"hint"* in letter from Sydney.—After lunch,
I wrote to N. S., to Paul (briefly), and chatted with various
people. Toward evening, I collected my things and sent them
to the "Itaka." At 9 Ted said that he was ready. I finished
letter to E. R. M., then I caught Ted via steamer. The port
was drenched in moonlight. "Marsina" large and gray. I went
to the front [of the ship] and lay down on a sail; China Straits;
I slept.

Friday, 11.30. Awoke at daybreak near East Cape.* Above
the water, palms and rocks shaded by the water. [. . .] Marvelous impression of nature and genuine atmosphere. View of
Normanby [Island] capped by Mount Bwebweso. Impression of
indescribable filth on this ship. Slept. Woke up refreshed near
[Ubui]. Read last letter from E. R. M. Began to write. Sketched
silhouettes of mountains and islands. Chatted with the boys
about ethnography of Normanby and Dobu. Dawson Straits.
Corrected my original impression. Arriving there, across from
us the steep shores of Fergusson [Island]; on this side, a tiny
island and a *knoll* covered with trees. We sailed between the
island and the *knoll*. A low shelf, gardens and jungles on it;
narrow entrance, like a lagoon. Then, wider view: on the other
side, first a steep coastline, the mountains retreat, a low plateau,
long and wide; to the right a [high] wall with many canyons
and peaks. Then new turn; Dobu, extinct volcano; Bwayo'u to
the left and distant ranges on Normanby beyond Dobu. I
climbed up the ladder, and enjoyed the marvelous landscape.

* Malinowski described this voyage in his general survey of the *kula* district, *Argonauts of the Western Pacific*, pp. 38-51.

THE   NORTHERN

TUMA I.

KAYLEULA I.   Kiriwina

TROBRIAND IS.

I WEST BRANCH OF THE N. MASSIM   KITAVA I.
(THE TROBRIAND NATIVES)   BOYOWA I.   IWA I.

VAKUTA I.

III THE AMPHLETT NATIVES

AMPHLETT IS.

NABWAGETA I.   GUMASILA I.
GOODENOUGH I.   DOMDOM I.
KWATOUTO

MT. KOYATABU

FERGUSSON I.   SANAROA I.

Collingwood Bay   D'ENTRECASTEAUX ISLANDS   Dawson Str.
DOBU I.

IV THE DOBU NATIVES

Goodenough Bay   NORMANBY I.

NEW   MT. BWEBWESO
GUINEA

East Cape

Milne Bay

V WEST BRANCH OF THE
MAILU I.
Orangerie Bay   SIDEA I.
BONA BONA I.   TUBETUBE
Gadogadoa   GROUP
Silosilo   BASILAKI I.
File Bay   ROGE'A I.
Farm Bay   SARIBA I.
SUAU I.   SAMARAI I.   S. MASSIM

WARI I.

THE   SOUTHERN

CORAL   SEA

MASSIM

II EAST BRANCH OF THE N. MASSIM

KWAYAWATA I.

GAWA I.

Dikoyas

MURUA (WOODLARK I.)

Sulogs

SOLOMON

SEA

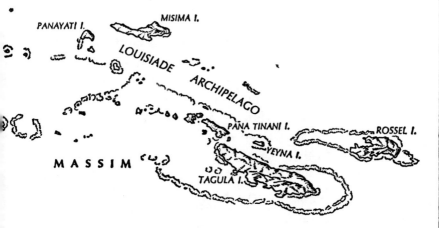

PANAYATI I.

MISIMA I.

LOUISIADE

ARCHIPELAGO

PANA TINANI I.

ROSSEL I.

YEYNA I.

MASSIM

TAGULA I.

Sunset; I went down, washed, dressed. Went to Scriven.—Effect of gold melting in a chalcedony bowl. We talked about the beauty of Dobu, and ethnology. He mentioned 2 stones [on which] they place sacrifices during *kula*.* Bought grammar. Return to ship. Abduction of Ogisa.† Trip to Bwayo'u. I went up the ladder again. Went ashore again, Ginger with the lamp and other *boys* —we went toward the dance. Moon amid palm groves, lemons and breadfruit. The villages are irregular, houses on pilings, but poorly built. I looked at some houses—was told that there is a celebration every time a new house is finished. *Canoes* of the Boyowa type; but no *kalipoulo*. I went back and turned in.

Saturday, 12.1. Early in the morning we sailed on past Dobu. The far end of the straits, where there are high mountains on both sides, looks beautiful. The sun rose slowly. I chatted with the *boys*, collecting geographical data about Goodenough & Fergusson islands. We approached Koyatabu,‡ covered with clouds. The Amphletts, before us, came up out of the sea. I took the rudder now and again. Wrote, and read E. R. M.'s letters. We had lunch. At 4, Gumasila. Rapture over the beautiful forms. Marvelous steep mountain covered with shaded vegetation, dotted here and there with huts. Below, tall palm tree bending over the shady water. Joy: I hear the word "Kiriwina" [another name for the Trobriands; more strictly, the northern province of Boyowa]. I get ready; little gray, pinkish huts. Photos. Feeling of ownership: It is I who will describe them or create them. Ashore; comical fences; miserable houses on pilings; [. . .]. The women ran away. Under each house implements for making pots. Yellow ocher pots lie under each house. —I try to talk to them; they run away or tell lies. *Canoes:* 4 or

* According to tradition, the two stones, Atu'a'ine and Aturamo'o, were men who had been turned to stone.

† A native who remained with him throughout this expedition.

‡ A large mountain on the north side of Fergusson Island, visible from as far away as the Trobriands. It was considered a sacred mountain.

6 *masawa*, small, built like *kalipoulo*, but they are called *kewo'u*.
—We go to Watobo'u. Koyatabu clearly visible, marvelous
forms. Wawima and Watobo'u move slowly away, disappearing
behind Koyatabu. Dark clouds. Only over Koyatabu a ring of
fantastic cumulus clouds, illumined from inside as though by a
blazing fire *like witches around a kettle in which there glows
some demoniacal fire.* Fairylike impression of something real.
This group is like the most beautiful part of the Queensland
coast, but I do not have the feeling of wilderness—attractive,
but formless. Here I have a distinct feeling of life crammed in.
Here I could settle down *sack and pack.*—I look at the marvelous view to the southwest. The steep rocks of Gumasila. Then I
look at Nabwageta and Bilibaloa and try to decide where the
view would be the loveliest.—Arrival in Bilibaloa—a wall, waves
smashing against it; we come in slowly, the forms become more
and more distinct, the waves louder; we drop anchor. We eat. I
take a *dinghy* ashore; tired. We pass a village; we joke about
[. . .]. The moon rises. We come back: rocks, the dark forms of
the trees. The village is deserted. 1 *masawa*. Miserable houses;
the trunks of the trees look like ladders. I examine the interior
of one house: 2 *lagims*. We cross the water to Watobo'u. There
I wait; a deserted house set among mangroves. Big drum. I beat
on it. Return.

Sunday 2. I get up feeling poorly. Gray day. *Sprawling
forms of* Watobo'u & Wawima. I sketch in outline the various
views. Nabwageta. Gentle low hill, and a fairly large village on
the sand beach. Also stone walls. Little houses are scattered
among the trees. The women don't run away. I buy 3 curios.
An old woman under a house makes a little curio. Wind and
rain. We leave. I look—above the low western hill you can see
the gray sea. Clouds rush by overhead. . . . A dark cloud in
the direction of Boyowa. Elated—my plans are taking shape.
Then I lie down and doze; rain (after unfurling of sail and

rolling up the *awning*). Ginger makes my bed. I sit on a sail, which has been rolled up and tied. A little tired, but I don't lose courage—am resisting the temptation to read novels. The Amphletts move away. My bones ache horribly.—We eat a frugal dinner. Ted works on the engine and is not too talkative. We catch some fish.—Little islands appear. I want to get to my destination, but I feel well. The sea turns deep green. The subtle thin line of the horizon breaks up, grows thicker, as though drawn with a blunt pencil. Then the line takes on dimension and color—a bright gray-green. The *boys* reel off names: Nanoula, Yabuanu (?), [Muwa]. Palms and other trees seem to be growing out of the water: Vakuta, Giribwa; we are in a lagoon. The broad [lines] of Kayleula; the whole island in front of me. I chat with Ted about a number of things, about Waite,* about the anti-Germans, Osborne, Stead's *Review*.† I wash, dress, getting ready to meet George. Campbell's *whaleboat*. We admire the Muwa plantations.—Three houses on the beach. We take the *dinghy*. George in a yellow shirt and *khaki* trousers. The house is right on the water. Natives and women in calico on the front veranda. The rear veranda (without view on the sea!) is reserved for George. George, very amiable with me, pitilessly upbraids Ted in my presence: for loss of ships, for failure to buy things in Samarai, etc. He told me stories about Brudo,‡ who *underestimates* his losses. I read Bulletins. Very sleepy.

Monday 3. Gomaya;§ I give him some tobacco; he *cadges* more.

* Theodor Waite, German anthropologist, an early (1821-1864) student of primitive thought, who believed in racial equality and in the bad effects of environment. His most important work was *Anthropologie der Naturvölker*.

† William Thomas Stead's *Review of Reviews* (established in 1890).

‡ Mr. and Mrs. Raffael Brudo, French pearl traders in the Trobriand area, became good friends of Malinowski's.

§ Gomaya, a Sinaketan who was one of Malinowski's first informants in Kiriwina; he is described as a notorious scoundrel in *The Sexual Life of Savages*.

News: Gilayviyaka* and M'tabalu† died; To'uluwa‡ and Bagi-
do'u§ living. Knows nothing about Vakuta. With his doglike
face, Gomaya amuses and attracts me. His feelings for me are
utilitarian rather than sentimental. After lunch we left on the
"Itaka." I chatted with George. Once again I was on the green
lagoon with the familiar views—Kayleula, the lagoon with the
canal along it; Kavataria; Losuya. We went ashore; saw the
jetty where I had walked and felt so empty, so unhappy, looking
to the south, ships on which the *prisoners* work, betel palms, the
"plantation" of fruit trees; [. . .]. Campbell seemed less loathsome now than he had before (than I had expected). [He acted
as judge] in the trial of William; I waited, nervous and impatient.—Decent, though he makes petty objections; but he *signed*
my boy *on* without guarantors.—We sailed to Gusaweta; we
got stuck in the mud. *Canoes* from Teyava took my things. At
night we sailed around the well-known bend. Billy‖ had gone to
Kiribi [a nearby trading post of Hancock's]. I checked my
things, went back to the ship, and then ashore again.

Tuesday 4. In the morning had breakfast here in Gusaweta. I
got the rest of my things off the ship; planned to meet Ted in
Lobu'a; went ashore. I went through Teyava. All this time
(from my arrival until today, Friday) I have not been too

* Gilayviyaka, a son of the chief, whose affair with one of his father's
wives had caused a grave scandal.

† M'tabalu, aged chief of Kasana'i.

‡ To'uluwa, chief of Kiriwina province and thus the highest ranking chief
of the Trobriands, lived in Omarakana and was a valued friend and informant of Malinowski's.

§ Bagido'u was the eldest son of the sister of To'uluwa, and thus the heir-
apparent to the chieftanship. His dramatic expulsion of the chief's favorite
son two years before is described in *The Sexual Life of Savages*.

‖ Billy Hancock, a trader in the Trobriand area, was a close friend of
Malinowski's, who frequently stayed in his home at Gusaweta. He disappeared
under mysterious circumstances in Samarai in the late 1920's. His wife was
living in Sinaketa as late as 1951.

alert, and my first impressions of the natives are very dim.
A kind of emotional lethargy; the first night I heard the distant
noise of a *walam* in the village. Then I saw them on Billy's
veranda; acquaintances from these villages and from the interior. But I did not react too strongly.—In Gusaweta I began
to sort out my things. At about 4:30 Billy arrived. What
George had told me about him—although it's an obvious
slander—spoiled the pleasure of first impression. He has a
nasal voice—looks very young and healthy. We talked about
photography, pearls, Verrebely, the war. We sat together in
the evening, chatting.

Wednesday 5. Felt rotten all day, read trashy novels. They did
not hold my attention, nor was I interested in the natives. Didn't
even feel like talking with Bill. . . .

Thursday 6. In the morning, I had a talk with Cameron. Looked
at his *camera*. Then (with a definite hangover) finished reading
Brewster's Millions [a novel by George Barr McCutcheon].
Then packed. Billy went to Norman Campbell's. In the evening
I had a talk with Bill. With some reluctance I went to the
village of Tukwa'ukwa. I couldn't imagine what I'd do there. I
struck up a conversation with one of the natives, then sat down,
and a group gathered around me. We talked and I tried to
understand their language. Then I proposed *kukwanebu*. An
old woman began to speak. They chattered after a pause—a
horrible racket. Then one man began to speak loudly—almost
shouting, saying indecent things, and the whole village roared
with laughter. Jokes were continually repeated, everybody
laughed. I felt a bit vulgar. I went back home. Talked with
Bill. Took more quinine and calomel.

Friday 7. In the morning (monstrous rain at night), boats out
fishing near Boymapo'u. I saw the triangular nets. Then I heard

ta'uya. Three boats returned from Vakuta. I went to the village, looked at *soulavas.* Speculated whether I am myself or my younger brother. Talk about *kula.* Breakfast. Dawdle with packing. In the evening went to Tukwa'ukwa by way of Olivilevi. Gymnastics; [Ogisa] held the lamp; he was scared. Return. In the upper village, natives showed me nets and talked about fishing. *Kukwanebu.* Feeling of absurdity less intense. Strong impression that my information about fishing is very inadequate. Back home, talked with Bill, who pointed out errors in my article.

Saturday 8. Got up late, felt rotten, took enema. At about 11 I went out; I heard cries; [people from] Kapwapu were bringing *uri* to Teyava. I sat with the natives, talked, took pictures. Went back. Billy corrected and supplemented my notes about *wasi.* At Teyava, an old man talked a great deal about fishes, but I did not understand him too well. Then we moved to his *bwayma.* Talked about *lili'u.* They kept questioning me about the war.— In the evening I talked with the policeman about *bwaga'u, lili'u,* and *yoyova.* I was irritated by their laughing. Billy again told me a number of interesting things. Took quinine and calomel.

Sunday 9. Slept well. . . . I felt well. Billy said we'd better set out for Kiribi at once, leave that same afternoon. I packed quickly (I am more interested in drawing [*kens*] than in ethnography, let alone packing.) I made lists of the linen I shall need and things indispensable to my [nomadic] life. After lunch finished packing in a hurry and at 3:20 we left. I was tired, but I had a residual *joie de vivre.* I gazed at the waters green as grass, the mangrove forests with their soft shadows and intense greens, the flying fish, the underwater plants. Arrival; house surrounded by palms; the deep cavernous shadows between the trunks designate clearings in the mangrove forest. Near the house a *bwayma;* then a tin *shithouse.* A jumble; I wanted to take pictures of it. Ilumedoi ignored me. I went ashore on the sandy beach and wrote a letter to E. R. M., but without great enthusiasm. I went back for lunch. Then talk with Billy. In the evening I sat with Ilumedoi and Moliasi;* the latter showed me a horrible abscess on his leg. We talked about *bwaga'u,* and *yoyova,* about M'tabalu's wives who ran away, and about the fact that Kasana'i had no ruler; about digging up mushrooms, about [. . .] *odila.* I only half understood Moliasi's talk. I could not sleep because of the endless chatter.

Monday 10. In the morning I finished letter to E. R. M. Reviewed my papers and notes about *kayasa,* and made a list of problems. I sat with a few natives, including some from Louya and Bwadela, and talked with them about *kayasa,* about going to Okayaulo.† But their information was vague, and they talked without concentration, just to "put me off." In the afternoon we talked again (don't remember what about). I read voraciously *Wheels of Anarchy* [a novel by Max Pemberton], and felt increasing aversion to these natives. Talk with Mick;‡ congeniality. "Mediterranean" when he sits crouching like Achilles in a drawing by Wyspianski. Greek-Turkish cuisine. [You can] *"smell the bloody hotel two miles away."* Mick's cosmopolitan ideas. *"Bloody German he no finish war."* Mick helps me in my

---

* Moliasi was a chief of secondary rank, ruler of the province of Tilataula and by tradition the enemy and main rival of the head chief, To'uluwa of Kiriwina province. Malinowski described him in *Argonauts of the Western Pacific* as "an old rogue."

† These were three of the villages in southern Boyowa where the women were said to practice an orgiastic form of *kayasa* during the weeding season. Because of the stories, men from other villages would not venture there at that season.

‡ Mick George, a Greek trader long resident in the Trobriands. Malinowski frequently stayed in his home.

ethnographic studies. *"Kayasa all same bloody market."* When I mentioned Ilumedoi and *mulukwausi: "they do not eat the insides, they only smell them."* All in all, we like Mick.—Gray-blue sea; *scirocco*, warm smell of the sea; bare, yellow huts; pink pastel houses on the rocks with faded roof tiles.—Monday evening I finished the novel; talked with Billy; sat for a moment with Ilumedoi and a garrulous female and talked about—? I listened to their chatter but I couldn't make out their language very clearly. (Took 3 calomels and *Epsom salts*.)

Tuesday 11. The [*giyopeulo*] came. I looked at and made drawings of *pwata'i*. Talked with [natives from] Tubowada. Wonderful men—I at once felt the difference in the quality of their information. After breakfast talked with a group of natives from Vakuta about *milamala*—before the [*giyopeulo*] recited his *lili'u* about Tudava.* But collecting information went badly [. . .]. In the afternoon I wrote down the story of Marianna on the veranda. At 5, I took the boat out for a row. After supper talked with the [*giyopeulo's*] sons and was struck by the high quality of their information. Seriously, scrupulously, and logically they explained the nature of *kayasa*, of communal work, and corrected my grammar. Then one of them recited the *Lili'u Dokonikan* better than anyone had done before. I made up my mind to go to Tubowada immediately once I got back from the Amphletts. Chatted a moment with Billy and went to bed.— Things Billy told me: Brudo has no *kaloma;* he went to Samarai, bought a cheap pearl, paid an exorbitant price. Norman Campbell is completely *"broke,"* even his ship was confiscated by Quinn, who had been taken into partnership. *Bill as a buffer: Brudo afraid to leave Kavataria & cannot lie in wait at Boymap'ou.* Camp. doesn't even know how to buy tobacco properly.

* Tudava is the hero of a cycle of stories recounted and analyzed in *Coral Gardens and Their Magic*, Vol. II.

Billy sent him several [*vidu*]; instead of sewing them into a belt, he gave them directly. N. C. is in good spirits, without *rancor*, content so long as he has betel. He drags himself [. . .] from one end of the veranda to the other. His wife steals as much as she can. Fellows remembered him as a *strapping youth, strong and energetic, but sweet.* I am definitely moved. I recall what E. R. M. said about [. . .]: *like a large Scotch terrier.* I thought about his possibilities. I always keep in mind Bill's basic problem: his marriage with Marianna; his love for their children. He treats Marianna as a native, stressing her bronze complexion. Today I thought that this was perhaps very clever on his part, that he expected the worst. At times I try— or rather have a [tendency] to feel in him an echo of my own longing for civilization, for a white woman. I have been trying to find out what brought him here. He was in *railway service; retrenchment; worked on mines with 2 Victorians; touch and go; Broken Hill* [in southwest Australia] *or Charles and Towers; from C.T. comes to N.G. to gold fields, loses 1,600 pounds on store in Yodda Cross South, spends 460. Returns with 140. Sets up this place.* B. H. speaks unfavorably about George Auerbach. Talks about the 60 lb of tobacco that G. A. refused to give him back, assuming that W. H. is in financial difficulties. Also, G. A. is supposed to have said that he would open a *bêche-de-mer* station in Teyava and Tukwa'ukwa to retaliate for Mick's having bought copra at Sinaketa. Billy threatens him with settling in Kanubumekwa.

Wednesday 12. Got up fairly late and began to write my diary when Billy called me. We set out. I felt tired all the time. The camera seemed too heavy. I reproached myself for not having mastered the ethnographic situation and Bill's presence hindered me a little. *After all*, he is not as interested as I am, in fact he thinks all this is rather silly. Once again my propensity for admiring marvelous landscapes (sometimes imaginary) played a trick on me.—E. R. M.'s co-operation in my investigation is not effective at a distance. Rather, I feel that I am playing a false role and that I must write to her that I am *disappointed with myself*. I formulated a letter to her in the afternoon, resting, after taking the *dinghy* out by myself. In Oburaku: we went to the [headman's] house (Towakayse). There we sat in the *bwayma*. Then the roasting of live pigs. Mixed feeling—cruelty and indignation. The carving of the pigs and the anatomical terms. Then we photographed a group with *nose-sticks*, and the *baku* with pigs. I took a *snapshot* of a group of men carving pigs. Then we sat and enjoyed the meal. I walked around the village looking for a place to put up a tent. We ate bananas and drank *coconut* milk. Then *sagali obukubaku*. Vanoikiriwina. I ran into acquaintances: a man from Kudokabilia who used to bring me eggs, dressed in a lady's nightgown. There was no one from Omarakana nor Kasana'i. *Sagali*, and all the villages were mentioned. Feeling of social bond in this act: the whole island as a unit: Kayleula and the other islands were not mentioned, but Kitava and Vakuta were.—Then it began to rain. We sat in the [headman's] *bwayma*. I took pictures of the village as a whole. 2 *canoes*. Billy left. I sat and drew [. . .]. Returned with Togugua in his boat. Sitting in the *dinghy* I enjoyed being alone. Then a dominant feeling of ethnographic disappointment came back. As I rowed I thought of E. R. M., of her enthusiasm about the boats on the Yarra [a river in Melbourne].—Back home, supper with Mick who repeated that Kiriwina had never seen such a *sagali*, and then makes excuses for not having given me tobacco. Dozed in an *armchair* on the veranda. Turned in at 8. —I slept well enough; my dreams took me far away from the Trobriands and ethnography—but where?—Oh yes. Two days ago I began to read *Tess of the d'Urbervilles*. This brings me closer to E. R. M. "*Maiden no more*." Thoughts about the extent of my obligation to her. I see her as my future wife, with a feeling of certainty, confidence, but without excitement. I think of N. S. fairly often. I showed pictures of her to Bill. Sad. I love her like a child, but I have no illusions and I am sure that she would not have been happy with me; and vice versa. A melody from *Samson and Delilah* reminds me of her. The line "Don't go" comes to mind, and I am in an amorous trance. I often long for culture—Paul and Hedy [Khuner] and their *home* (almost brings tears to my eyes); E. R. M. and M. H. W. and that atmosphere. Will those happy days in E. Malvern ever come back?—Beethoven's melodies. I am immensely attached to P. and H.

Thursday 13. Got up around 7, had morning tea; talked with Mick and told him that we'd leave at 11; wrote diary for last days under coconut tree, then went back. Brudo is back, didn't get *vaygu'a*. Br. is a pig. Formerly there were many *traders* here, they would gather evenings, *"playing and whoring."* He told me how exhausted he was; showed me how thin and flabby his body is. He can't even go to *shithouse*. Discussion about the necessity for large *shithouses*. He offered me a dinghy. I got my things together, settled business with Marianna. Felt marvelous physically. *Native canoe*, fills up with water. We moved to the dinghy. Arrival. I chose a place for the *tent*. Bomeran, a policeman, and a couple of *boys* helped me. I watched the *tent* a while and looked at the village a bit. I had the satisfaction of seeing a *tent* built. The pleasure of picnicking. Ilumedoi was there with his brothers and introduced me. I gave them three sticks of tobacco. I ate bananas. Then I drew a plan of the village, one of Ilumedoi's brothers being very helpful. I went back, inspected the tent, and supervised the unpacking. Then took a walk; thought of E. R. M.; reached the water and did Swedish gymnastics. I felt well; although the atmosphere is that of a Turkish bath, I was neither oppressed nor depressed. First Kiriwina walk [. . .]. Spiritual presence of E. R. M. I thought of writing a letter to N. S. to break everything off. I went back —dragging myself. Drank my supper. Then went for an evening *round*. Right next me—at about 6 meters—*iwalamsi*. What I heard was mainly, "*Latuyo, gedugedo bigadaigu*"—a melodious, monotonous chant—must have a narcotic effect on them. Then went to Towakayse. There I had to do a lot of urging before they were willing to talk. I spoke about *poulo;* then two fellows' *kukwanebu*. I was terribly sleepy. Went back, drank coffee. Turned in, but visions of tortoise-shell combs kept me awake. That night, rain. *Bulukwas* walking around my tent.

Friday 14. Rain. Got up at 6:30. I walked around the village, observed groups of natives. Went back; drank my breakfast; chatted on the veranda with the policemen and a few natives. Then to my *tent;* a few specific tasks: to correct the plan of the village, to copy the ethnographic diary; I did some of this but, though I felt well physically, resistance: the work did not interest me. Moreover, there was a torrential downpour; water leaked through the tent, made rivers. Also Pilapala was carrying on, and all this got on my nerves. At 12 natives came from Vilay-lima and Osapola. We talked about crabs, etc. This interview bored me, and did not go well. At 2 I ordered lunch—eggs and cocoa. I thought of Paul, and E. R. M. I thought of civilization with a *pang;* I rowed the Yarra as I read the newspapers, details about Melbourne. The house in Malvern seems now like paradise on earth. Throughout the time I was with them, I was doubtless happy (except for moods à la Dostoevsky and illness), particularly at the end when I wanted so much to stay in Melbourne until April. The war will surely end, and the idyl in Melbourne will be broken up; regrets and remorse.—In the afternoon I rested; walked around the village—preparations for *mona.* At 4:30 I watched the cooking of taro. Dropped dumplings; *excitement; buoysila urgowa.* I went from [pot] to [pot]. The excitement and the *buoysila urgowa* fascinated me. Walking and standing tired me, "I was dropping from exhaustion." *Sagali* in [Kaytabu]. I sat in the *bwayma* of a young woman of Sinaketa.—Went back to [Yasitine]. Dusk. Grayness. Dark-blue damp smoke rose among the palms, the gray, brown, or ocher houses took on warm tones. Enveloped in darkness the village seems smaller, more huddled, looms up out of the surrounding void. I lay for a while in my *tent.* Rowing in the dinghy, I was not without fears: that I might not find the village, that I'd run aground, that "something" was crawling out of the darkness. E. R. M. would like to see me now. When I look at women I think of their breasts and figure *in terms of* E. R. M. Went back, ate a very frugal supper, and lying on my bed talked with a policeman from Vakuta and a native in a yellow *lava lava* about various things (*poulo, tova'u*), also about Doketa and Gabena. He knew [Giblen], Subeta, and [Arse]. I slept well, though afraid that I'd feel rotten (afternoon skept. reaction?). Took cathartic comp.

Saturday 15. At about 6 in the morning, a deafening *walamsi* in two voices (Ginger says they don't howl so continuously at Sariba). I got up. At 6:30 the boats left. I went to shit in the mangroves; the only occasion when I am in contact with nature! . . . Big trees, hard shiny leaves, deep shadows on the ground covered with decaying leaves. I felt fine physically and this kept up the whole day. After breakfast (tea and biscuits) *v[illage]* census from 9 to 11, then I went back and made a new drawing of the village. Census: I sit on a chair, which the *gwadi* carry around the village. The *gwadi* also give the names of the inhabitants. Some they name despite mourning, but if it is *kala koulo kwaiwa'u,* they do not say the names. At 12 I went out in the *dinghy;* my tent was cold, it was hot in the sun. I rowed near the mangroves. Feeling strong and healthy. At 12:45, [Galuluva] and bread from Mick. I taught Ginger (yelling and swearing) how to fry. I ate an omelet made with lard. I lay down (am not reading novels). At 3:30 I began to work on genealogies [on the basis of the census data]. To'uluwa came, preceded by N. G.* Gave him tobacco. I asked him about his friends. Gilayviyaka died. Others came—Kalumwaywo,† [Micaidaili, Oricapa]. The last mentioned seems to have the most "human" manners. At all events, he is extremely pleasant, he has a fine mouth and beautiful eyes, a very modest expression. He is *the first gentleman of Kiriwina.* To'uluwa came. We greet each other as friends. He spoke about me and praised me. Despite everything there is a certain residue of sympathy. He stood over me with a half-ironical, half-indulgent smile, telling about my exploits. Joke about our *kula.‡* Then, in the tent, Dipapa, Kenoria.§ I went alone to Wawela. It was sultry, but I was energetic. The wilderness fascinated me. [. . .]; *giyovila;* Kenoria is pretty, has a wonderful figure. Impulse to "pat her on the belly." I mastered it. In the evening I rowed again, went to bed early.

Sunday 16. Slept late. *Taparoro* [*tapwaropo?*] (very short) near my tent, Tomwaya Lakwabulo‖ and a few other natives.

---

* Namwana Guya'u, the eldest son of To'uluwa and his favorite, one of the leading figures in Omarakana. Though he had been banished to another village, he often paid visits to attend his father.

† Kalumwaywo, mentioned in *Coral Gardens* as a strong and efficient gardener.

‡ During his previous stay in the Trobriands, Malinowski had persuaded To'uluwa to take him on a *kula* expedition to Kitava Island. The wind changed in mid-voyage and the canoes had to turn back. Malinowski felt that To'uluwa thought his presence had brought bad luck.

§ Son and daughter of To'uluwa.

‖ Tomwaya Lakwabulo, "the Seer," was one of Malinowski's major informants (see *The Sexual Life of Savages*).

154

Fairly good information about *poulo*. Before lunch rowed a awhile. After lunch at 2, census of the village. About 5, exhaustion (nervous)—could barely move. I went to Kiribwa (*tomakava* and *yamataulobwala*). Mick complained, very pessimistic. A desolate house, a lonely little ship—very sad. Books from E. R. M. I read some pieces by Stevenson. Rowed back all the way. Talked with a fellow about *poulo*, the plan for *mona* around here. I rowed energetically, and felt fine (I had eaten a marvelous loin of pork at Kiribwa). At about 8 drank *lemonade* and went to *Kway[utili]*. *Bwaga'u row*. I sat; the men told me about *katoulo*, *silami*, etc. *Village policeman* is very good informant. Went back to my tent at 10, washed my hair. Slept well.

12.17.17. Up at 6:30. Walked around the village. I sat listening to a *walam*, and talked with an old man in [Wakayse.] Then back to tent via Okinai, Oloolam (I tried to buy 2 *lagim*) *Vayoulo* was brought. Tomwaya Lakwabulo was carted in. T. L. gave me a *vocabulary* of the Tuma* language. Very guttural. Then *baloma*. Then Namwana Guya'u came back. I took out the *dinghy* as usual. After lunch I [carried] yellow calico and spoke about the *baloma*. I made a small *sagali*, Navavile.† I was *fed up* with the *niggers*‡ and with my work. I walked alone through the *raybwag*. Water. I felt strong and energetic. *I waded through* but the mud stopped me. During the walk the physical effort absorbed me, and I didn't think much. The

* Tuma, an island northwest of Boyowa, was also the spirit land, where the spirits of the dead dwelt.
† Navavile, an important informant from Oburaku.
‡ Webster's New International Dictionary, Second Edition, gives as the second meaning of this term: "Improperly or loosely, a member of any very dark-skinned race, as an East Indian, a Filipino, an Egyptian." It was the colloquial term commonly used by Europeans, at the time Malinowski was writing, to denote native peoples, many of whom, like the Melanesians, were, of course, not Negroes.

tropics have completely lost their extraordinary character for me; I cannot believe that I could feel better anywhere else. *Dinghy;* I felt so energetic that after coming back once I took it out again. Then stewed bananas (wonderful invention). Walked over to see Navavile. By then I was tired. At night, storm, but once again fell asleep quickly.—Rheumatic pains in knee almost gone without a trace—sometimes I feel I have a right leg.

12.18.18. [*sic*]. Got up at 7. Cold wind—I put on an extra shirt and underdrawers (t = 24.5° [about 76° F.]). Chalcedony-colored sky with patches of tea-rose; sea of the same color, with green reflections.—In the morning I reread a few pages of this diary, and I thought of E. R. M., P. & H., and Mim. I resolved: to bring order into my notes and to improve my system. Yesterday while walking I thought about the "preface" to my book: Jan Kubary* as a concrete methodologist. Mikluho-Maclay† as a new type. Marett's‡ comparison: *early ethnographers as prospectors.* I thought about my present attitude toward ethnogr. work and the natives. My dislike of them, my longing for civilization.—After breakfast, I looked over my notes, annotated and organized them. It didn't go too well, I was stale and slightly foggy. Occasionally I slowed down. Ideal P. J. Black (aped by Greenwood?) with stony slowness and phlegmatic ways. At 12, when the sun emerged I went out in the boat. My headache and sluggishness were dispelled by *exercise.* Had some general ideas (jotted them down in the back of the book) about sociology, Rivers, etc. After lunch (fried fish—my own culinary invention) jotted down my ideas, at about 3 went to [Tub-

---

* J. S. Kubary, author of *Ethnographische Beiträge zur Kenntnis des Karolinen Archipels.*

† Baron Nicolai Mikluho-Maclay, Russian explorer and ethnologist who made several expeditions to New Guinea, the Malay Peninsula, and the Philippines during the 1870's and 1880's.

‡ R. R. Marett, English anthropologist (1866-1943).

waba] and made a genealogical census (not amusing!), then with the policeman to Lubwoila (*sapi*)—I was tired, but I walked briskly and felt better. Then took out the boat. In the middle, I stopped, listened, heard rustlings at the bottom of the boat—*funk*. It got dark; I thought of N. S. and about the letter I *must** write her. It was dark—clouds with dirty-bronze reflections, sheets of rain over the sea. In the west *pilapala* rumbling and *kavikavila* flickered. Sadness. I thought of E. R. M. —if she were here, would I be freed of my longings and my melancholy? Exhaustion. I lay down. Natives came, Kadilakula and Nayowa, and others. I talked about *poulo, wasi, gimwali*, etc. Went to sleep very late; read Stevenson's letters.

12.19.17. Got up at 7. Yesterday, under the mosquito net, dirty thoughts: Mrs. [H. P.]; Mrs. C. and even Mrs. W. . . . I thought that even if E. R. M. had been here, this would not have satisfied me. Dirty thoughts about C. R. The doctrine of this man [Ceran] that you're doing a woman a favor if you deflower her. (Solomon Hirschband). I even thought of seducing M. Shook all this off. . . . Today got up at 7— sluggish; I lay under the mosquito net and wanted to read a book instead of working. I got up and made the *rounds* of the village. Breakfast. *Gimwali*. I resolved absolutely to avoid all lecherous thoughts, and in my work to finish the census, if possible, today. At about 9 I went to Kaytabu where I took the census with a bearded old man. Monotonous, stupid work, but indispensable. Toward the end I was exhausted, panting for breath. Then took out the *dinghy*. For lunch—*crab* with cucumbers. What I eat at present: morning, cocoa; lunch relatively varied, and almost always *fresh food*. Supper very light, banana compote, *momyapu;* once I ate a lot of fish and felt no ill effects. Tendency to constipation (iodine or arsenic?). In the

---

* Underlined in original.

afternoon (it took me 2 hrs. to eat the *crab!*), at 3, census in the *obukubaku*. At five went to Wawela with a young fellow from Kaytabu (Mwanusa) and Morovato.* I did not feel too buoyant and feared that the walk would tire me. But not at all; when I saw the sea I cried with joy: transparent water with a dark steely sheen in the distance and a line of black and white breakers—*gaping black when they vault and then white with foam*— this created a kind of background of holiday spirits, which I miss here on the lagoon. A coconut grove, the gently curving bay with its green vegetation, which rises like an amphitheater above the sandy beach. The coast stretches on into the distance toward Vakuta, pandanus trees with broad leaves along the shore. We went in the boat. I thought of E. R. M. I feel a mystical link between her and this view, particularly because of the line of breaking waves. I am happy at the thought that I'll live here.

Broad street in Wawela. Kovala Koya right in front of me. I walked across, chose a site for my *tent*—right beyond the village, under palm trees. I'll need to *babayva* a piece of *odila*. Two or three abandoned *obukubaki*. This rundown village presents a sad sight. A Kitavan hut. Naguayluva, living in an isolated hut. At night, a little tired, but not exhausted, I sang, to a Wagner melody, the words "Kiss my ass" to chase away *mulukwausi*. I tried to separate from my companions but they were apparently nervous, and the road was bad, too. Tomakapu didn't wait, but went straight to the village. Trick for chasing away *fireflies* (the *fireflies* in the *raybwag* are magnificent). Almost fell into the water, but a *black* helped me across. Storm was gathering. Noise of rain and wind. Marvelous sheet of rain hanging over the sea *like a curtain*, coming closer. (Yesterday while rowing I thought of E. R. M. and our sociological plans; I thought that I would not have the right to compel her to stay with me, since our roles are reversed: my sacrifice is that usually made by the

* Morovato, a reliable informant cited in *The Sexual Life of Savages*.

woman, and hers that by the man, for it is she who is exposing herself to danger.) Yesterday, returning from Wawela I had some ethnological ideas, but I cannot remember what they were.[*] They had a bearing on the general theoretical "sauce" in which my concrete observations are to be dressed up. At about 9 I withdrew under the mosquito net and chatted a while with Niyova.[†] I fell asleep with some difficulty.

[*] *Naturmythus, Naturkontakt, Naturvölker* [religion of nature, contact with nature, primitive peoples]. [Malinowski's footnote.]

Thursday, 12.20. I got up at 6 (awoke at 5:30). I didn't feel very buoyant. Made the *rounds* of the village. Tomakapu gave me explanations concerning the sacred grove near his house. It had been raining all night; mud. Everybody was in the village. The *policeman* joined me at 9, I set to work with him. At 10:30 they decided to go for a *poulo* and I set out with them. *Megwa* in the house of Yosala Gawa. I felt again the joy of being with real *Naturmenschen*. Rode in a boat. Many observations. I learn a great deal. General *Stimmung* [atmosphere], style, in which I observe tabu. Technology of the hunt, which would have required weeks of research. Opened-up horizons filled me with joy. We made a *cruise around this part of the lagoon*—as far as Kiribi, and then to Boymapo'u. Extraordinary sight of fishes darting through the air, jumping into nets. I rowed with them. I removed my shirt and had a kind of sun bath. The water attracted me, I wanted to bathe, but somehow I did not—why? Because of my lack of energy and initiative, which had done me so much harm. Then, this began to weary me; hunger. The charm of open expanses gave way to feeling of absolute emptiness. We returned [by way of] Kaytuvi and Kwabulo; [Towoma Katabayluve] at the mouth of the *waya.*—A boat from Billy with [my

[†] Niyova, a native of Oburaku whom Malinowski thought a sound informant.

shoes and billycans]. I went back, had lunch (at 3 or 4!). Then, around 5, I went to Tudaga where I took a census. I came back; the sunset was a blazing brick color. Some *natives* observed a *Tumadawa* fish and 12 or 13 boats set out in pursuit of it. I tried to catch up with them, but I felt a bit tired. I put down my oars, and I thought of N. S., and of South Australia. S. A. is to me one of the most charming parts of the world. The intense feelings I had going back there last time. N. S. and my love affair with her is the soul of this paradise. Now, with N. S. lost, the paradise too is lost. I don't want to go back there, ever. I thought about all this and composed a letter to her in my mind. I don't want to lose her friendship.—Beyond doubt, my love for her was one of the purest, most romantic things in my life. Friendship for her? If she were healthy, strong? *No**—her way of taking life would be impossible for me. Entirely impossible. We would have talked to each other as though shouting from different rooms. And yet I feel regrets. If I could cancel it all out, and never possess her soul? This fatal urge to get to the bottom, to achieve absolute spiritual mastery. I certainly sinned against her, I heartlessly sacrificed her to a more secure relationship.—I felt poorly when I returned. Drank tea only. I chatted a bit, but without any specific aim. Enema. . . . Slept well.

Friday, 12.21. Awoke late, at 7. Dreams in which S. I. W. [Stanislaw Ignacy ("Staś") Witkiewicz] and old W. [Staś's father] are mixed up. Also, Judge Herbert, and others.—Rain; violent shit near the graves. I resolved never again to take cathartics compound!—Laziness: I'd like to break the monotony, to *"take a day off."* This is one of my worst tendencies! But I shall do the opposite: finish some routine tasks, "the ethnographic diary," rewrite my census notes and yesterday's

---

* Underlined in original.

impressions. This morning I felt poorly; my hands were numb
(= tired heart); fogginess; general weakness, "touching bottom
in the stream of vitality."—I thought of E. R. M., about a letter
to her.—After breakfast, Tomwaya Lakwabulo, his little stories
about the other world. The *baloma* language. When I ask him a
question, there is a short pause before he answers, and *a shifty
look in his eyes*. He reminds me a little of Sir Oliver Lodge.—
Then I wrote down my impressions of yesterday's expedition.
Then to Walasi, where I took a census. . . . I was very tired;
after lunch (fish and taro) went to bed. Woke up around 4 very
tired. I thought of a passage from [R. L.] Stevenson's letters in
which he speaks of a heroic struggle against illness and exhaustion.—Then in a boat to Kwabulo. I asked questions concerning
the names of the trees and the lagoon and decided to study the
language systematically, compiling a *vocabulary*. *Waya* Kwabulo—a shaded narrow streamlet between groups of mangroves.
In Kwabulo—afternoon atmosphere—the cool dusk on the black
earth and golden-green gleams [. . .]. Inspected Inuvayla'u's
kwila.* Bought bananas, *momyapus*, one stone. Return. Intense
glow in the west—golden red, surrounded by the monotonous
liquid blue of sky and sea. I planned to make a drawing of the
clouds for E. R. M., and other drawings for her—in addition to
the silhouette of the mountains I sketched aboard the "Itaka."
I was again alone—emptiness of moonlit night on the lagoon. I
rowed vigorously and thought about—? Came back very tired.
Drank tea and went to bed, without eating anything, after a talk
with Morovato Kariwabu, about fishing, the names of trees, etc.
—All that day longing for civilization. I thought about friends
in Melbourne. At night in the *dinghy*, pleasantly ambitious
thought: I'll surely be "an eminent Polish scholar." This will be

* Stone landmarks associated with the legend of Inuvayla'u, told in *The
Sexual Life of Savages*.

my last ethnological escapade. After that, I'll devote myself to
constructive sociology: methodology, political economy, etc.,
and in Poland I can realize my ambitions better than anywhere
else.—Strong contrast between my dreams of a civilized life and
my life with the savages. I resolve to eliminate the elements
(components) of laziness and sloth from my present life. Don't
read novels unless this is necessary. Try *not** to forget creative
ideas.

Saturday, 12.22. Woke up very late (slept badly, 3 gr. of calomel the night before). Under the mosquito net I thought about
relation between the historical *point of view* ([. . .] causality
as in respect of *extraordinary*, singular things) and the sociological point of view (in respect of normal course of things, the
sociological *law* in the sense of the laws of physics, chemistry).
"Historicists" à la Rivers = investigate geology and geological
"history," ignoring the laws of physics and chemistry. The
physics and chemistry of history and ethnography = social
psychology. Sociological mechanics and chemistry = the individual soul in relation to collective creations.—In the morning I
walked to *sopi* and thought about language as a product of collective psychology. As a *"system of social ideas."* Language is
an objective creation, and as such it corresponds to the *institution* in the equation: social imagination = institution + individual ideas. On the other hand, language is an instrument, a
vehicle for individual ideas, and as such it must be considered
first when I study the other component of the equation. Then I
worked on fishing terms (mainly [with Morovato, Yosala Gawa,
Kariwabu, and Toyodala). I *overhauled* the sketch I had written
spontaneously. Results satisfactory. Slept after lunch. Also before lunch—on the whole I did not feel too strong, but better

* Underlined in original.

than on Friday. On Friday I had Stevenson-type reactions. On
Saturday, after taking 10 gr. of quinine, 3 gr. of calomel and
Epsom salts, I felt fairly well, but exhausted. At 4 I decided to
go to Kiribwa; I engaged Morovato and [Weirove]; brief census
at Oloolam; we set out at 5, I rowed *a good deal.* Mick much
better; we talked about his condition, and ate scorched soup of
[*kwabu*]. Sunset in a gamut of scarlets and ochers. We came
back by moonlight. Discussed the geography of the lagoon with
Morovato. I rowed vigorously. Gorged myself with bananas and
rice. I am quite drowsy, get under the mosquito net. *"Subver-
sive"* thoughts—I resolved to control them. But [gone] too
far. Slept very badly. Weak heart, numb hands.

Sunday, 12.23. Day set aside for writing Christmas letters. In
the morning diarrhea. Then straight back to the *tent.* Read
Stevenson a little. Under the mosquito net wrote the easiest and
the most trivial letters—Dim Dim, Bruno, etc.— At about 12
watched making of *Saipwana* in the village. Then came back,
slept, wrote more letters. Very tired, I lay down and dozed,
woke up still tired but stronger. *Crab* with cucumbers. Then
a short rest. The *niggers* were noisy—everybody idle because
it was Sunday. I wrote to P. & H., began a letter to E. R. M.,
planned a letter to N. S.—At about 6, on the lagoon. Marvelously translucent evening. Children sail in a boat and sing.
I am full of yearnings and think about Melbourne (?). Some
worries about E. R. M.—when I realize what threatens her I am
drenched in cold sweat. I think of how much she has suffered,
waiting for news of C. E. M.—At moments I lose sight of her.
Sensually, she has not succeeded in subjugating me. I rowed as
far as Kaytuvi, returned by moonlight; lost in reverie, clouds,
water. General aversion for *niggers,* for the monotony—feel
imprisoned. [Prospect of] tomorrow's walk to Billy and visit
to Gusaweta not too pleasant. In the evening *kayaku* and lin-

guistic terms—all around, singing (obscene song from Okay-koda) Fell asleep quickly around 10.

Monday 24. Got up at 7, walked around the village. *Kumaidona tomuota bilousi wapoulo* [everyone has gone fishing]. This annoyed me a little. *Kilesi Imkuba ivita vatusi Saipwana.* I decided to take pictures. I blundered with the camera, at about 10 —spoiled something, spoiled one roll of film. Rage and mortification. *Up against fate. After all it will probably do its work.* Photographed females. Returned in a state of irritation. Nevertheless I wrote E. R. M. Am hoping to get letter from her. Gradually she came back to me. I began to "feel her" again. Lunch (still irritated, gave my order to Ginger with tears in my voice). Then I wrote some more, rather an effort, but I felt there were many things I should tell her. At 4:30 Wilkes and Izod appeared on the horizon. I was decidedly displeased, they bothered me. *In fact,* they spoiled my afternoon walk. I showed them Inuvayla'u's *kwila* in Kwabulo. What is terrible is that I am unable to free myself completely from the atmosphere created by *foreign bodies:* their presence takes away from the scientific value and personal pleasure of my walk. I saw and felt the utter drabness of the Kiriwina villages; I saw them through their eyes (it's fine to have this ability), but I forgot to look at them with my own.—The conversation: criticizing the government, especially Murray. The poetic trip through the mangroves spoiled by the chatter. Wilkes likes to tell stories. An obtuse egoist underneath his shell of refinement. Izod quite pleasant. Priest hasn't arrived yet; probably drinking with the Auerbachs. —Talk with Billy about photographs, a bottle of *whiskey.—* Mick spoke about his *countrymen.* Went to bed at 10. Intense, deeply emotional thoughts (sensuality of the most refined kind) about E. R. M. Feeling that I'd like to have her as my wife and the idea of having sensual pleasure with other women has *quelque*

TUMA I.

OPEN SEA
(WALUM)

KIRIWINA

Kaybola • • M'tava
Kudokabilia • • Liluta
Tubowada • • Omarakana • Kwaybwaga
Kabululo • ⊙ • Tilakaywa
TILATAULA Kabwaku ⊙ • Wakayse • Yourawotu
Okaykoda • Kaulagu
Obowada
Obweria

8°30'S   8°30'S

Kaduwaga •   Lobu'a • Kela
                KUBOMA • Kudukway • Kapwapu
KAYLEULA I.   Gusaweta   ⊙ Olivilevi
        Bwoytalu • Teyava • Tukwa'ukwa
        Osaysaya • • Vilaylima
Wabutuma •   Kavateria • Osapola
                KULUMATA • LUBA • Dubwaga
        BOYMAPO'U I.   • Kwabulo
MANUWATA I.   • Oburaku
                                Wawela
KUYAWA I.
                        BOYOWA I.   KITAVA I.
        NUBIYAM I.   Kudayuri •
                                                Kumwageya •
        TROBRIAND LAGOON   Kaulasi •
        (WADOM)   Sinaketa •
                                • Bwadela
                                Louya •
                                        • Kumilabwaga
                        KAYBWAGINA
        MUWA I.
YAGA I.   • Okayaulo

                        Susuwa Beach
                NANOULA I.   Giribwa
                                        • Giribwa Pt.
                        Giribwa Str.
                                        Osikwey • • Okina'i
                                        VAKUTA I. ⊙ Vakuta
                                                • Kaulaka

TROBRIAND ISLANDS
                        SEA ARM OF PILOLU
        Scale of Miles
0   5   10

151°E

chose de funeste. I thought about our moments together, and how I never obtained the true reward which the very fact of possessing her must give me. I missed her—I wanted to have her near me again. Visions of her with her hair down. Does intense longing always lead to extremes? Perhaps only under mosquito netting.—Woke up at night, full of lecherous thoughts about, *of all the people imaginable,* my landlord's wife! This must stop! That I am not absolutely sure that I might not seduce my best friend's wife, that after such a strong surge of longing for E. R. M., that this could happen—*c'est un peu trop!* This has got to stop once and for all.—Yesterday I felt fine during the day. Completely forgot it was Christmas Eve. But just now, this very morning, when I couldn't sleep, Mother was thinking of me and was missing me. My God, my God, how terrible it is to live in a continuous ethical conflict. My failure to think seriously about Mother, Staś, Poland—about their sufferings there and about Poland's ordeal—is disgusting!

Tuesday 25. I crawled out from under my mosquito net before sunrise. Billy, bath, talk about Ted: Ted had gone to Gilmour* and told him, "*I have the clap.*" "*What is clap?*" "*Bloody pocks.*" Gilmour gave him some medicines.—Ted spent on drink the £80 Murphy had loaned George and lied to George that he would pay him back. Ted has pustules on his penis. Bill asked where—"*on the bloody cock.*"—After breakfast I sat under a tree and wrote a letter to E. R. M. Ogisa kept chasing the flies. I felt immensely closer to her; the letter was easier to write. Entirely different feelings. Then I moved on nearer to the house and went on writing. Lunch with Mick. The fools came back with Bill. At 3 I went back to my letter. At 5 I dressed and

---

* Rev. M. K. Gilmour, then at the nearby Methodist mission at Oiabia. In *Argonauts* Malinowski says that he was "fully acquainted with the facts of the *kula*."

went to Olivilevi via Tukwa'ukwa. I felt fairly well, but sweated profusely. Dinner. Ride in a *dinghy* with Ginger and Gomera'u. The latter gave me valuable information about *bwaga'u* and Ta'ukuripokapoka.*—Violent aversion to listening to him; I simply rejected inwardly all the marvelous things he had to tell me. The main ethnographic difficulty is to overcome this. I drank claret. Talked with Billy Priest who vociferated against his *boss*. I retired under my mosquito net and turned my thoughts again to E. R. M.

12.26. In the morning mad *scramble* with letters. Difficulties in writing to N. S. Official letters concerning extension of leave. After lunch, talk with Wilkes, who turns out to be an amateur of colored women and says that some districts in Nigeria are *"very bad."* His admiration for Conrad mortified me. After they were gone I looked at *war pictures* for half an hour, and then began to look over my own things. Unpacked *foodstuffs* and got it all sorted out with Ginger's help. This will enable me to figure out what and how I should eat, etc. Then in a *dinghy* on the *creek* with E. R. M.'s spirit. I was very energetic, and felt in good shape (I had relaxed—my ethnographic work is† hard). In the evening talked about pearls with Bill. He told me about deals between Stone and [Graham], and about Verrebely who was offended because George Auerbach had learned that V. *came up £100 on his original price.*

12.27. Got up fairly late. Planned to go over my papers and begin work. But the packing took a long time. After lunch I again rummaged in my things. At about 4 went with Bill to Mission Station. There, Taylor—young, handsome, pleasant—

---

* A mythological being and an expert in evil. The witches are said to meet him at night for dancing and orgies.
† Underlined in original.

and Brudo, very friendly and polite. Return with Bill. Depressed by what I have seen in Losuya: rotten people and life [. . .]. I shudder at the thought of how life looks from their point of view. Campbell, Symons. [. . .] £1.1.—stupid, unpleasant jokes about my *Austrian nationality.*—Loathsome, and the effect is depressing. These fellows have such fabulous *opportunities*—the sea, ships, the *jungle,* power over the natives—and don't do a thing! Supper with Bill. Bootlicking letter to Symons. At 8:30 went to Oburaku. At first I felt *out of sorts,* and if I hadn't been convinced that a walk would do me good, my nervous state would probably have resulted in total exhaustion. Between Olivilevi and Vilaylima I was very energetic; then somewhat tired, but not too much. A shallow lagoon; an amusing fellow from Osaysaya carried me, the dark bare earth with mangrove roots like a section of vegetation. Fish leaping all around. Thoughts, feeling, and moods: no interest in ethnology. In the morning when I had packed up and was wandering around Gusaweta, constant longing for E. R. M. (The previous evening, violent surge of longing when I looked at her photos.) Strong feeling of her personality; she is my wife *de facto* and I should think of her as my wife. As for ethnology: I see the life of the natives as utterly devoid of interest or importance, something as remote from me as the life of a dog. During the walk, I made it a point of honor to think about what I am here to do. About the need to collect many documents. I have a general idea about their life and some acquaintance with their language, and if I can only somehow "document" all this, I'll have valuable material.—Must concentrate on my ambitions and work to some purpose. Must organize the linguistic material and collect documents, find better ways of studying the life of women, *gugu'a,* and system of "social representations." Strong spiritual impulse. I looked through my books and took Rivers, German books, poems; outside of my work, I must lead an intellectual life, and live in seclusion, with E. R. M. for my *companion*. I visualize the happiness of possessing her so intensely that I am seized with polycratic fear lest something so perfect actually come true.—Nonetheless, knowing that she loves me, is thinking of me, that everything I feel for her is reciprocated, I am happy.

12.28. When I got back to my tent, at 12:30, I found Ogisa, Tomakapu and the boys asleep. Ginger made my bed, I drank 2 *bwaybways* and, tired, turned in. Slept a long time, until 10:30. Got up. Great longing for E. R. M.—I read her letters. Disorganization in my work. No desire to do anything. I decided to review *census* and to take up linguistics, to devote ½ hour daily to study of language. All preparations completed by 12:30. Classified notes on village *census* (results very poor). Lunch at 2. Read Swinburne (restlessness). Then again v[illage] c[ensus] (I felt weak, exhausted, my brain didn't function properly). Then disorganization; I read Swinburne, *Villette*. Wrote letters to E. R. M. (great longing). (Angry with Ginger.) Strong feeling of the importance of my relationship with E. R. M. Took out the *dinghy*. I thought little, but tried to *steel my thoughts for work*. Return. After supper, Gomera'u and Ginger.—Evaluation of that day: I was doubtless tired by my walk the day before. Laziness, sluggishness. No strength when I took the boat out. Effect of giving up tobacco and of small amounts of alcohol?—*Weltschmerz* moods but with a distinct focusing on E. R. M. Except for low output, nothing to reproach myself with.

12.29. Slept until 9. Eyes tired (field of vision like a screen). Got up at once. Cold, gray day, sky and sea diluted Saxe blue. Put drops in my eyes. Tendency to think of E. R. M., desire to write her and to reread her letters. Gomera'u was waiting—I set to

work with him. Long morning session; Toyodala* related a
lili'u. Continued in the afternoon; at 5 went to Kiribi with Gomera'u. I did a lot of the rowing. Billy, Mick, the "Kayona" to
leave tomorrow. Wrote letters to E. R. M., Smith, Mrs. Gofton,
and Aumüller.—I was tired (eyes, and nerves), and turned in.
All day long constantly thought about E. R. M., sharing my
plans with her, thinking of her with tenderness, deep friendship,
and passion.

12.30. Got up at 6, at daybreak (had taken calomel the night
before), and finished letter to E. R. M. (read her letters with an
entirely different feeling, intenser than before); at 9 I sent
Ginger out (the one-legged [Medo'u] *funks* Samarai). Edited
the *lili'u* I had taken down the day before (rainy day). After
lunch I went to the *poulo*, took pictures; then along the creek
to Kaytuvi—mangroves, gay, cheerful impression. (Contrast:
mangroves at low tide really a monstrous swamp; at high tide,
they are smiling at life.) In the evening saw Yosala Gawa;
talked about *kula*, about Kudayuri† (an old man, but he recited
a *lili'u*).—The story made me very sleepy. Back, annoyed by
Ogisa's stupidity. Under the mosquito net, I thought of E. R. M.
affectionately and passionately.

12.31.17. Last day of this year—a year that may turn out to be
immensely important in my life if E. R. M. becomes my wife. In
the morning, under the mosquito net, thought very intensely
about E. R. M.—At 8:30 everybody left for the *poulo*. I walked
around the village, getting informants together. A very poor
group (Narubutau, Niyova, [Taburabi, Bobau]), the two last

* Toyodala, an important informant in Oburaku (see *The Sexual Life of
Savages*).

† Kudayuri, a village of Kitava Island. The myth of the Flying Canoe of
Kudayuri is told in *Argonauts of the Western Pacific*.

mentioned old men about the best.—Despair and impatience. But I kept my temper and struggled on. After lunch—around 1, everybody back. Yosala Gawa and Toyodala; I copied the *megwa* and began to translate. At 5 tired; I did a bit of linguistics; seized with violent longing for E. R. M. Last day of 1917. Sea slightly choppy; mysterious, disquieting, drifting light and shadow alternate continually, coming and going. The sky clear overhead, on the horizon the golden glow of sunset between flaky clouds; between the sea and the sky, the black belt of mangroves. At first, thought about Baldwin and prepared retaliation (I'll present the collection and reproach him with the promise he did not keep). Then thought of E. R. M. "What is she doing?— and what if—she is not there?" Horrible feeling. I thought of her and of C. E. M. About the war. I also had some constructive thoughts about grammar. I went back. Navavile gave me *megwa* (very good). Wrote letter to E. R. M. All I have felt and planned to say vanishes when I stare at the blank sheet of paper. The lagoon calm as a mirror, drenched with the light of the rising moon; palms bending over the water. I was feeling very well physically, as though the tropics don't bother me at all; I long for E. R. M. rather than for civilization.

1.1.18. Awoke at 7. The air was pure, slightly colored, a warm pink tone [. . .]. Mangroves clearly outlined, with soft bunches of green vegetation and patchy shadows. I was awakened by the cries of natives leaving [. . .] for Oiabia [a Methodist mission near Losuya]. I got up, thinking of the New Year—my heart tightened—*17*, symbol of a period, symbol of how numbers implacably impose themselves upon life itself. Thought about E. R. M. Wrote diary. I had some essential thoughts about keeping a diary and adding depth to my life. . . . Ideas about the historical value of the diary. I concentrated, felt fine. Worked on linguistics, with good results. Then the *balomas*. Tired—

from quarter to one—napped for ½ an hour. Then superintended grilling of chop (*damned hard*), then *kayaku*, talk about the *balomas*. At 5 *bum off*; shaved, collected my things and rowed to Bill's place. The stars sparkled (after a blazing sunset)—I rowed vigorously, thinking about linguistics. Also about the stars, and spoke to the stars about E. R. M.—Billy, tea. Told me about Oiabia; Brudo with wife and children, Thursday Islanders who danced afterward. He told me that Geo. Auerbach wants to buy up Harrison's *trading site* in Vakuta. He spoke about "*jumping a claim on the gold fields*" and "*tin-drumming.*" Then I questioned him about ethnographic material—about menstruation, conception, birth. We sat around a while, and I went to bed at 12. Mick coughed horribly; then a child squealed.—Rotten night.

1.2.18. Felt fine, in spite of it. Got out at 7 from under the *tainamo*. Typical *Stimmung* of Bill's house. Went to the *small house*. I had my tea at a table which Bill's children had messed up horribly. Then began to take pictures. Fellows from Omarakana. Bill and I went to Teyava. Returned; lunch; then back again. Used up 6 rolls of film. Although it was hot, I was quite energetic, and on coming back I would have occupied myself with the language if I had had the time. Worked on my photographs. After supper, collected my things (injection of streptococci); ate too much, but I rowed all the way and was back in 1 hour and 45 min. Tea with a drop of brandy, talk with a few savages—at 11 went to bed, thinking of E. R. M.

Introspection: I realize once again how materialistic my sense reactions are: my desire for the bottle of *ginger beer* is acutely tempting; the concealed eagerness with which I fetch a bottle of brandy and am waiting for the bottles from Samarai; and finally I succumb to the temptation of smoking again. There is nothing really bad in all this. Sensual enjoyment of the world

is merely a lower form of artistic enjoyment. What is important
is to be quite clear in one's mind about it, and not to let it
interfere with essential things. (Remember how you over-
indulged when you stayed with the Khuners.) On the other hand
I am perfectly capable of an all but ascetic life. The main thing
is that it should *not matter*.

1.3.18. Morning—the same *Stimmung* on the lagoon. Blue sky
with warm pink tones, little violet clouds. The lagoon smooth,
disturbed only by changing reflections of the clouds. As usual,
under the mosquito net, I try to collect myself and get ready to
work. I am trying to "deepen" my diary, I have been doing it
almost every day, but so far my diary hasn't gone very deep!—
At 7 I got out from under the mosquito net. Diary, breakfast,
looked over my papers. T. L. [Tomwaya Lakwabula] near my
tent. At 10 began to work (*baloma*, reincarnation, conception).
At about 12:30, very tired, took a nap. At 1:30 got up and
superintended *bulukwa*, which was very tasty. At 3 I went back
to work, but I was tired and sluggish. At 4, Reuma, prelimi-
naries of the *kula*, and testing (*échantillons* [samples of]),
mwasila. At 5 very tired (down to the bottom of consciousness,
intellectual fluid all *dried up*); I lay down; "Tiresias" by Swinburne. Wrote to E. R. M.—At 6 took out the *dinghy*. Undressed down to my truss; fragment of associations: thought
of marriage to E. R. M. B. Sp. is also cool toward her—will he
break with her? Lady Sp.—what attitude will she take? I
thought with indignation of her anti-Austrian-Polish attitude—
I made up a long speech pointing out the ignominy of such an
attitude. *I screw myself up to a pitch of indignation.* Then I
remind myself that all she really cares about is *public opinion.*
"*Wahn, alles Wahn*" [all is delusion]. I thought about R. Wagner—would he be a violent Anglophobe today? A Russian dance
tune comes to mind: vision of Juliet and Olga in the E. Malvern

Studio. Yearning for what used to be. Thought of Ivanova. Then the stars came out. I picked out different constellations. Briefly, I asked myself: To what extent am I living in the starlit darkness—like Swinburne's Tiresias? E. R. M. is always with me. I thought a long time about the trip with the boat I was planning to take. I decided to load the camera so I could take pictures, and I told myself which ones I'd take. (And then I forgot to load the camera!) In the evening from 8 to 9 drank tea. Then talked about various things. From 10:30 to 11 wrote to E. R. M. Then thought of her under the mosquito net. Will I ever go back to Cairns and walk along the parade? Will I ever see E. R. M.? *Death, the blear-eyed visitor, I am ready to meet.* —In the dinghy, strong desire to have a family, to marry E. R. M., to settle down.

1.4.18. Got up as usual and came out at 7 from under the *tainamo.* Once again smooth waters, clouds—dark violet cumulus clouds in the firmament and white fluffy ones on the horizon. Strong [*rualimina*] gusts, rain—the sea a glassy green, a little dirty. Then the dull green glow of the mangroves through the thinning rain, the sun comes out, fine weather, and little white clouds in the sky and over the water.—But back to ethnography!—Began to work at 9, but very soon tired. I worked with inferior informants and I *"overhauled"* my data with the help of 2 fellows. Boba'u not bad as informant, after all.—At 11 stopped, exhausted, I wrote to E. R. M. (nasty rain, I put away my papers); went out in a boat, but without energy, "no *punch.*"—Returned, ate taro. At about 3 I resumed work. [Tibabayila] very bad informant. Then again wrote to E. R. M. . . . I thought about Józek Koscielski, and how I would describe him; son of a member of the *Herrenhaus* and friend of the Kaiser's; Bloch's grandson—I remember my conversation with him in Berlin (I met those two, Morszlyn, Koscielski, through

Jan Wlodek). Then I thought of Miss [Weissenhof], and whether I would impress her now. I imagined meetings with various Polish men and women. If I married E. R. M., I would be estranged from Polishness. This discourages me more than anything else when I think of marrying E. R. M.—And how about her? Then I looked at the sea and the sky and my thoughts returned to E. R. M. Sadness at the thought that I might never see her again.—I went back; supper; read *T[ess] o[f the] d'U[rbervilles]* in which I am beginning to find something. The theme of false sexual [appropriation] very strong, but the *treatment?* Short talk with natives, but no great results. Under the *tainamo*, thought of E. R. M. I want her very deeply and intensely. My thoughts do not deviate into any lecherous impasse. When leaving I put some vaseline on my hands; this trivial association aroused in me sensual longing, deep, sentimental.—I thought of my return; the fervor of our glances. The absolute value of her body.

1.5.18. Damp, rainy, stormy day. In the morning sky and lagoon *bien électrique*. At 10 began to work. Tokabaylisa finished his *lili'u*. I slowed down around 10; ate a betel nut and then took the dinghy out around 12:45 (felt the need for exercise). After lunch went back to work with Yosala Gawa, and 2 hours of translating his *megwa "do for me."* At 4:30 I went to the *water hole* and for 4 minutes ran vigorously. At 6 I went back, then rowed as far as Boymapo'u, and back. After supper, Navavile spoke about [*Kum'*]; I wrote down traditions, as I heard them from him. Wrote a few lines to E. R. M. Under the mosquito net fell asleep quickly.

The deeper current of life. In the morning I worked but I also worked on the diary, etc., without any need for special stimulation. I do this spontaneously to some extent, *as a matter of course*. The work itself does not go well. Perhaps I am not A-1

physically. (I was somewhat depressed on Thursday.) The most
important thing would be to eliminate *elements of worry out of
my work.* To have a feeling *of the ultimate mastery of things.*
Writing down information, I have (1) a pedantic feeling that I
must do *a certain measure (3pages, 2 hours, fill out a blank
space in Chap. X or Y)*, (2) too great a desire to skip wherever
possible.

Toward the end of the day's work hidden longings come to
the surface, and visions as well: yesterday I saw the western
end of Albert Street, where the broad boulevard cuts across it
toward Lonsdale St. Longing for E. R. M. *follows.* During my
walk to the *sopi* I felt the need to run away from the *niggers*,
but I can't remember what I thought about. In the boat: impressions of Joan Weigall, and longing for elegant, well-dressed
women. E. R. M. momentarily eclipsed. At moments I long violently to go *South* again. How would I feel if for some reason
E. R. M. were not waiting for me there? I simply can't think
about it.—Miscellaneous associations: My future with E. R. M.
—in [. . .] in Poland? I think about Molly and how I should
write her a New Year's letter! Surely she would still speak to
me. It is one of my traits that I think about people who are
hostile to me more than I do about friendly ones. All those whom
I have to convince, rape, subjugate (Joan, Lady Sp., Baldie,
Molly) rather than the Khuners, Mim, the Pecks, the Stirlings.
—This morning (1.6.18) it occurred to me that the purpose in
keeping a diary and trying to control one's life and thoughts at
every moment must be to consolidate life, to integrate one's
thinking, to avoid fragmenting themes.—Also gives a chance for
reflection, like my observations about people who don't like me.

Return from Boymapo'u, marvelous phosphorescence making the fishes light up. Looked at Venus, thinking of E. R. M.
and about my work, and planning attack on documents, etc.

1.6.18. Sunday. Got up at 8. *Bapopu.* At 10 began to work

—many people around because it was Sunday. Chiefly Navavile. Talked mainly about *bwaga'u* and similar things. At 1 took the boat out. Annoyed by discovery that one oar had a crack in it. Did some linguistics. Then monstrous rain. Two fellows in my *tent*. When the flaps are down, it is so dark that reading or writing is out of the question. I moved my table to the other side of the tent and got [Mwanusa] to come; he gave me *megwa*. (Oh yes, on the way I looked into the hut where [Weirove's] wife, almost a child, was crying because he had beat her up. I thought of E. R. M., association: marriage and spiritual harmony.) Gloomy, rainy day. I remembered days like this at St. Vigeans, and suddenly longed for N. S.—Gradually my nerves got worse; females began to howl (*walam*) in nearby houses. I went to Navavile's, he was out. I got Niyova, who doesn't turn out to be a good informant about [*bugwaywo*]. Checked relationship terms. Then (discouraged by the cracked oar, I did not go out in the dinghy) went to *sopi*. Strenuous gymnastics. I was pensive; thought about diary and integrating life throughout the day; till I tried to master a fit of depression that assailed me at 4-5. At 5 I went out; tried to control and observe my thoughts. On the whole, I am composed, and preoccupied by the need for physical *exercise*. Planning to clear a piece of ground where I can do my gymnastics. I did Swedish exercises *à plusieurs reprises:* there is a stretch of way with a somewhat lower *odila* —there the view is broader and more pleasant. I ran and exercised here. Then to the pond where I sat down to rest. A palm leaf nips my *unu'unu*. I thought about how her hair was always *in the way*. Deep longing. Thought of N. S. and composed a *final letter* [in my mind]. This time I must not put it off. It's hard—I hate to hurt her, but I must write, once and for all. Also thought about Paul and Hedy.—Yesterday and today I had difficulties with taking pictures; characteristic helplessness, one of the main difficulties in my work. In the evening, I went

back, sat and dried myself at the fire—completely changed outlook after strenuous gymnastics, the discomforts of camping
now seem *good fun*. Frying taro. Wrote letters to C. G. S. [Se-
ligman], P. & H. Then short *kayaku* in [Sugwaywo]; young females, blackened, with shaven heads, one of them a *nakubukwabuya* with an animal-like, brutishly sensual face. I shudder at the thought of copulating with her. Thought of E. R. M—
While walking I thought that if E. R. M. left me for some handsome fellow with a simple soul, that would be the only thing that
could make me go back to simple love à la N. S. But this won't
happen.

1.7.18. Got up at 5:45. Went around the village. Everything
normal. Nearly everyone at the *bagula*. A few *nakaka'us* and
tobwabwa'us painting themselves black. Some eating cold *kaulo*.
I went to the *babopopu* and then took a short walk. I tried to
prepare myself for the gathering and get ready to take pictures. Also thought about the diary. This morning right after
getting up thought of E. R. M., then walking through the village—associations?—Oh yes, on my way to *babopopu* I observed that I was walking with my toes turned outward—like
E. R. M. when she had chilblains. Then, from 8 to 12 went over
the questionnaire with Morovato and Kariwabu. Strong *pangs* of
longing for E. R. M. as I went over the questions and plans we
had looked at together, with which she had helped me.—At 12:30
Swedish exercises, brief but effective. (In the morning the *boys*
took away Mick's *dinghy*.) All day I kept asking whether anyone had seen Gilmour's boat—but no. Also, in the morning, incident with a snake which was swimming near the village—*tauva'u*.
In the afternoon worked alone on linguistics—fairly well. At 5
went with Ginger through the *raybwag* to [. . .]. I felt strong
and walked along smartly, the physical effort did not bother me.
At moments I ran. I sat by the sea. Bathed in the warm water

which is shallow and full of stones. Went back with a lamp. I was eating taro when someone brought me the *mailbag*. Nervous *strain rather* than feeling of happiness. I sorted the letters: Mother first, then the less important ones—Lila, Mim, Paul, the Mayos—then E. R. M. Passage about Charles made the strongest impression on me, depressed me, and even alienated me. Moment of longing for N. S. I read her letter last, actually fearing the deeper *passages* which I formerly would have looked for.— Sat up late until almost 12. Slept badly (sea bathing or *excitement* by the letters?) In brief, I was entirely shaken—*hors des gonds* [unhinged]. Have some very important things to write E. R. M. Also to give a not too cruel but definitive *hint* to N. S.— N. S. weighs on my conscience—I am sorry for her but I don't long for her.—E. R. M. letters are considerably more subjective. I am transported—entirely, in a trance, drunk—the *niggers* don't exist. I don't even want to eat or drink.

1.8.18. Got up at 7. Wrote a few less important letters (to P. & H., and the Mayos), and then began a letter to E. R. M. (no desire to write the diary). I wrote from about 10 to 5; with short breaks for lunch, etc., during which I reread her letters and thought about her. At moments strong emotions. At moments, when I wrote about the suffragettes and about the Gilbraiths and touched on controversial matters, I felt a certain *ruffledness*. In the end I was exhausted and felt the need for a brisk walk. On the whole, neither when I read her letter nor when I wrote to her, were my feelings intensified.—I cannot say that *her real self, as brought home by her letters* is infinitely closer to me than her *Double. There is always a process of adaptation—the Double is the result.*—And yet her letters, her short stories, her spirit in reading the newspapers absorb me almost exclusively. Mad longing (restless, unresigned) for her, a longing I did not feel for the *Double.* Only I am thrown off

balance, and to this I always react negatively.—*In the evening,
expedition to Dubwaga.* Went from Kwabulo to Dubwaga thinking about her, about Charles, about ultimate things: it is easier
to love those who are not alive than the living. I wrote some
more to her and went to bed.

1.9.18. In the morning, diary etc. Then the short story. At first
dislike, then gradually better, at moments really moved me; on
the whole, very good—only I am too much involved personally
to throw off a certain diffidence with respect to my enthusiasm.
At 11, Navavile—violent tearful longing for her. Feeling of in-
completeness. *Haunting feeling.* After lunch, read newspapers
until 3:30; then translated Navavile's *megwa.* Then with Ginger on the lagoon.

"*The red sunset was just dying away under a belt of black
clouds, the long stretch of mangrove reflected in the water also
standing in rigid darkness against sky and water. The heavy
soiled red light seemed oozing through the luminous patch in the
West. It floated and trembled with the slow motion of the waves,
and encased in the black frame of clouds and shore it seemed as
stifled and stifling as the tepid air, which rolled along in clammy,
indolent puffs. I felt it clinging to my bare skin rather than
beating against it.*"—Then Swedish gymnastics. The short
story. The problem of heroism. Strong feeling of dejection.
Charles and I. At moments sad because I cannot subject myself
to a test. I recalled my superstitious feeling that if E. R. M.
fell in love with me, I would have *mala sombra* in N[ew] G[uinea].
—For one moment I thought that there is no room for me
in her heart in the shadow of his fame. I wished he would come
back and that I had never met her. Then thought about myself.
Strong fatalistic feeling that "*nolentem fata trahunt, volentem
ducunt*" [fate drags the unwilling, leads the willing]. A teasing
poem occurs to me. I thought about E. R. M.'s mysticism, her

belief that fate sent her and broke her to give happiness to
Charles. *"Mysticism not fatalism."* For a moment I looked Destiny in the eyes. I know that if I had had to go to war, I would
have gone calmly and without too much inner fuss. Now: place
my everyday life in that heroic frame; be ruthless in relation to
appetites and weakness; not to yield to depressions and such
digressions as the inability to take photos. Shake off clumsiness,
yearning, sentimentalism. My love for E. R. M. can be, must be,
based on the feeling that she has faith in my heroism, that if I
had been called to the colors, I would not have tried to get out of
it. And I too must have faith in myself, otherwise I won't get
anywhere. To fight, to keep going, to be ready at any moment,
without depressions and premonitions!—Philosophical happiness: "Whatever may happen—it won't affect me," feeling that
the straight road leads to the tomb, where I can't take along
either sorrows or joys, hopes or fears, and that every moment of
life is full of what will be and what was.

1.10.18. Very bad night. Nerves, heart. (Smoke too much?)
Thought of E. R. M. and distinct, definitive regret (not the first
time?) that I cannot put myself to the test. Composed
(mentally) letter to N. S.—Got up, wrote diary, collected my
things, so as to be ready to leave by 10. Ready around 11, when
a strong *yavata* blew up; furious, but I must expect rain and
wind. Read and corrected letter to E. R. M. Around 12 fine
weather, calm. I ate *momyapu* and went in a small *waga* to Kwabulo, and from there walked to Gusaweta, via Vilaylima. There
Billy bought a large pearl. Then we talked. Read bulletins;
slightly relaxed. Billy gave me some ethnographical data. After
supper I went to Losuya—all that time strong feelings for
E. R. M.—In Losuya, friendly talk with Camp[bell], and in Oiabia with Gilmour. The latter very amiable, we discussed things
and chatted. I got nervous, quite unnecessarily. Then pleasant

feeling that I am alone again, that I can return to E. R. M. in my thoughts. But a certain fatigue and instinct against "tele-sentimental monomania." I tried to think more normally. I lost my way and walked to Kapwapu; storm on the distant horizon. I came back, slept badly. All that time: problem of maintaining inner purity in relation to her, clearly realizing this can be done. I realize that purity in deeds depends on purity of thought, and I resolve to watch myself right down to the deepest instincts. On the other hand, my deep, immensely tender and passionate love for her crystallizes into a strong feeling of the value of her person, and I feel that I really desire only her. I can repress occasional violent whoring impulses by realizing that it would get me nowhere, that even if I possessed women under these con-ditions, I would merely be sloshing in the mud. The most impor-tant thing is to have a strong aversion to sloshing in the mud (onanism, whoring, etc.). And to seek out everything that builds up such an aversion. A Nietzsche aphorism comes to mind: *Ihr höchstes Glück ist bei einem Weibe zu liegen* [Your greatest happiness is to lie with a woman]. My feeling for E. R. M. is something absolutely different: *mein Leib und Seele mit der ihri-gen zu verschmelzen* [to fuse my body and soul with hers].—On the other hand, I try to struggle against sentimental effusions and nihilistic yearnings, etc. I go back mentally to that moment of deep concentration when I longed for a heroic life, when I looked "destiny in the eyes": a life leading through the wilder-ness to happiness, through happiness to sorrow and despair. I love her deeply; I feel that she is the only woman made to be my wife. Will fate once again play a trick on us? Whatever may happen—*nolentem fata trahunt, volentem ducunt!*

1.11.18. After very bad night, got up with *stiff neck.* I looked over some bulletins, keeping an eye out for anything touching E. R. M. or her clan—also political dispatches. Thinking of her

continuously. Referendum a failure; sorry for our Charles.
Then I read letters from N. S. and I wrote her. Hard going; in
spite of noises and interruptions, I kept myself in hand, and was
cheered by the feeling that I was now strong enough not "to get
nervous." Interruption for lunch. But after writing (I was a
little less drastic than I had intended to be) felt greatly relieved. Although the feeling that I wronged her and that I would
hurt her now is horrible. But this had to happen. I feel I have
done something that had to be done. First step. And perhaps I
have done it so as to hurt N. S. as little as possible.

After lunch, I went back to my letter to E. R. M. I read my
letter to her; then hers, and I wrote again, very tenderly and
passionately. I miss her terribly and I have the worst premonitions. I feel rotten at the thought that I may never see her
again. Evening: Billy told me *stories*, then we developed photographs—*Stories: Copulating king is suspected of having a baby
on his mamba. Billy lives with a woman (on her forearm tattoo:
Billy). C. K. comes into the store, talks to her in good English
about return to God, etc., & invites her to come down and live at
Mission Station. Billy hears and translates: "He talk you come
live along him along Mission Station." "You talk him: he go to
buggery." C. K. turns round and struts out. . . . Hon. X. Y.
Walsh, always drunk. Ernie Oates and Billy. Billy arranges
with woman to come up to Bogi. They all come down after
a month to the beach, estuary of Yodda. There police camp on
one side, J. St. Russell gives order that the police does not detain
the woman. Word comes that they did in spite of that. An expedition to catch. Walsh (Lady Northcote's brother) drunk, falls
down. Catch two girls and corporal. Court: R. with his legs up
owing to clap in balls. W. stone drunk. Ernie translates
interrogative tense into imperative. Girl acquiesces in having
been bought for Billy. (B. says she'd have preferred the police-*

*man every time.) The corporal flogged by Walsh, girls locked
up in the store, but by 11 P.M. they are with Ernie and Billy.—
Trouble about woman on the Yodda. Just over 50 miles. Monck-
ton* comes to Kokoda. Miners [say] "Fuck him." Billy Little
("The G.'s pimp") repeats it to Monckton. M. struts in,
in marching order, "right, left," "right, left," the miners mock
him. B. H. writes then a letter to a chap who comes and meets
M. halfway and treats him politely. M. makes no row about it
after that.*

Saturday, 1.12.18. Morning, I asked Billy and *Mrs.* to help me
with my work. *Mrs.* told me nothing of interest. Then I looked
over notes on grammar. In the afternoon, tired, rain and sultry.
Read Locke† and again did some grammar, without great results. In the evening went to do exercises. Went back, wrote
letter to E. R. M. Throughout those days, most intense, immensely deep love and longing for E. R. M. Resolution to be
pure. I must have no lecherous or sentimental thoughts about
any other woman. "Woman" = E. R. M. Leafing through Foote,
I feel an aversion to all lechery, and the above equation exists
for me.

Sunday, 1.13.18. Awoke at 5—. . . Thought, with feeling of
happiness, about existence of E. R. M. Like music. Then woke
up late, weakened. Read stories by Locke and thought of
E. R. M.—Waiting for Gilmour. At about 4, when I finished
the stories, began to pack. Gilmour came; talk. Then he went.
I talked with him about grammar and planned possible collabo-

* Charles A. W. Monckton, a New Zealander who came to New Guinea
in 1895 and became resident magistrate of Samarai in 1897 and of Kokoda
in 1903. He led the Waria-Lakekamu patrol, an important exploratory expedition.

† William J. Locke, popular British novelist of the time.

ration. We talked about Bromilow.* I gave him my last letter
to E. R. M. Before that I had made out my will with Bill.—
After supper I got ready. Scared in the badly unbalanced boat.
Stars. Thought about grammar.—E. R. M. all the time—under
the *tainamo* surge of physical longing for E. R. M. passes
gradually into indiscriminate lecherousness. . . . Except for
Saturday afternoon, these last days we had marvelous weather,
east winds and calm, clear skies, a little hot despite everything.

1.14.18. This morning I lay under the *tainamo*, spoiling
myself a bit; but then I had not slept decently for a long time—
I never can sleep properly in Gusaweta. I must get back to
work. I am in full swing in linguistics. Get at it, strike while the
iron is hot! Once again a clear, fine day. I worked on the terminology of gardens; Navavile came and helped. Very tired at
12:45, took a nap. After lunch worked on terminology, *waga*,
and then I wrote down the main points of the *waga*, with the
help of informants. Work under *high tension*. Head very tired.
At 5, Ginger, I, and Toysenegila went to [*Lum'*]. So exhausted
nervously that I didn't even long for her much. A few questions I
asked Toysenegila finished me off. I walked like an automaton.
Smooth road to the sea. Bathing; I am getting used to the contact of the water, though it still gets on my nerves. Then, on my
way back, depressed about E. R. M. Over the glassy-green sea,
the gathering shadows of the night in the eastern sky, pink
clouds overhead. I gazed southward and toward the passage in
Giribwa. Somehow lacking enthusiasm and expression for the
view, *I conjure* [up] her picture—and somehow don't react to it.
Exactly the same longing for longing as I had in Melbourne
when I "*fell out of love.*" She suddenly vanished from the hori-

---

* Rev. W. E. Bromilow, the first missionary in Dobu; his observations on
some of the native customs, in the records of the Australian Association for
the Advancement of Science, was apparently the only written account of the
Dobuans at the time Malinowski wrote *Argonauts of the Western Pacific.*

zon. Lost all meaning. Absolute void, the whole world is under
my nose, solid, but it holds nothing for me. This is result of
exhaustion. Did some exercises. In the evening, Tylor (I would
have turned in at 9 had it not been for that *bastard*). After he
had left, sudden longing for E. R. M. Under the *tainamo*
monstrous physical longing.

1.15.18. Clear and transparent sky. Strong, deep feeling for
E. R. M. "My wife" *de facto* and *de sentimento*. I think that
after we're married we'll be able to tell Molly about our present
relationship. I think of N. S.—only of how I must *break the
news* to her. I am very much attracted to her and interested in
her health, but I don't think of her as a woman. In the morning
worked on the dictionary, *canoes*—the same subject as yesterday with other informants—learned extremely interesting details about construction of *kalipoulo*. Work does not go bril-
liantly but I keep on without pressure and *I let the time do the
rest*. I feel the effect of salt on bones and muscles. At 11 gymnastics. Then nap before lunch. I am not smoking and feel much
better. After lunch the same subject. After 5 to *raybwag* with
Ginger. Collected information from Niyova. Tired. Stayed too
long in the water; came back exhausted, heart pounding; but I
walked slowly and took frequent rests hoping the pounding
would abate. (Hope proves justified today 1/16.) Thought of
E. R. M., imagining what it would be like with her here. More
and more clearly feel that this would be *"perfect happiness."* (I
imagine asking Seligman how he was with his wife in the tropics.)—Back, I listened to their chatter, ate, wrote a few lines
to E. R. M., and went to bed. . . .

1.16.18. Got up at 7:15. Went out for gymnastics; sky with
cumulus clouds, between them patches of blue. Deep shadows under the palms and other trees, strange shapes and colors. I went

into a coconut grove. There thought about the meaning of a diary: changes in life's course, *readjustment of values*—the content of ethics—based on introduction of harmony. The taming of my lusts, the elimination of lecherousness, concentrating on E. R. M. gives me happiness, contentment much greater than just letting go does. Utilitarian hedonism, if we don't forget other instincts (social instincts) is the only rational system: the happiness of the individual in harmony with the happiness of the collectivity (that this must be the *Grundton* [keynote] of instinct, can be deduced a priori, from the fact "*homo animal socialis*").—I think of the value of the diary (*with direct reference to* E. R. M.): grasping the deeper currents in contrast to mere *ripples;* conversation with oneself, and glimpse of the content of life.—Obviously something has to be sacrificed—you don't get anything for nothing, but what is in question is a choice.—Planning a letter to E. R. M. about these ideas; need for real solitude.—Went back full of lofty thoughts: life must proceed at a slow pace if it is to run deep. Either the reflection of fleeting shimmering gleams on the rippling changing surface, or the immense smile of the depths—depends on the point of view. One should force oneself to look at the emptiness of the surface without illusion. Feeling that systematic though monotonous work with a purpose should be enough for me. I felt a nirvanalike contentment with existence ("nothing is happening"), looking at the damp leaves and the shaded interior of the Australian jungle.—Axiom: the continual craving for change is the result of our inability to feel the plenitude of happiness; if we captured our moments of happiness, we would not need change.

Back to my tent; bathing in the sea felt in my bones; inability to concentrate; mental standstill. I fought against it, but work did not go well. At 11:30 I stopped and went out for exercise. Went back, wrote E. R. M.—Then lunch; read *Tess of the d'Urb.* Intensity of my thinking about E. R. M. not diminished since Christmas.—Then Yasala Gawa; talked about *bwaga'u.* At 5 tired; ½ hour of linguistics. It was getting dark, I went to Lubwoyla, did gymnastic exercises in the rain. Controlled my nerves, recalling heroic impulses. The moon and stars between little clouds; I thought how necessary it was to adjust mentally to gymnastics; gymnastics as an essential form of solitude and mental concentration. Whatever may happen, I must never neglect gymnastics 3 times a day. On returning I felt fine and took part in conversation with the *niggers,* I also felt mentally balanced, but my longing for E. R. M. not diminished. (I made observations about *kadumilaguwa valu.*) I wrote her a few lines and went to bed. Thought of her with passion.

1.17.18. Woke up at 7:30: After writing diary went to *sopi* for gymnastics, under the palms, near the mangroves. Running, then very intensive exercises. Also, planned the day and *steel my thoughts.* Gymnastics removed slackness but introduced a certain nervous tension, *nervous irritability,* insomnia which I have not had for a long time. Worked 2 hours in the morning; Campbell arrived; this irritated and depressed me—like a customs search on the border; a little afraid he might cause me some unpleasantness; then again *bother,* waste of time, and I don't like him personally. Talk during which I was expansive. Then a short letter to E. R. M. Gymnastics; I tried to concentrate, to take the proper attitude toward the Bulgarian:* "he doesn't exist so far as I am concerned." Gymnastics calmed my nerves, restored my balance and put me in an excellent mood.—With gymnastics and a regular mode of life I should keep healthy and carry out my scientific plans. The only danger is overstraining my heart. Ergo: take intellectual work, everyday difficulties,

---

* This may be an allusion to the conventionally heroic Bulgarian soldier depicted in Shaw's play *Arms and the Man.*

efforts lightly, "not take them to heart." Absolutely eliminate personal rancors, *excitements*, etc. Cultivate *sense of humor* (not the English one, but my own, B. M. + E. R. M.).

Then lunch with a fellow and talk—about what?—In the afternoon: I lay down for a quarter of an hour, and started work—*bwaga'u* business. At about 5 stopped, was fed up. Excited, impossible to concentrate. Ate pineapple, drank tea, wrote E. R. M., took a walk; intensive gymnastics. Gymnastics should be a time of concentration and solitude; something that gives me an opportunity to escape from the *niggers* and my own agitation. Supper with a fellow who told me stupid anecdotes, not interesting at all, about Kiriwinian ethnology. I listened and dozed and nodded: what a brute. Short letter to E. R. M. I thought about her intensely again: the only woman for me, the incarnation of everything a woman can give me. Some fellow sang during the night, this annoyed me, I couldn't fall asleep. Slept badly.

1.18.18. Up late, 7:30. Gymnastics in the clearing near the mangroves. Strength, intensity, *irritability rather than* [*sentiment*]. Thought about E. R. M.: a traveling companion rather than star *leading my destinies*. But she is always with me. At moments I think my longing for her is less strong, but then am suddenly dominated by it. I thought about N. S., about Adelaide, the city and the country will always be *Paradise Lost* to me: old Stirling, very faithful, the mother, and the whole [camp]. Then I went back; irritated by the impudence of Navavile and the Wawela fellows (they had eaten too much betel nut). Decided to spend the day reviewing my notes and listing problems. This went slowly at first, then specific problems emerged.—After lunch, [*Tapi Bobau*]. Strong wind; I closed *tent*, and we began to recite *silami*, when Billy arrived. I was

somewhat bored and irritated by this interruption, but I greeted
him with *bonne mine à mauvais jeu* and we chatted (I like him
personally), then we went to Kiribi. Mick and B. furious at N.
Camp[bell] who spoiled four cases of benzine, when going to
Yaga [Island], where he has "plantations," and then dragged
Kavataria *canoes* behind him. Billy also told me an anecdote,
how N. C. was showing [*beku*], which his wife's father and
grandfather owned; he licked *right along* it with his tongue and
wept drunkenly. I did not feel A-1 in Kiribi and did not [go to
the] *kayaka* with Moliasi. On our way back, the *waga* shipped
water. Beautiful moon, I sat in front of the *canoe*, Toyodala
punted, Ginger scooped the water. In the evening I changed the
dressing on Towakayse's penis. Then read E. R. M. letters from
Crandon. I understand her emotions about C. E. M.: she sees the
tragic past in the light of her feeling for me. *As if from a safe
shore.* Her letters to me don't grow stale. I looked at pictures of
her. I'd like to send them to Mother.

1.19.18 First really nasty day. At night, storm with furious
thunder and downpour, so that the ground shook. Also a gale. I
woke up and it took me a long time to fall asleep again. Naturally, I thought about E. R. M. Got up at 8:30, wrote diary
under pressure, for I learned that a fellow had died in Kwabulo.
Went there in a boat, with Tomwaya Lakwabulo and [Wayesi],
and talked with them about D[eath] & B[urial], but without
positive results. In Kwabulo: enormous puddles, people just
coming back from funeral. I went to the house: outburst of
howling. I went to the grave and talked about the cutting of
trees and the wrecking of houses after a man's death.—I sat on
the *baku*, and bought *momyapu* and *waywo*. Began to feel rotten, quite low after return. Lunch at 1; then read *Tess of d'U.*
Thought of E. R. M., although I see T. of U. more like N.S.

than like E. R. M.—Marked passages which I'd like to send Elsie. The novel absorbed me [and I idled away]. I sat by the water. At moments almost unbearable longing for E. R. M.—or is it for civilization?—I walked around the village, but feeling feverish I came back. Not in a mood to write letters; tried to read *T. of d'U.* but my eyes were tired.—I felt that if she were here, she'd be comfort. I wondered what I had been doing a year ago?—At night a wind of such force that I feared it would blow over the tent. Took calomel + [*local veg.*]. + quinine + aspirin in the evening. At about 2 A.M. [had to run out].—When I came back I chased lecherous thoughts. E. R. M. is my *de facto* wife. The night before I thought that if we met now we would *exchange vows* and put our relationship *on a firm basis*. It's as if we had contracted a *clandestine marriage*.—All the time, the indefinite, vague longing and the need to commune with her.

1.20.18. Nasty day. Up at 8:30. Started to work fairly late. Wrote down songs from Weirove. Then read *Tess d'U.* Ginger came to tell me that Toyodala's wife was sick. I went there; interesting and diverting scene. I thought *in personal terms* about E. R. M. and myself—which of the two of us will die before the other? "When you contract new ties, you assume new burdens." But I wouldn't exchange all the cares resulting from love for the barren severity of egoism.—Then ate frugal lunch (taro). (Before then I had photographed a group bringing in [*vayewo*].)—Again read *Tess of the d'U.*, finished it. It made on me a strong, though unpleasant impression: the dramatic, despairing denouement is not justified. Then walked around the village; the natives eating *towamoto* on the occasion of [*vayewo*], first the men, then the women. Then, I sat near Naruya's house; talked about *mulukwausi* and *kayga'u*. Then drank tea (did not eat), also took *ula'ula* to the *baloma*, listened to his *megwa*. Turned in at 10.

1.21.18 (Monday). Third day of bad weather. Stayed in bed until 9. Strange dreams. I was inspecting the theater of war. German establishments run by Englishmen. Some sort of monstrous, fat, piggish mask, a German [. . .] or something of the sort.— Dreamed of E. R. M.—I was engaged to some woman who was betraying me and of whom I was jealous. I recalled that I was engaged to E. R. M.—In the morning, characteristic *irritability:* the *niggers* got on my nerves.—There had been raging storms the two nights before. Last night was calm, and I slept better. Today, sky overcast, rain on and off. No wind, very sticky.—Began to work at about 11, mostly writing record of previous day's events. In afternoon, discussed this record with the fellows. I had begun to feel better by noon, and in the afternoon I worked fairly well. At noon I started a letter to M. H. W., but didn't finish it. After work lay on bed and rested. It was raining.—The silvery dimness of a moonlit night. I went to Missionary [. . .]. Among the palms smoky vapors swirling as in a cauldron and the air exactly like a Turkish bath. Took a short walk, thinking about E. R. M. Half-dreamy mood. Through the swirling monstrosity of this Turkish bath flit memories of morbid moods in Omarakana. Then I felt a certain relief: began to look at all this—through all this—from outside: *Ende gut, alles gut* [All's well that ends well]. But if *this* were to be the end—feeling that I am choking, that the claws of death are strangling me alive.—After some light gymnastics felt incomparably better and freer in this thick soup. After supper and making *a round round the village* (I upbraided them for not sending me back *ula'ula of the baloma*), began to write a letter to E. R. M., but I stopped because of my eyes; then sat a moment by the sea, content with the stagnation and solitude, when I heard that Ineykoya's [Toyodala's wife] condition was worse—she was groaning loudly. I went to see: she had another hemorrhage, groaned horribly, and was apparently

dying. I thought of the horrible torment of a hemorrhage and of
N. S. and suddenly felt that I was deserting her. I also felt that
I wanted to be with her at any cost, to allay her sufferings.
Strong reaction. I also thought of E. R. M. and in my nervous
disarray I told myself: *"the shadow of death is between us and
it will separate us."* My betrayal of N. S. confronted me in all
its starkness.—Over the hut in which my lamp was glowing, tall
palms, thick white clouds, through which the moonlight filtered.
Kabwaku sings melodiously and clearly.—Death—all this is
like an ebb tide, a flowing off into nothingness, extinction.
Through all this, the cruel *customs* of the *niggers*—who were
again washing her, preparing her for death.—For the first
half of the day I was dejected and almost did not believe in the possibility of health. Then *I buck up* and *I hope.*
Planned letters to Dr. Stowell and to Spencer. Then I thought
about my theory of religion, in relation to my Polish book.

1.22.18. Tuesday. Very bad night; woke up and felt stifled under
the mosquito net (had gorged myself with fish). Got up late; did
not exercise. Felt incomparably better. Started to work. I decided to deal with *kayga'u*, about which I had had an interesting
discussion with Tokabawivila and Molilakwa; worked with the
latter that day (from 9 to 12:30) (Ginger and Ogisa left with
Medo'u to get wood). I sat with Molilakwa and two girls (his
daughter and Kavala, 7 years). Purely fatherly feelings, then
spoiled, and I directed my thoughts at E. R. M. to shake off *lewdness.* After lunch (fish and taro) I wrote to E. R. M., rested.
Then took pictures, then again with Molilakwa. Tired. I sat by
the calm sea, resting, *not* * longing. Then in moonlight, gymnastics. Humming songs, an impulse to compose—seizing upon a
musical idea and expressing it in my own melody. If I had an
instrument—even a piano—I might have been able to compose,

* Underlined in original.

poorly, without originality, like my poems? Thought of E. R. M. —and that I'd like to "sing" for her what she told me in Belgrave Gully. Then gymnastics; I was nervous and felt *"jumpy."* But I mastered this, and exercised well. Thought about photography. Came back composed, "stony"—ordered a *waga* from Narubuta'u. Then supper; I wanted to record my ethnographic observations. Unnecessary row with Karigudu. Principle: never lose temper. If a fellow goes too far, send him away calmly and don't have anything further to do with him. Also, it would have been better never to give anything for Kaukweda, and not to encourage *kayaku* in my tent.—Later, however, I clearly realized the stupidity of my behavior and the vanity of being angry and insisting on "points of honor." I tried to control myself as quickly as possible, and was successful after a while. Went to a *kayaku* in a house at Vitabu. Then observed a delegation in front of the house in the *obukubaku*, to which Ineykoya had been carried. Went back, drank tea, and turned in. Thought about Ineykoya and N. S. Strongest remorse I ever had (next to the one I had when Ineykoya had hemorrhage). What if her health were really ruined? (Stella, Madge, who will not leave Craig.) At moments I really think that I'll have to go back to her. On the other hand, strong physical attraction to N. S., stronger than ever before. I think of her physique (*am I gross?*)—imagining her body vividly in every detail.

1.23.18. Wednesday. Got up fairly late; went out for gymnastics. I intended to concentrate and think about my work, but somehow nothing came of it. I am still a bit unhappy about N. S., and E. R. M. is on the wane. But for all that, tendency not to let a whim of the moment spoil really essential things. Had not *unaccountable moods induced a mad recklessness, my tempo in Tristan-Isolde incident* would have been considerably slower, and I would have been happier. My feelings for E. R. M. are

deep and based upon a definite engagement. I should take the
surface ups and downs for what they are, though there is no
reason to ignore them altogether. The richness of life this
implies can be [conceived of] as *experimental thinking. E.g.*,
in the physiology of sex—experimental thoughts, but the
moment they pass into the organism and become "physiolog-
ical," to be rejected. E. R. M. is my wife. As for N. S. I have
done nothing wrong, for during the critical period (March-May
1916) I had no other feelings or thoughts.—After lunch I
shaved and was about to work with Niyova when *mail* was
brought me.—Emotional turmoil. I finished shaving. Short letter
from C. G. S.—Ernest P. K.—Mim. Then long letter and diary
from E. R. M. I read her letter slowly, and this time the *real*
E. R. M. is better than her *Double.* But the diary somehow vexed
me. My portrait in it is not sympathetic, as I see it. I don't like
this fellow and I feel that she does not love me. Also, a feeling
that that period, as she describes it, is growing paler, becoming
gray.—Also, the apology of [Diering] and Jim, whom I like
very much, peeved me a little. It gave me the feeling *that it
might never have been.* In fact the crisis came too soon, and we
were unprepared. I acted too brutally. The error of too great
freedom.—Went to the beach and sat there. N. S. gives me terrible guilt feelings. I went out in a *canoe.* Painful feeling that
all this is spoiled, that this fundamental error casts a shadow
over my life, over my relation with E. R. M. I shouldn't have
started anything with her before definitively breaking with N. S.
In the evening, characteristic dissatisfaction and restlessness,
associated with mail day—this craving for strong and complicated impressions, *feeling for points of contact with the absent
ones. This sudden rush of presence,* need for a *condensed dose of
a friend's personality.*—I reread those letters from N. S. which
are especially beautiful and affectionate and simply howled with
despair. Then I walked through the village and looked at Iney-

koya. "*Desertion in the face of the enemy.*" Perhaps for the first time since I left Australia, distinct feeling that if N. S.'s health or life depended on it, I would have to sacrifice E. R. M.—myself—and go back to N. S.—More clearly than ever I feel that I love them both.—Only the illness of N. S.—which up to now has been—is now the strongest link. Aesthetically, I should never go back to Australia. Death, the ebb tide of reality, does not seem as terrible as a few days ago.—Sat up late, read letters again. Went to bed very depressed and fell asleep quickly, *sleeping my misery over.* I dreamed about C. R.

Thursday. 1.24. Morning, gymnastics with very mixed feelings, Molilakwa and *lili'u tokabitam.* After lunch took photographs of men roasting fish and carving a canoe prow in the village. Then worked a bit and set out for Gusaweta. The trip. Read beginning of E. R. M.'s diary; it vexed me. Looked with pleasure at the mangroves and the lagoon; I "was alone" and felt no desire to go back. For the last few days, until the *mail* came, *native life and native society* had come to seem almost enough to me. At Billy's, a bit of gymnastics, *developing* photos, mortified by the poor results. To bed at 12 (felt rotten).

I think, or rather I am in a mental turmoil, about the letters. I don't want to write E. R. M. about it. It wouldn't be fair. In the worst case, if N. S.'s health required it, E. R. M. would accept *the inevitable.*

Comprehension of one aspect of history: *A being endowed with memory must be understood through its history. Physics (Geschlossene systeme* [closed systems]). *Biology (heredity). Individual psychology. Sociology.—Must we accept a collective soul in order to treat history really seriously?*

1.25.18. Friday. Gusaweta. I cannot write the diary. Dissipation, I take up novel reading. Developing films, and thinking

about a number of things. Radical longing only for E. R. M.—
Intellectual and emotional turmoil abates. Exhaustion, headache. Impulse to go back to Oburaku. I went back; I went out
rowing. Echoes of Elsie, Mim, Paul, Hedy, Bronio [Broniowski].
Coming closer to E. R. M. in my thoughts, but I am still "alone."
. . . Went to see Toyadala. He is clearly more hopeful. I sat
and dozed. Read a few passages in E. R. M.'s diary. Jim and
[Diering] again annoyed me. I felt *shouldered out*. My role in
her life is too faint. Went to bed; at moments so peeved I
couldn't think. Basic reaction: "I want to be alone." But I know
au fond this is only momentary. Also joyful feeling persists
through all this—now she is in love with me.

During the night Ineykoya died. Got up at 3:30 and went
there. Deep impression. *I lose my nerve*. All my despair, after
all those killed in the war, hangs over this miserable Melanesian
hut. I thought of E. R. M., Jim, and Charles. Then went back
under my mosquito net and couldn't fall asleep and thought a
great deal of E. R. M. My *misgivings à propos* Dostoevskian
feelings. Doubts about whether she is still the "complete woman"
for me—I decide to keep them to myself.

Saturday, 1.26.18. Up at 8:30 with headache. Went to see Toyodala. Same difficulties as during the night because of personal
relationship. Went with handkerchief and pretended I was
weeping. Then gave him a *stick* of tobacco. Women dancing on
[o]bukubaku.

Mon Tue Wed Thu Fri Saturday

Sunday 1/27; 28; 29; 30; 31; 1; 2.

Written at Gusaweta, 2.5.18.

After lunch, and short rest, worked with one of the fellows
who reported that Kivi buy *waywo*. Photographs. Palms cut.

Massage. After supper, the *yawali*. Very tired, sat and dozed. Slept heavily.

1.27. Sunday. Woke up sick. Skull aching. Feeling that something is "wrong." Diagnosis: Tuberculosis (Ineykoya); *blackwater; antrum;* teeth. Subjectively I am very indifferent, I don't believe in the possibility of danger, but if I died, it would be *an excellent way out of the muddle.* Somewhat resentful feelings about E. R. M.—In the afternoon read her diary. Posed before the *niggers.*

1.28. Monday. I feel worse. In the afternoon collapse. Shivering. Took quinine and aspirin. Beginning to believe in the hypothesis that I am about to die. I am indifferent. Fever, lack of vitality; rotten physical condition. No desire to live, I don't regret any loss. Feeling this is a good time to die. Alone, calm, *air of finality.* In the evening Elaitia came.

1.29.18. Tuesday. The quinine is effective: headache, weakness. I don't feel much better. Collapse in the afternoon. Wrote to Billy. Took an enema—this relieved me at once. Then calomel and general purge. Effervescent salts, which turns out to be my salvation. Unable even to read E. R. M. diary these days.

1.30. Wednesday. A little better. Afternoon, Marian. Got milk from Billy.

1.31. Thursday. Much better. Belief that I'll recover. Subjective emptiness, depression. E. R. M.: a certain resentment, unjustified. Complication with N. S. weighs heavily on me.—Losing my affection for Ginger who steals tobacco. Letter from Bill, parcel from Kiribi. Uncertainty whether "Kayona" brought *mail.*

2.1.18. Friday. Much better, but still not too able to read. In the afternoon, Billy. *Mail.* Cara, Cathie.—E. R. M., strong emotions: loving letter; then vexation; Baldwin's slanders. Annoyed by the latter, chiefly his dirty spying.—Took a walk: everything looked deserted, dead. Heterogeneous feelings, like gusts of wind coming from every direction at once, which do not combine but throw me back and forth from one mood to another; half-dreamy feeling of unimportance of existence.

2.2.18. Saturday. Letters to N. S. and E. R. M. Very slow and very hard. Day wore on slowly, lazily and emptily. Ground has been taken out from under me.

2.3.18. Sunday. All morning read Conrad. At 4 to Gusaweta. Despair over monotony of existence; back and forth between Oburaku and Gusaweta. In spite of it, the salty, damp smell of the sea, the *exercise* of rowing, and the marvelous pastel colors of the landscape fill me with joy, or rather give me pangs of pleasure. Planned new excursions and expeditions. Decided to go to Amphletts* with the "Kayona" if it waits about 10 days. At Gusaweta we talked. I shaved and went to bed at 9.

2.4. Monday. The Toyodala film. Read *Glory of Clementina Wing* (very weak). Subconsciously E. R. M. coming back to the surface. Felt spiritual need for her. In the evening we developed plates. Turned in at 9:30. Woke up during the night; thought about E. R. M. deeply and passionately.

2.5. Tuesday. Read in the morning. Then walked in the direction of Kapwapu. First attempt to concentrate. Then wrote diary. After lunch read E. R. M.'s letters and wrote to her. Also

* During the next few weeks, Malinowski witnessed a number of events that were part of an *uvulaku* (large-scale, competitive *kula*) between Sinaketa and Dobu. The previous fall the Sinaketans had made their *uvulaku* to Dobu, and now the Dobuans were due to make theirs. Their canoes would set out toward the end of March for a *kula* in the Amphletts, after which the Amphlettans would join them for the expedition to Vakuta and finally to Sinaketa, where they were due early in April. In preparation for the event, the Vakutans sailed to Kitava for a *kula* and returned with a supply of arm-shells. To'uluwa of Kiriwina also made an expedition to Kitava for the arm-shells, and the Sinaketans then made an inland *kula* to Omarakana in order to obtain them in exchange. Thus the hosts in Vakuta and Sinaketa were well supplied with suitable gifts when their visitors arrived from Dobu. These transactions are described in detail in *Argonauts of the Western Pacific*.

in the evening. All this period lived literally from day to day. Impulse to read trashy novels. Through all this strong, unexpressed longing for E. R. M. Now I really can say she is the only woman for me.

2.6. Wednesday. In the morning read *Secret Agent*. Finished with feeling of disgust: poor, unnecessary, drawn out. Then shuffled back and forth in my room like a bear in a cage. Reread *Half-Caste*. Main criticism: the story is not dramatic. "Plot." I'd like her to give a plot. I don't write her, although I think of her and about the problem of telling our secret to Molly. Ornu'a. At 4 I start packing. Left at 6, without knowing what for—neither my work nor Oburaku attract me. I began to row—*bump*. Pushed the boat through mud and stones; prospect of spending night on lagoon; happiness in the form of a bed. Despite everything I display some grit on this occasion, without me Ginger would have given up. Arrival at 9. Straight to bed.

2.7. Thursday. Feel incomparably better in Oburaku. At once lost all desire to read.

Written Monday, 2.11.18.
    Thursday, 2.7. A bit of gymnastics in the morning—but didn't feel *up to it*. Then work. In the afternoon, very irritable —at 4 had to stop, at 6 went to bed. Took at once large amount of calomel. Next day (or perhaps same evening) shivers, then fever—105°—scared—"*Piss he black.*" Afraid of *blackwater*. Sitting on the beach that day thought about E. R. M.—and felt rotten, felt *pang* at the thought I might never see her again.
    Friday, 2.8. *Ut supra*—all day long, felt rotten. Temperature down with the help of aspirin, then quinine. Headache. All day in bed: no aches. Temperature lowers my *vitality*. Death

(outcome I thought very likely—*blackwater*) did not frighten me.

Saturday, 2.9. Felt better in the morning. In the afternoon read *Villette* [novel by Charlotte Brontë], fascinates me. Went to the beach; cool; kept reading. Shivering; warmed myself by the fire with Elaitia. Went back, could not eat much. Fever again, temperature went up slowly to 103°. Ginger had belly-ache and refused to work. Compresses on chest (hypothesis of effect on lungs, because of *sudden jumps in temperature*).— Hypothesis of septicemia: had eaten stale soup with [. . .], maggoty and *mouldy* rice. Sleepless night, splitting headache. Purged myself with salts, enema. A little better; in the morning quinine.

2.10. Sunday. Quinine in the morning; took no food or drink. Felt better. The quinine did not depress me too much. Read *Villette*. Thought about E. R. M. but without too much enthusiasm. Once again almost sleepless night, or more accurately, I woke up at 1 and did not go back to sleep until 6. Learned that little Charlie died; dejection. Letter to Billy. Thought about Sir B. Sp. and the various forms in which *I shall take action*. Also thought about my behavior toward N. S. and E. R. M. and couldn't look upon it as *correct*. In relation to E. R. M. my conduct was more outrageous, but since *to her I intend to stick*, weaker guilt feelings.

2.11. Better. Ate 1 toast for lunch. Read *Villette*; has for me the same *charm of quiet fascination* as *Pride and Prejudice*. Feminine tact, intuition, grasp of *inwardness of things* and longing for life. Thought a great deal about E. R. M., at moments without enthusiasm, occasionally with surges of passion. Jarring *mood of convalescence*, like drifting clouds *blown by conflicting winds*. No solid ground to stand on. In the morning fresh N.W. wind, fine weather, marvelous smell of the sea; I felt life smiling again; felt *the fetters of sickness* and was uncertain whether that promise would come true. Got up, walked a little around the village. I was horribly hungry: visions of *vol-au-vents de volaille*, French chophouses in Soho, etc., attract me more than the loftiest spiritual joys. Moments of frightful longing to get out of this rotten hole.

Written 2.13.18 (Wednesday).

Feeling better from day to day, although I am weak; sweat at night, need for quinine, and the abscess on the foot prevent me from being certain that I'll get well, and my physical and intellectual weakness have blunted my faculties. I have no strong vital "thread." Up until yesterday had been reading *Villette* all day long. Eating, too, plays a great role in my present outlook. Tuesday morning the fellows went on a *poulo*. Pouring rain, so naturally got up in a rotten mood; everything in my bed was drenched with sweat, night almost sleepless, worry. I bought a lot of fish, at noon boiled them. Drank fish soup avidly. In the evening, short walk and a bit of rowing. Letter from Billy: George is sick, goes to Samarai. Altruistically sorry; egoistically vexed. Finished letter to E. R. M. (my head very tired, had a hard time writing). The *boys* went to Kiribi, I sat and chatted with Niyova and other fellows.—Slept fairly well, but sweated profusely.—This morning, rainy, damp. Again had a few sleepless hours. Got up despite the cold and my depressed mood, began to work with Navavile. But I was unable to write: my head didn't function properly. Read *Villette* a while. In afternoon worked again, and rowed.

Dulled emotional state. Think of E. R. M. relatively little, but this still means very often. The moment I got to work, agitation and *homesickness* vanished. My temperature was 103 Saturday night, 101 on Sunday, 99.2 Monday and Tuesday, just

98.6 this morning and at 5 P.M. Swollen and painful bubo bothers me a bit. Planning to move to Kaybola beach in a week or so.

2.14.18. Yesterday evening listened to Molilakwa's stories. Felt sleepy at 9:30 and lay down. Woke up at 11.30; hot compresses on bubo, enema. Then lecherous thoughts about Rasputin's system; and I wondered how I would discuss it with A. M. B. Rotten psychological state. . . . Slept badly, sweated again. Got up 8:30; did not feel well, could not think either sentimentally or synthetically, but felt I could start working and that this was my only hope for breaking out of this prison mood. Wrote down *bwaga'u*. Then Molilakwa Kuigau. Made *rough sketch*, then, after lunch, copied it. Excellent system! In the afternoon worked from 3 to 5, first copying, then with Navavile and Niyova I again worked on *mukwausi*. At 5:30 to Kiribi—emotionally dull, only the silhouette of the Koya, dark in the gray clouds and the leaden waters, cheered me: the road to the south. Satisfaction with the day's work. Rowed a bit. At Kiribi, Ilumedoi, Mick. Vexed to hear that Billy wouldn't be back for 2 weeks or more—he closed store and house. Went back—lay down on bench in the back; sleepy melancholy.

Today many thoughts about N. S. Had a dream: We are living in the Little Square. Mother. I return. N. S. is there. Mother surprised and reproachful because I am not married to N. S. "She has only two weeks left to live." I, too, was very sad. This sadness filters from dream to waking state. Remorse; sadness. Effect of *Villette* on me is that I feel *how wicked I am.*

2.15.18 (Friday). In the morning took a walk, very tired and grumpy. Need quinine (?). Took 5 gr. The fellows brought fish. Couldn't find decent informants. Began to write down *bwaga'u*, and to make outline of *"Disease and Death."* Felt rotten. Again took a walk. Then came the fellows with whom I am compiling dictionary. After lunch I lay down but did not sleep. Finished *Villette*. The end weaker than the beginning and middle. Best: Her way of struggling against fate and her hunger for happiness. After lunch went to see Toyodala and worked on theme of *Waribu*. Back, read Swinburne, took the boat out. Rowed vigorously; felt better. All that day, I was apathetic; thought of N. S. as *paradise lost*. Didn't think much about E. R. M. though am convinced that if she had been *paradise lost*, I'd have been very unhappy. After supper went to see the *nakaka'u*, where I made new observations on *Waribu*. Then Mokaylepa told long *kukwanebu*, in the middle of which I felt terribly sleepy. Turned in. Woke up because I had taken cathartic compound, couldn't fall asleep afterward. Thought about E. R. M. with passion. Dream: I am in Germany, 2 crippled cavalry officers; met them in some hotel. Walking with them in some German city. Fraternizing with them. I express my sympathy for Germany and German culture, and tell them I was a *Kriegsgefangener* [prisoner of war] in England.

2.16.18. Saturday. On the whole, I am much stronger, I sleep better, although still sweating at night (but less than before). I can also row for more than an hour. I am disposed to work, the work absorbs me and on awakening I make plans, also during walks and in the boat. I am quite apathetic and oppressed by a heavy melancholy. Feeling that E. R. M. is waiting for me, that I could give her my work—that she would share it with me—helps me and gives me everything love can give—this yearning for happiness—pure as gold, pure as crystal, lies before me like some treasure under an evil spell; I can see it, but it does not rejoice my eyes.—This will pass, and the truth and the deep values will endure.—In the morning woke up late, after 9. Wrote diary and fumbled among my papers (wrote down con-

versations and observations). Then walked until 11:30. Morovato and Kariwabu: I attacked problem of *sagali* and *mourning*.
After lunch, same subject with the same informants. At 5 went
to see Toyodala and obtained some additional data. Rowing, one
hour; deep melancholy, murky thoughts which I don't recall.—
Homesickness for civilization doesn't torment me these days. In
the evening rather big supper, then Navavile, and looked at
Tomwaya Lakwabulo.* Turned in at 11; woke up before daybreak (sweating), thought about E. R. M. Dreamed about her:
she and Mim and I sitting together; she is writing a letter;
tender feelings.—Also, in the evening under mosquito netting,
ugly, coldly lecherous thoughts about L. P. I said to myself: "I
don't regret my sins of the past, I wish I had committed more!"

2.17. Sunday. Up at 7:30 after short but fairly good night.
Still sweating at night—some sort of process undoubtedly going
on in my organism. Right after getting up I walked to the *sopi;*
still disposed to work, I made plans and drew up some problems.
During the day I thought a few times about E. R. M., but it was
more intellectual than spontaneous. Still, clear realization of
what she means to me clearly provoked an emotional upsurge. In
the evening I thought about what would happen if C. E. M.
came back—and at once I longed for her and felt how much she
meant to me. This disgusting trait of mine—that whatever I
possess with certainty loses all attraction for me—is one of my
basic misfortunes. In the boat, after a long moment of deep, dull
melancholy I thought about the possibility of a professorship in
[Wolobrook] (!) and planned lectures, receptions, etc., with
E. R. M. as my wife.—In the evening, back from the boat, dull
but satisfied fatigue; I lay down and let my thoughts wander
sluggishly.

* The seer was presumably in one of his lengthy trances, described in *The
Sexual Life of Savages.*

Events: after my walk, breakfast, etc., began to write. Navavile prepared *daymas*. I watched him; then he made a *megwa*
on the *daymas*. Then visited a garden with Morovato. After
lunch (3:30!) I wrote down *sagali* and *Waribu*. Then took out
boat; Swinburne's poems. Thoughts as above. Evening; I ate,
rested, dragged myself to a *bwayma* where I talked with
Bo'usari.* Namyobe'i† and Tomwaya Lakwabulo. Then Yasala
Gawa. Listened to T. L. outside a door. Went back.

2.18. Monday. After fairly good night (sweating but not too
violently), got up physically weakened and mentally dull. Village preparing for *ula'ula*. I was *in the mood for working.*—
Took a walk, then inspected [*soba*]. Breakfast. I went to
Towakayse's. He prepared a small *sagali* (*vila vila*), and I pa-
tiently watched their sluggish, slow fumbling. Went back. With
Kariwabu I wrote down main points of *ula'ula*. About 12, utter exhaustion. I lay on my bed as if dead, then felt better, got
up and read *Kipps* [a novel by H. G. Wells]. Then wrote,
looked over my papers; at 4:30 again exhausted. It was raining,
I could not go to the lagoon. I sat or lay, again dull feeling,
total ebbing of physical and mental strength. Then short walk.
Trivial thoughts. Counted months before moment of liberation.
Strange nervousness: shying like a horse at every shadow, every
rustle in the jungle. Went back in my thoughts and emotions to
Annie; thought that if I went back through S[outh] A[us-
tralia] I might live with her. *No*‡—emotional; I am *de facto*
married and have no right even to think of it. After I came back,

* Bo'usari, an attractive native girl from Oburaku who had left two hus-
bands and was looking for a third.
† Namyobe'i was a spirit woman dwelling in Tuma (the Trobriand after-
world), whom Tomwaya Lakwabulo had married on one of his visits there
(made during his trances).
‡ Underlined in original.

ate large quantities of taro, read *Kipps*. At 9 so exhausted that I retired under mosquito netting.

2.19. Slept and stayed in bed until 8:30. I took no quinine yesterday, and did not sweat at night. But this morning horribly weak physically and intellectually. Could barely drag myself. No energy for work or anything. Thought affectionately about E. R. M. but in the same anemic tone as about other things.—That day, like the two preceding ones, overcast; drizzle and sudden downpours. Got to work late, after reading *Kipps*. Began to question Morovato at 11. Recalled my abscess and dressed it, then shaved—it was 12:35 by then, but I rested and felt like working. I went to the *"bushes"* in the rain; then Niyova, with whom I worked on *"small stuff"*—problems and *queries*. At 4:30 took out the dinghy—rowed too vigorously. I tried to collect myself, to get out of my lethargy and melancholy. Read Swinburne; thought about E. R. M. and the need to work intensively if I am to keep my *self-respect*. I told myself that although my work was not amusing and not glamorous, it was not entirely pointless. Went back; rest; supper—completely exhausted. Nevertheless I went to see the *nakaka'u* and gave her [. . .] and worked a little on *Saipwana* and *lisala dabu*. Via Molilakwa's, where I almost fell asleep, went back home.

2.20. Woke up early. Thoughts about E. R. M. in a sensual way; then deviation to L. P. which I mastered. Clear, sunny day, light northwest breeze. Stayed in bed until 8:30. Got up again feeling as though I had been put through a wringer. I'll have to eat less or earlier in the evening. Morning: Morovato came; I did *sagali* with him, finished it; but many points still left open. At 12:45, very tired; lay on my bed, then read *Kipps*—a little too long—during and after lunch (*experiment* with *tinned oysters*). Then collected my papers and went to see *Ribu*

Nakaka'u and *Tobuaka'u*, where I made a couple of discoveries concerning *terms of relationship and adopted friendship*, or rather *veyola*. Then went back; rain and storm made boat trip difficult. Read *Kipps*. Then went [. . .] along *karikeda* to Kiribi. Once again I thought about Baldwin Spencer and Seligman, planned letters and prepared *attitudes*. Then recalled that this theme is taboo. Went back and ate supper; went via Tomwaya Lakwabulo, who returned to Tuma, to Reuma's *bwayma* and talked there. Irritated by Muayoulo's talk about insufficient pay. Evening—had too strong tea—couldn't fall asleep. Thought about E. R. M. and my anti-B. feelings: desire to shake Anglo-Saxon dust off my sandals. Certain admiration for German culture. In the evening—or was it at night—I again thought of E. R. M. with tenderness and passion; again deviation and setting myself straight.

> *"For the more you have known of the others*
> *The less you will settle to one."*

These lines vex me.—During the night obscene dream about some monstrously coarse and disgustingly sexy *barmaids*—2 of them—whom I pawed *all over*.

2.21. Woke up early and couldn't sleep. Strong northwester. Made up my mind *not** to go to Gusaweta, and to write a few letters before I go. Felt fairly well [. . .]. After breakfast went out to find informants. Molilakwa, whom I wanted to question about *kabitam*, had gone for a walk. Engaged Mokaylepa and Mosibuadaribu. First looked over my papers and copied scattered notations. Then *poulo* with Muayoulo, and the two mentioned above. Not bad but M. again irritated me. Then brief paddling in the *dinghy* in strong wind. After lunch felt poorly, I began to write letters, but stopped several times to rest—could

* Underlined in original.

it be that *tinned food* again affected me? I was irritated by the *niggers* and homesick. Wrote letters to Seligman, Mim, P. & H., E. R. M., and as usual letter to her aroused my slumbering feelings. Wrote until 6, then the *dinghy*. Blood-colored sunset, wind, waves. I felt weak, could not row far. A small stretch toward Kiribi. Thoughts about theoretical not sentimental matters— but what were they? Oh yes—I was telling Strong in the presence of E. R. M. that England was the embodiment of self-assurance, status quo, the whole world *in the palm of their hands*. Lack of enthusiasm, idealism, purpose. The Germans have a purpose, possibly lousy and thwarted, but there is *élan*, there is a sense of mission. Conservatives [preaching] to "democrats"; democrats [allying themselves] with Prussianism—the whole thing is a confusion of ideas. The episode with Baldwin etc. makes me decidedly an Anglo-Saxon- —not *"phobe"* perhaps, but it eliminates my *"philia."*—When I came back I lay on the bed, exhausted; then supper, then wrote to E. R. M. At about 9 so tired I crawled under the mosquito netting; slept fairly well. Dream about Mr. Wallace who loves *modern music;* in the dream I recalled some themes from R. Strauss.—By morning I [. . .]. My thought went back to Tośka; then fatal thoughts about Mecklen[burgh] Square; shook them off in the name of E. R. M. I must "air" the other things.

2.22. Cold, overcast day. The northwester is weaker but still blowing. Decided to go to Gusaweta. In the boat—sea, wind, change—the horizon a little clearer—I feel that I must find another place to live. Furious wind; I row with Ginger. Gusaweta deserted, sad; no *mail*. Mick scared me by saying that the "Marsina" is to be taken off the run. Wrote letters, read *Zeppelin Nights* [a novel by Violet Hunt and Ford Madox Ford]. Rain, wind. Turned in at 8 but couldn't sleep. Bad night.

2.23. Saturday. Gusaweta. Wrote letters, read the novel. Left at 4. Ted. "30%." I felt so low that even the company of those fellows was pleasant. Learned that the "Marsina" will not be taken off the run and that we'll have a *monthly boat* [. . .] Misima. Went back to Gusaweta with Ted. One half bottle claret. Ted again developed his anthropological theories. At 12 to bed. Slept badly.

2.24. Sunday. Got up late. Veranda flooded by rains. Day cold, overcast like the day before. Read—finished *Zeppelin Nights.* Strong upsurge of pro-British feelings and regrets that I am not in the war. Also thoughts about E. R. M. Wrote her additional letter.—New idea: possibly I was vexed on learning that she loved me because I did not feel worthy of her. Had I been in khaki and going off to war, *ce serait une autre chose.* But her love for me simply devaluated her. Then I lost my head and all sense of value and began to treat the whole thing as an ordinary *love adventure.*—All that day I felt rotten.— Went back to Oburaku at 4. Had no strength to concentrate on feeling of solitude. Began to read *All for a Scrap of Paper* [subtitled *A Romance of the Present War,* by J. Hocking]— and finished it by 10. A very inferior novel but the patriotic tone moved me; I thought of E. R. M.; vague feeling that my lack of heroism was cause of her devaluation. I loved her in relation to C. E. M. and I believed in her eternal faithfulness. If I felt worthy of him . . .

2.25. Monday. Slept until 8:30, felt rotten. Began to work around 11 when I was told that Billy was in Gusaweta and I got a letter from him. I went there with Morovato. Billy: the illness, Samarai—he was not too badly depressed. Read a number of *Life.* Went back; raging wind; had continually to scoop out the *waga*. In the afternoon, from 3:30 to 6, in spite of exhaustion, *village census*. Then went to the beach and sat there, tired. In the evening, after supper, wind. The palms swayed, the leaves like arms flailing madly, or wild locks of hair tossed in passion. The *niggers* sat in front of their huts; Iluwaka'i sang the *megwa;* part of the village was emigrating to [Borwanai]. Kadilakula sat bravely and performed the *megwa*. I sat next to him. We talked about the *megwa* and then about the wind and the rain. Then about *vilamalia*—and about hunting.—I smeared my bubo with iodine, and went to bed.—Waiting impatiently for tomorrow's mail. Letters from E. R. M. *offset by the remorse connected with N. S.*

2.26. Fresh cold wind from northwest; felt better than day before, although gorged myself with *kaimagi*. Palm and [*Kum'*] chopped down early in the morning. Inspected them and wanted to eat *palm cabbage*. Ginger didn't appear until 10. I worked on the palm, gathered informants, and attacked the *kabitam problems*. Ginger arrived. I was excited but I worked until 1. Then *lunch* and I opened the letters. First, the [less personal] ones. A friendly letter from C. G. S., from Miss Hadley; very nice letters from the Khuners. E. R. M. again about the B. Spencer business. Taken aback. I read on.—I went to the *odila*. I made up my mind to write final letter to N. S., and to Sir Edward,* to England. Then I read E. R. M.'s letters to the end; although I don't trust the promise given by B. Sp., I feel in the end completely calm and happy. I am again *in touch with* E. R. M. and this makes me happy. There is not the slightest doubt: we are engaged and I'll marry her as soon as possible. Read her letters until 5, then took out the *dinghy*. I thought about her and felt

---

* Possibly a reference to Sir Edward Burnett Tylor (1832-1917), a founder of British anthropology. If so, word of his death had not yet reached Malinowski.

happy, and the longing and the desire to run away from her pass—apparently I feel healthier. I went back, my eyes smarting, but I was relaxed. After supper I forgot my worries preparing coconut [salad], then went to the sea and talked with Navavile. Then to the village, Molilakwa, Yasala Gawa. Back at 12. I composed final letter to N. S.

2.27. General tone: calm, smiling contentment—thought a great deal about B. Sp. and means of defense, about C. G. S. [Seligman], R. M.* and E. C. S.†—I am happy that my relation with E. R. M. is taking ever clearer shape, and I feel a much closer tie to her. I also have a feeling of certainty that no more ideal wife could be imagined. But I don't think about her very much or very intensely. I think a great deal about N. S.—I keep composing letters to her in order to clear up the situation once and for all. Possibly the interference of B. Sp. contributes to this, compels me to reach a decision, to take decisive steps, and to some extent gratifies me.—Got up still sleepy and not feeling very well. Diary; read letters and part of a novel. Then the women, census. Then Kadilakula's *megwa*. After lunch, rest, then again Kadilakula and translation. My head bursting with fatigue—I left a few expressions unfinished at the end. Took the *dinghy* to Kiribi, rowing vigorously. Melancholy sight of Mick sitting there, wasting away, watching the gray lagoon; swirling clouds [conceal] the southwest—his window on the world. Empty house. Squatting with towel in hand on the crumbling veranda. Excellent setting for a novel. But what about the plot? I would have to introduce Brudo working hard to become a millionaire; transform Billy,

* Robert Mond, scientist and philanthropist who gave, through the University of London, the Robert Mond Travelling Scholarship, which Malinowski used on his field trips—£250 per annum for five years.

† Professor E. C. Stirling of Adelaide, a close professional associate of Malinowski's and editor of his Mailu study.

George and Edward Auerbach? M[ick] G[eorge] before advent of government. Fights against the blacks, becomes absolute master. Benevolent despotism. Then comes "government"—Moreton, à la De Moleyns—a drunk, good-natured, *irresponsible* usurper. Threatens Mick with *capital punishment.* Property deed made out crookedly, inaccurately: *drinking bout;* Edw. A. comes into it now.—Then, plot. Brudo tries to get rid of Mick.— First describe a *slump* in Mick's fortunes, then their sudden *rise.* Then unsaddled. Rage; he is dragged to prison; dies.

I went back. Rowed again. Didn't think much, for all that time mentally exhausted. The moon rises. Return. Supper (again *palm cabbage*). *Kayaku* in front of Molilakwa's house—women only. Then saw Towakayse. We talked about Gumasila and Domdom [both islands in the Amphletts]. Came back very sleepy and fell asleep quickly.

2.28. Thursday. In the morning—awakened by shouts of natives at an early hour so that I haven't slept enough. In spite of it, felt fine, and took morning walk without getting tired. Wrote diary *with elation.* After breakfast read some of E. R. M.'s letters—I love her very much, and am calmly, cheerfully happy. My good health, too, contributes to this. But just now I am *not* in love. Nonetheless I feel none of the metaphysical sadness, forsakenness, pessimism which I normally feel. At free moments I compose letters to Sir Edw., Sir James, C. G. S., and Atlee Hunt (in the evening, in the *dinghy*). But all this without rage and without pessimism. I think more about these things than about E. R. M. personally, but this does not spoil my taste for ethnological work nor my feeling for E. R. M., nor my optimism. Health, health!

I worked well all day until I was utterly tired. Did unpleasant tasks—a map of the sea and the grounds. Today I should finish (i.e., March 1) as well as do as much as I can on the genealogy. I spent the morning with Morovato, Bobau, and Muayoulo. Talked also about habits of fishes. After lunch wrote and made drawings, assisted by Niyova. Terribly tired. Ate pineapple.—At 5:30 went out to get palm cabbage. At 6 dinghy, dark red sea. Back at 7 and [cut] cabbage, at 8 taro, and squabble over who burned the pot (*billycan*). Then the fellows told very indecent *kukwanebu*. Didawina,* Sugeluma, [Kailavasi].—Went to sleep at 11. . . .

March 1, 1918. The fellows woke me at 8, also I had to get up for other reasons. I now sleep without a blanket or other warming things and feel better this way. After a walk, during which I drew up decisive letters in my mind to N. S. and E. S., worked with Mosibuadaribu, who explained [. . .], but I felt rotten, and his information about L. T. was unsatisfactory. After an unsuccessful attempt to take a nap, and lunch, Yasala Gawa and Morovato; very tired, could barely speak. At 5, I stopped and lay down. There could be no question of writing to E. R. M., not even reading—(after lunch I read E. R. M.'s letter and a bit of *Cadoresse*). *In the dinghy I thought about* E. R. M., our plans for marriage. The idea that we'll be married soon makes me happy.—I came back, ate a great deal, gorged myself. Inspected a burrow, termites. Went to bed at 10. Iluwaka'i's *kukwanebu*. (All evening long was irritated by the fact that I couldn't beat up Bo'uriosi without starting a row.) —In the afternoon decided to go to Sinaketa.—Tendency to work to exhaustion and inability to sleep; work under high pressure. Calm love for E. R. M., I read her letters like the Scriptures.

March 2. Excursion to Sinaketa. In the morning, rain and windy. But I am determined to go anyway. Joy of being on the

* Possibly Digawina, heroine of a story told in *The Sexual Life of Savages*.

sea again. Glassy green waves around Sinaketa. Made a sketch of the *waga*, did not think of anything except the present moment. Naturally thought about E. R. M.—how wonderful it would be to have her here.—Two hours. George A[uerbach] seemed somewhat less cordial at first. Wrote to E. R. M.—this put him in a somewhat better mood. After lunch furious hurricane, rain; I worry about the tent, I imagine it blown away, my papers scattered, my MS. destroyed.—I finished letter to E. R. M., wrote to C. G. S. and P. & H. At 4:30 went to see the Brudos. Raffael—young, with a nervous, intelligent, pleasant face. Amiable, sincere and straightforward. Talked about politics and the war. His views are similar to mine. Invited me warmly to visit them, even to stay overnight. I have the impression that he is the only man whose company *would bring me in contact with civilization.* I find him extremely sympathetic as a person, as well as his views and manners.—Went back to George's; the villages of Sinaketa over the green sea; the cold violet outlines of the huts *against the orange transparencies of the western sky. Light almost afloat, suspended in the air.* George showed me his pearls. Then we talked about Raffael. . . . Before then we had talked politics and I had criticized Hughes and had expressed moderate anti-German opinions.— In the evening, after supper (abundant—pork, potatoes, custard), I asked George whether he doesn't have something against Ted so that I could be an [intermediary]. Very polite and friendly protestations. At 9:30 the *waga* made ready, at about 10 departure. Thought about E. R. M. (had been thinking about her since I left Brudo). I dozed. Row with Ginger at Oburaku. This spoiled my night and humor and I recognized I was in the wrong.

March 3. Sunday. Rain and wind at night and in the morning. Got up late (8:30), gray, damp. Wrote diary; tension between

the *boys* and me. I was edgy, tense; in addition, intense stomach-
ache, overeating—I couldn't eat a thing. From 11 to 1 a bit of
work with Muayoulo and [Wayei] and [*vagila, kuna, dodewo*].
Around 1, I was tired, felt I had not worked hard enough. At 1,
letter to E. R. M.—There could be no doubt I was tired. After
—or rather during—lunch I went to see Mrs. Cambol [. . .]
and *sagali* at Morovato's (crab and fish, no vegetables). Then
sat and watched [. . .] *saipwana*. Furious wind, we put up mats
for protection. Jokes about going to Tuma and marrying them
[the spirits] all. Thought about E. R. M. and wanted to
tell her about all this. Then the indecencies of Nanabo *kukwanebu*. We left at about 4. Dark, rainy, windy. My eyes hurt me,
no question of writing or reading in the tent. I went to Tomakapu's house and talked—physically I felt broken, and I was
sleepy. Then went back to the tent, and to bed at 8:30. Ginger's
kukwanebu got on my nerves. Slept fairly well (*Dover powder*),
thought about E. R. M. physically, and once again felt that she
was my only woman and my wife.—I want to write her that we
must get married soon.

March 4. Monday. Awakened by their shouting at 6:30. Ginger
again got on my nerves (*Tropenkoller?* [tropical frenzy]). I
got up—decided to shake off that lightheadedness. Walked to
sopi. Am stronger physically—I thought about ethnogr. work.
Also, thought with pride about my work: better than Sp. & G.'s
[Spencer and Gillen*], better than all the others. Should I write
to Frazer and Seligman? I collected myself: all that matters is
what I am doing right now. Breakfast: struggle with the termites; Mwagwaya and Medo'u; talk; diary. All the time
thought about E. R. M.; in love with her.

Worked with M. and M. until 11—no, until 12. Then to the

---

* F. J. Gillen, coauthor with Spencer of several major studies up to this
time.

village, to get informants, but no luck. Around 1, went for a walk to relax. Thought about E. R. M., also about *Lettres persanes, Letters of a Chinaman.* Plan *"History of Uto-pias"* and cynical criticisms *à la Swift.* Thought about developing this idea in a letter to E. R. M.—After lunch terribly tired, couldn't even write E. R. M. Tried to nap, in vain; *desultory reading of Cadoresse.* Then [Mobaymoni] came, and I worked with him and Niyova, slowly and lazily, on miscellaneous questions. At 5:30 walk around the village. From 6:15 to 7:30, out in the boat. No appetite. Irritated by theft of Billy's book. Also stolen is Zola's *Dr. Pascal,* for I did not see this book yesterday. Read Stead * as an opiate. Turned in late, at 10:30; furious at all these pigs.

March 5. Anniversary of departure from Port Moresby for Sydney two years ago. At 6 in the morning *dinghy* wasn't there. Vexed and mortified—£14. Morovato found [. . .]. Then went for a walk and composed letter to Frazer. (Yesterday composed letters to Hunt.) Fearing obsession on the score of B. Sp. accusations—I controlled myself and thought about ethnographic method: apart from the question of the "social dimension," relig:ous images and faith, there is the problem of "actual definition" of rules of custom. There is a rule, given in a certain way; a *fixed and set* rule—all informants agree it is so and not otherwise; this rule to be verified. Furthermore, the mythological way of describing certain phenomena, e.g., *a hurricane, shipwreck,* etc.: tendency to "schematize" facts. And then, two kinds of understanding: observation and magic causality. *Luya* falls: *mulukwausi* sat on top. A man is fishing and *pilapala* hits him: revenge of *tauva'u,* for the [*mini*] of Wawela killed him. *Silami* as the ground of sickness. Also wounds. *Kariyala—side by side*

* William Thomas Stead, well-known English journalist and author, founder of the *Review of Reviews* (1890).

with natural explanation of things. Today I must finish census; copy all [. . .] also go over my notes and see what still needs to be completed.—in the morning I read a little in Stead's magazine and *Papuan Times,* and a novel. Began to work at 11. Don't remember the rest of the day! As usual, took out dinghy; recalled anniversary of trip to Sydney from Port Morseby. In the evening wrote letter to E. R. M.—I love her with a strong passionate love. I ought to think of her as my wife.

March 6. *Sagali* in Kaytuvi. On my way there I mentally noted intimate and picturesque details. Thought about E. R. M. and referred material to her. In Kaytuvi I worked honestly for 3 hours, with camera and notebook, and learned a great deal, lots of concrete details. New theoretical point: (1) Definition of a given ceremony, spontaneously formulated by the Negroes. (2) Definition arrived at after they have been "pumped" by *leading questions.* (3) Definition arrived at by interpretation of concrete data.—Came back to the tent tired but not broken or exhausted. Read *Cadoresse* for an hour; from 4:30 to 6 talked about the *sagali* with Morovato and Kadilakula. Fatigue: I forget terms, I speak slowly; three seconds later I have forgotten what I had in mind. Then in the *dinghy*—what did I think about? At all events, not about letters to potentates and N. S., for I recalled them and was vexed by this. Went back. Too tired even to write down [story of] Digawina. Talked with the fellows about general matters. Morovato and Iluwaka'i. Read *Cadoresse* for a while. Then to bed. At night awakened by dogs howling. Took *Dover powder.* Wind in the morning. Thought about E. R. M. and missed her. Felt strong but pure passion for her. . . .

March 7. Thursday. Got up late; rain; dampness. After breakfast read *Cadoresse.* Thought about E. R. M. Moments of violent longing: *only to see her luminous, lithe body again.* At moments discouraged by my strong hatred for England and the English. Began to work alone at 11:30 and worked well until 1, recording my impressions of the *sagali*. After lunch felt worse. Worked a little with Muayoulo and Iluwaka'i (wrote down *kukwanebu*). Read issues of Bulletin. At 5 made rounds of the village; at 6 went to Kiribi, where I felt tired. Marianna gave me *gulukwa*. On my way back, I scraped my foot on the *waga*, applied Goulard's cerate; half-dozed on chair. Read E. R. M. letters and some *Cadoresse*. To bed at 11. Slept fairly well.

March 8. Got up at 8. Fine weather, the rippled surface of the water green, transparent. I felt fine, certain contentment with *surroundings* and work. *Round the village.* Marianna's *saipwana*. Then walked to *sopi*. Thought of publishing my photographs in an album with explanatory notes. Breakfasted late. I decided to take a few decent pictures. Loaded both cameras and discovered probable cause of fogginess in ¼ *plate camera.* Took picture of *saipwana;* then of a small sailboat. I wasn't too "*brilliant*" and worked lazily. After lunch, interviewed Marianna: the "Kayona" will sail next week. Started to *wind up my affairs* in Oburaku. Translated *song from* Tuma. Then dark; in the boat drew up plan for collecting things:

To be left: (1) papers, MS. and letters. Take only *general file.*

                     (2) [Bulunakao] bag.

To take: 200 sheets of paper and other things needed for work.

                   Cameras. 12 rolls and 3 *dozen plates* and equipment for developing films.

                   Food for 6 weeks.

                   Pharmacy: Extra aspirin and what I have here!

To be done: Instructions for Billy and my will.
Letters (1) C. G. S. (2) R. Mond. (3) J.
Frazer. (4) A. Hunt. (5) N. S. and E. S.

On coming back (in the boat I had looked at the stars and thought this had to be done before they all vanish) I worked on the stars, chiefly with Morovato, but also with Mobaymoni and Wayei. Went to bed at 11:30. Slept well after 5 gr. aspirin.

March 9. Saturday. After morning walk, breakfast, etc. drew up letter to E. R. M.—or rather, realized I had a great deal to tell her. But I began to work: Morovato eluded me and Karigudu did nothing in his absence. Furious, I went to the village (the whole gang came from Kaytuvi to play *cricket*). [*Ibodem:*] *saipwana*. Then Morovato came, helped, I finished the *saipwana* and the translation. After lunch, I read *The Village that Voted the Earth Flat* and I understood what E. R. M. thought about it. Then census with a blind woman and Mwagwaya. M. is very good informant. Worked to the point of exhaustion. At 6 I left. Drew up a letter to Hunt, but I was tired; terribly dejected, and the prospect of trip to Gumasila doesn't comfort me. Concrete formula of life: *"Mate with her, beget children, write books, die"*—what is it in comparison with cosmic ambitions? To possess the sea and the stars and the universe—or at least to encompass them in one's thoughts? To express the attraction, the force that compels me to plunge my spirit into reality. Something greater than curiosity and more essential than thought.—I felt the need to express this in a poem, and to send it to Elsie.—Went back. After supper, again census, until 10. To bed at 10:30.

March 10. Sunday. Felt it was my duty to go to Wawela. Shook off natural laziness and made up my mind to go. Brief walk, during which planned move to Gusaweta. Since yesterday have been vexed by Billy's attitude: his letters are laconic and he does not invite me to come to Gusaweta or on the "Kayona." At 9:30 I went to Wawela via *raybwag*. At first very tired; sweating, the sun beat down. I asked the names of trees; Morovato, as usual with *niggers* on such occasions, answered reluctantly.— View of the sea delightful, in spite of fatigue. In Wawela I gave orders not to remove [. . .] and took pictures with the Graflex. Then, rain. Talk with Kwalakayu (a decent fellow, rather obliging). Watched the making of a *waga*. Lunch on the beach: roasted [*tanimewa*] with boiled yam, coconut; then I got up my courage and ate *towamoto* (very tasty). *Picnic* mood on the sand by the open sea. Thought all the time about E. R. M.— here in this place, and with a much freer existence than in Oburaku. I'd like to have her with me here much more than in Oburaku. I felt sleepy and dozed. Return to Kiribi. Enormous deep jungle. Then broad view of the sea past Boymopo'u. Something like a Mediterranean mood on the sea. Mick alone, looked better. Leafed through illustrated issue of *Mailu*. Said good-by to him and went in his *waga* to Oburaku. Morovato was *sulky* and relatively unpleasant. Began to write letter to E. R. M.—the sun set. *Dinghy*. I think I must first finish *business points:* N. S., E. S., Atlee Hunt, *etc.* After supper (the *niggers* came and were friendly—taboo) I wrote rough draft of letter to N. S.— very difficult! Turned in (irritated).

March 11. Monday. Packed—everything finished by 12. I have no sentimental feelings about this period—I am glad that the Oburaku *niggers* are behind me, and that I'll never again live in this village. Looking for a *waga* in the village irritated me. Morovato helped me loyally to the end. Sailing in intense heat; I rowed a great deal; uncertainty about Billy's attitude. In Gusaweta, Billy, *absolutely all right*. We developed photographs. A lot of letters for me, which I read with no great eagerness, for I

am not so interested in what is going on, and am preoccupied
with all I have to do. E. R. M.'s letters made no great impression
on me. Letters from C. G. S. and Mrs. S. very affectionate. I
think a great deal about writing N. S. and I am incapable of
reading her letters.

March 12. Tuesday. Packing. I am quite energetic and systematic. Continue packing after lunch. Tired by evening. Finished
everything by lamplight. At 9 sat with Bill and chatted a bit.
Didn't attend to will, or letters. Bill developed three rolls, all of
them good. Only the picture of the two of us is bad. I don't
recall what were my main thoughts and feelings these two days.
I am not terribly happy that I am going (*no*;* I am glad that I
broke the foul monotony of life in Oburaku, that I have only 5
months more in Kiriwina, and that I'll live in the fabulous world
of the little islands).

March 13. Wednesday. 6 A.M. Final packing. Somewhat worried
about "30%," he may be in difficulties. Walked to Losuya.
Bought 4 combs at Bwoytalu. "30%" was decent: loaned me Bulletins. The little cabin on the "Kayona"; my things. "Tonight
I'll be in Gumasila." † Cruised back and forth between Losuya
and Oiabia. Mangroves west of Kavataria. Across the *passage.*
Sea choppy.—Lay in cabin, slightly seasick. Boymapo'u, Boyowa in a light mist; indentation in the coast where Oburaku is
situated. Drank coffee, dozed—thoughts wander. "Freedom and
mastering of space." Ha ha! I wake up—Koyatabu, Domdom,
and Gumasila. Pink and green pastel colors. Night falls. We
pass close by a little coral island, the sea smashing against it.
Quite dark—Gumasila a black spot. Looking for anchorage.

* Underlined in original.
† Gumasila, one of the Amphlett Islands, was one of the destinations of
the *kula* expedition from Dobu.

Somebody's hat falls overboard. Cruising. Aroused by cries. *Squall.* A sail torn. I realize the situation is serious. Scared—I tremble with fear! Superstition comes to the surface: 13; premonitions about Amphletts. I think of E. R. M.—she is sleeping peacefully and I'll never see her again. Characteristic insincerity and pessimism based on superstition: I am afraid to be optimistic because I believe this brings *bad luck.*

March 14. Thursday. Woke up about 11 between Sanaroa and Garea. Broken and discouraged by seasickness, having lost hope that I'll ever get to Nabwageta. South wind. We cruise near Sanaroa. Strong currents cross here, winds, choppy seas, characteristic noises. We sail around the sand bank and enter a calm *inlet.* I sit tired, feeling no hunger, only thirst. I ["emerge"] from my impressions. Monauya is in a fairly pessimistic mood. (Serious, composed face. Reminds me of Ahuia.) Slept till 5. Trip to Giligili. [Storch.] I tell him my story of the last days, he tells me his. Shows me the ship. Tells me a second time how he became paralyzed, and tells me his symptoms. A blond; face of the Dying Gaul—pendant, tow-colored mustache; thin, no paunch. Simple, no affectation or fakery (à la Geo. Auerb., Brudo, etc.), likable. We express political opinions. Then gramophone. I drink tea and eat XX [. . .] with *black currant jam.* Went back. S. + and Gr. Bear [Southern Cross and Great Bear]. E. R. M. Southern hemisphere incomparably more beautiful than the northern.

Friday 15. Got up early. Wrote E. R. M. Went ashore. The fellows tie the *waga.* Then after lunch to a large village and a hill. *Pitcher plants* and orchids. Lovely view. *Flat mangrove belt dissolves itself into a maze of inlets and islets.* Koyatabu invisible. Cold wind. Return. In the evening talk with Monauya.

—Dirty thoughts (trying to struggle against them by thinking
of E. R. M., but unsuccessfully). . . .

Saturday 16. In the morning, expedition: I want to go to Sanaroa. But immediately after landing in the village, I feel very
weak. Preparing of sago. Return. Read E. R. M.'s letters and
newspapers for February 4-19. Then with Ogisa in the dinghy.
Marvelous view. Koyatabu visible. Matterhorn and Wetterhorn
above the mangroves. Evening again with Monauya. Then to
bed, very tired and sleepy. . . .

Sunday 17. Woke up. Resolved to carry out moral reform: it
isn't difficult to be decent in a state of grace. Only when you lack
strength and dirty thoughts assail you—only then is moral
stamina put to the test.—After breakfast, sailed up the creek
with Ogisa. Line of tall white trunks above intense green. Then
the jungle; [*lalang*] *grass* to the right, sago. I looked at a *sago
swamp* and *temporary shelter*. Return. Wrote E. R. M. Read.
Ate lunch, then read again until dark—true, I read [Rev. C. W.]
Abel and [Pöch], but still!—In the evening *dinghy*. On the
north (above Sanaroa), south (above [Mount] Bwebweso),
and east, swirling white cumulus clouds piled up in several lay-
ers, on the background of black stratus. Rowed to the western
tip of Sanaroa. Feared that strong northwester might blow me
away from the shore. Also the current. Could hear the noise of
foaming eddies. Above Bwebweso constant thunder and lightning. I was seized with panic. Tried to *"steel my nerve,"* but
only half-succeeded. Sat for a long time watching the dark
clouds and the sparks flashing between them. I thought a bit
about work—but how? After I came back talked with Monauya
about *kula*. Turned in at 9. Slept well.

Monday 18. Woke up at 6. I lay thinking about E. R. M. Day
before, in the *dinghy*, had thought about her and the need for
spiritual purity. This morning I shuddered at the thought
of betraying her. Also thought about Kiriwina and about my
work. I must hurry, to be sure to finish! Yesterday I felt rotten
—I ascribe this to terribly sultry atmosphere. Today feeling of
tension and pressure on eyeballs; terrible sluggishness and the
same unpleasant smell of a *particle out of my mouth* I used to
have, before oper. of Andrew. Could this be the liver? I threw up
in Gumasila; the taste of blood [. . .]. Also I have a somewhat
congested throat and nose.—Around 7 we folded my tent aboard
ship and set out. I still felt rotten, and this prevented me from
enjoying this excursion. Sanaroa unfolded slowly as a broad and
extensive plain—a green ribbon—to the right, and a belt of low
but complicated (ergo, [broad]) hills. Koyatabu in clouds. The
green hills on Fergusson [Island] came closer; outlines of individual trees. The wind had almost completely abated. I went
down to the cabin and read [*The*] *Englishman* [an English literary journal], which I finished. I don't associate this with
E. R. M.; aroused anglophobic feelings in me. I thought about
this and about the complications it might have created in my feelings for E. R. M. We passed 2 *launches*. Strong wind. I didn't
feel too well. I lay on the roof of my cabin and looked at the landscape. Garea Bay, and to the southeast, Koyatabu came into
view. The flat shore line in the back leads directly to Begasi and
Deidei. [Extinct] little volcano drawn out into a broad ridge.
I observed it—tall trees covered with white blossoms—the physical inaccessibility of the tropics. The dark-green water, the
bronze-colored rocks, the white foam, the green trees—all this is
fairylike but silent and threatening rather than eloquent and
inviting.—An unseen voice from a *launch* invites me. I shaved,
read a piece from *Maud Diver*. Monstrous downpour. I talked.

Donovan annoyed me: "respect more in the German trenches."
I went back and set out for the village in a *dinghy*. We changed
anchorage because we were almost on a reef. Night fell; thunder; dark clouds.—I went to the "village." A single, miserable
hut; a few pigmylike fellows and women. They had nothing to
sell. They kept scratching themselves and almost all had [*sepuma*]. The little house on pillars was very primitive; the floor
and walls of sago sticks and bark; a pot from Amphletts the
most magnificent possession.—Another village: a couple of huts;
the men fairly tall. Broad faces. The women's faces pleasant,
not the perennial whorish expression of the Kiriwina women.
Some of the inhabitants had gone on a *sago-making expedition*.
Previously they had lived in the hills (out of fear of the Dobuans?). We killed a snake. I went back, slept well.

Tuesday, March 19. Mother's name day. Thought about Mother
from morning and decided to write letter. Also thought that
landing on Amphletts that day should bring luck. In the
morning, Monauya and I went to the village. Clear day. Trees
right next to the water among bronze-colored rocks. A few
palms right by the water, once again that inaccessibility. I
walked a few hundred yards. Gigantic dark trees. Struck by the
number and size of gardens. Next to the houses on pillars, [some
with] roofs on the ground, open to one side, very primitive no
doubt. The inhabitants didn't run away nor were they insolent.
Strong wind. Domdom is closer than I thought—in two hours
we'll be there! I sat and this time enjoyed magnificent view at
the foot of Koyatabu. A broad chain of islands; to the left,
mountain in the mist, steep profiles running down into the water; the sea cut at bottom by the horizon and on top by the plain
(*level roof*) of clouds bring to mind the Canary Islands. (O
mother, Mother, will we ever travel again by *carretera* [high-

way] from Tacoronte to Icod de los Vinos?)—In the morning that day, moment of intense reflection: need for intellectual work and continuity. I made plans concerning Amphletts—linguistic, technological, etc.—My thoughts got confused and mixed by impressions of the landscape; the wind had abated, and it was as though we were tied, at a few hundred meters perhaps a kilometer from a little island covered with *lalang* and jungle, but uninhabited. I felt fairly well and struggled against inner emptiness. The view was magnificent: the pyramid of Domdom with the cupola on top between lateral extensions at the foot; Gumasila with the double hump. The three cupolas of Nabwageta, further along on the wooded hills of Kwatouto and Yabwaya—all this with the shores of Fergusson in the background.—The silence of the sea and the absence of wind wearied me (I could not write the diary, let alone letters to M. and E. R. M.).—I got out *Letters of a Chinaman*, when the wind rose, [*Boremana*] and we sailed on to Gumasila. 2 *masawas* vanished behind an islet. —We reached Gumasila on a foaming, choppy sea. No possibility of landing. We sailed around: a calm bay, a tiny but attractive village. Seemingly deserted. We landed in about an hour, put the things on the beach among *wagas* and [pigs]. Dogs *nosed about*. My friend Kipela appeared and offered his services. Talked with him: a certain ability to lie and unpredictability in this fellow, but he speaks very good *pidgin*. I slept outside a little house, my things were put in the huts. Almost no place for the tent.

Wednesday, March 20. After getting out of my cage (*tainamo* squeezed between *stretcher* and the low ceiling of the house), I walked around the village, looking for a site for the tent. I made the acquaintance of an old gentleman and dragged him to the tent in process of being put up. Until two o'clock I divided my time between talking with him and superintending the tent (with frequent irritations). Then cocoa and *biscuits* (I had had no breakfast); the little dictionary with another fellow (I don't remember his name). Then with rain pouring down every minute we set out in the dinghy. I felt that to live in this world was worth all the trouble involved: a steep wall of mountain with perpendicular cracks where lush vegetation was growing, tiny waterfalls, the noise of water. Ten minutes after a violent downpour, the noise of mountain torrents, and right next to the tent the murky foaming waters mingle with the green depths of the bay.—We went out in the *dinghy;* to the south the shores of our bay lie low at the foot of hills covered with *lalang grass;* northward, the hills rise to a mountain summit; there are two gigantic rocks that cut across the sandy beach. Then, right above, the sheer cliff with the cracks in it; then again the semicircular bay, and the gardens of the little village above it. We sailed between outcroppings of rock offshore (furious wind and rain). The village is deserted. Picturesque view of a belt of pyramid-shaped hills; Domdom *veiled with gray rain.* The massive stone terraces glisten under the moisture. At moments I have a voluptuous feeling ("mixed identity of circumstances")—the gray sea, the mist-covered greenness of the island opposite, and the long, stone terraces have something of the air of a northern fishing village. The dark [mass] of the island rising behind [creates] a strange mood, such as I have never experienced before. The little houses in the village attract me, as well as intrigue me ethnologically. There is also the difficulty of doing research under these conditions. The fellows are unpleasant and answer my questions with obvious reluctance. If I did not have my Kiriwina assets, I should never accomplish anything here!—I inspected the houses: one in mourning; they strike me as very old, very "deep-rooted" houses, in contrast to the Trobriand Islands, where the houses

and *establishment* are new.—We went back and I ate taro;
very tired, I went to bed at 9 and fell asleep. Before, I sat a
while and looked at the *landscape.*—[. . .].

Thursday 21. Slept a long time—"catching up on my sleep"—
I feel I needed it. I feel a little knocked out; but not unwell.
Rain, chilly (76° = 24.5°C), continually [changing] wind. The
view from my tent, just a few steps from the sea—bounded on
the left by the green wall of the bay and a rock, and the prow of
a wrecked *waga* at the right—is fabulous.—Wrote diary, neg-
lected since departure from Sanaroa. I must draw up a system
of investigation on the Amphletts. In the morning I wrote a long
time, started ethnogr. fairly late. Worked at first with Anaibutuna and Tovasana,* who are not bad, but not *first-class informants.* After lunch Kipela and an old man; I got annoyed with
the latter and chased him away. For a moment I was afraid that
this would spoil my business, then Kipela successfully resolved
the difficulties. At 6, in the *dinghy* with Ginger to *lalang* peninsula. Once again joy when I am on the deep green waters, and
the island covered with dense green vegetation gradually reveals
itself. The lower arm of the bay runs toward a few little red and
black rocks (*just a bunch of warm blood-stained red in the
dark brown*), wrapped in verdant plumes. The luxuriance surrounding the crevices, suspended over bare rocks, climbing up
the bare walls, gives the landscape a specific tropical character.
There emerges the rounded top of the island, covered with
lalang. Apparently the line between *lalang* and jungle depends on the nature of the soil, for the low hills of Nabwageta
are covered with jungle, while here the low peninsula [is covered
with] *lalang.*—I feel strong and healthy and crave a long walk.

---

* Tovasana was the main headman in the Amphletts; Malinowski was
staying in his village, Nu'agasi on Gumasila, and used him as an informant
(see *Argonauts of the Western Pacific,* particularly Chapter XI).

Through a short col—rock: *breccia*, very coarse-grained, cohesive, rusty-blood-colored agglomerate which determines the overall coloring of the rocks. We tried unsuccessfully to make our way through the little rock and the trees coming down to the water; we took the dinghy back to the promontory, and along the sandy beach to the bushes. There, surrounded with *taboo palms*. Then again view of the beach through fallen tree trunks. I rowed coming back. Such pleasure to explore, to make contact with the tropics. Thought about E. R. M., about telling her all this. When we got back Ginger told me about *gora* in Sariba, and we planned ethnographic research in Sariba for next year— in fact 4 months would be enough! Then short talk with Tobawona and Kipela; important discovery about the heterogeneity of *megwas*—a pleasant moment for an ethnographer! After supper did excellent work on the language. Tobawona my best informant.—Went to bed; again thought about Donovan's insult and tried to master it—but the most important thing is the lesson that I should be more careful with this scum.

Main themes of life: joyous relief at living peacefully, without being persecuted by rascals, incomparably easier relationship with the natives.—Ginger has been somewhat tamed; he is less *cheeky*, though he doesn't work properly. Happiness, fullness of life (yesterday, because I felt healthier) as a result of the new surroundings, new work, new type of work. My tent, a few steps from the water, always has the sound of gentle plashing, and the noise of torrents up above in the lofty green wall.—Emotionally: calm attachment to E. R. M.; thoughts about Mother; last night sensual-emotional throwback to N. S. Since Donovan, anti-English feelings, more accurately, anti-nationalistic feelings. Intellectually: comparative ideas (Melanesian histories) concerning the situation of these fellows. Yesterday I understood the charm of *"survey study"* à la Rivers, the encompassing of broad areas as a single whole. But this projection of space onto time (two-dimensional or rather multi-dimensional entity) is very dangerous.

Friday 22. Main currents of life: Ethnogr. work which goes very well, *thanks to* Tobawona.—Got up at 9 ([. . .]!); rain, hence nothing came of planned excursion to Domdom. In the morning wrote diary carefully, then to the village; all the *Sine-sine* in their huts. Tobaw. came. Worked on death and belief in *Tuma;* it went very well. In the afternoon (violent downpour opened *creek* to the sea) again Tobaw. *et Co.* This kind of work —superficial, without going into details—is much lighter and more amusing than the work in Kiriwina. At 6 we set out for Gumawana.* Black cloud on the northern horizon. In the dinghy I sketched a plan of the village. Tob. unwilling to land. The fellows sat dully on stones, *independent, sulky, unfriendly—true islanders!* Then I got ashore, walked among the houses. Again spellbound by the picturesque village. A black shadow slowly strangling the yellowish light blended with the silvery glow of the moon behind clouds. Domdom: a big *tilted pyramid,* 2 replicas to the left, 1 to the right—*a chain of almost geometrical uniformity, yet impressive and rhythmic.* Returned fairly late; threatening clouds approach. Rocks all around. To the left, the dark, complicated, richly decked wall of Gumasila; to the right Omea (Domdom), *the* [*top*] *overbridged by the dark cloud.* Koyatabu visible, blue, cut only on top by a line of little white clouds. We sailed around a stone. Distant view of Nabwageta and clear outlines of smaller islands. Behind the promontory, a rain cloud. I felt a curious desire to be caught in a real rain once without any protection. I began to roar out a Wagner melody. The cloud—or rather rain—moved closer and covered us like a white sheet. Exactly like a cold *shower bath;* wind. The dinghy

---

* Gumawana was the large village of Gumasila, around a point of land from Nu'agasi.

filled with water. My watch, fear of *tabekusi.* Back home; I dried
myself off.—Work on the dictionary. Could not fall asleep for a
long time; thoughts offensive to E. R. M., struggled against
them—most dangerous those about N. S. But when I got to the
point of imagining giving up E. R. M., I realized this would be
impossible. Fearing I had caught cold, I took *Dov*[*er*]
pow[*der*], quin[ine], and asp[irin]. Slept well.

Saturday 23. Equinox. Woke up at 9, a bit uncertain as to how
I'd feel. Epsom salts, tea. Worked with Tobawona, who is going
stale on me, and who left in the middle to go fishing; Kipela
stayed on, and he was not too bad.—After lunch (read a weak
story by Kipling) set out for Gumawana; a boat with Nab.
[natives from Nabwageta?] had gone there and a *mwadare* is
supposed to take place. (In the morning many boats went out on
a fishing expedition.) Kipela, Anaibutuma, and I. As usual, joy;
I planned photographs, looked at the sea bottom. Right before
Gumaw. I realized that "I had forgotten the keys"—dismayed,
but controlled myself. *Census.* Continued happiness at the surroundings: delighted in the view of Koyatabu; sketched Domdom. I was given sago.—We went to Sarakeikeine. Looked at
Gumawana—immensely beautiful silhouette. Two rocks rise up
out of the vegetation, *like two truncated pillars out of a heap of
overgrown ruins.* The sea striving, advancing in orderly rows of
long smooth waves. I rowed. At moments I didn't know which
way to look—at the exquisite silhouette of Gumasila or the vig-
orous harmonies of Domdom, or the symphony of pastel colors
on the distant mountains of the big island.—Sarakeikeine.
Flights of birds against the clouds dotting them like buckshot.
We startled flocks of *dawata* and pigeons (*bunebune*). The cliff
—a red conglomerate on the southeast, and northwest hollowed
out into a deep vault—grottoes; on the other sides, steep.—We
went back. I recalled night with Gilmour when we dropped an-

chor here. "*Mere rocks*" he [said], and with dark, sharp profiles. I had imagined them as sheer black volcanic cliffs—and the villages had seemed pasted on to the steep side, near the water. This accounts partly for my longing for these islands.— I thought about this *in terms of a letter to* E. R. M. (The previous day, returning with Tobaw. before the rain, when the light was simply magical, to E. R. M.: *This is quite like a symphony.*) I recalled Szymberski and his island. We were near Domdom.—We turned back. The big island vanished in the dark. Mixed light of dusk and moon rising between the islands. I rowed. Echo. Again planned ethnogr. work.—Supper, dictionary. I walked around gazing at the stars. Mars glowed red through a break in the clouds. The moon overhead.

Sunday, 3.24. First clear morning. Koyatabu clearly visible. I could see the top covered with *lalang.* The [wind] from the west rising up to the very top and cutting across it with shadows. A steep green slope plunging down a slanting wall that is plowed by deep, narrow furrows (dark narrow ribbons) along a single deep hollow on the left: a waterfall. Yesterday, when the whole sky was covered by thick dark stratus clouds, Koyatabu was in the sun against the clear sky on the horizon. For the first time I understood the effect of phosphorescence: the same as the effect of moonlight: light more concentrated *in** a small area than *around** it. (Thought about how to formulate this for E. R. M.) Today got up at 8, took a walk, delighted in the view extending as far as the pointed peak (replica of Koyatabu) and mountains of Goodenough. I was afraid that everybody might go out on *poulo,* for the water was calm and there was no wind or rain.—Still happy with the surroundings. I want no change, nor news, I am not bored. The smells (yesterday moss, seaweed, and flowers, the wind was

* Underlined in original.

from the island; today the fragrance of tuberoses on the beach),
the rustling stream, the jungle, the shady wall with its sump-
tuous covering of tropical trees.—In the morning all the fellows
went out on *poulo*. Kipela and the *old man*—fairly slow. At
about 1, Kaduwaga men & Kuyawa men—*kula.** Came to*
Nab[wageta] yesterday. Came [in] small canoe: 2 bu. of taro,
1 yams. Nonchalance in coming; nonchalance in receiving them
displayed by old man. Then they come & sit on the canoe. Con-
versation: jocular haggling, lying about the soulava. Then give
it. Then they go to other end & they [taloi] the men. (I eat my
rice and kippers & read my Kipling at intervals.) I sit with them
& listen to their conversation, then drag out some information.—
Then dinghy (sketch of map), inspection of garden: amount of
work done in terracing, draining, & clearing their patches.
Then proceed in moonlight. Unexpected luminosity of moon,
coming out from behind the hill. Along the coast. Again formu-
late description about "the soft distinction of Gumaw." & the
harsh but lulling rhythm of Domdom. "Lights and shadows on
the soft full forms seem to have intensity & weight & press
against each other. The shadows float in places over the surface
of the dense bush in places they sink, in places they tear out
large cavities."—Then encounter with man who gives a sample
of monikiniki (in Boyowan) and tells ab[out] tomorrow's kula.
Then turn round from the stone (I row) along the village, back
to our place. Evening (from 10 to 11) Tobawona etc. Explana-
tion of kula, stars, some myths.—Night full of dreams, Cracow.
Thoughts, tender and passionate, of E. R. M.

Monday, 3.25. That day Gumasila and Nu'agasi men left for
kula at Boyowa.† Whether because of *secretiveness* or supersti-

* This visit of an expedition from two islands west of Boyowa is described
in detail in *Argonauts*, pages 269-72.

† The Amphlett canoes accompanied those from Dobu at the *kula* at
Sinaketa early in April.

tion, they always conceal their departures from me (Mailu, Omarakana, here).—Got up at 9, as usual. Did not notice anything (the day before, Kipela had been washing and cleaning himself up—was this for a last visit to his fiancée or part of the *kula* program?). Went to Gumawana (peeved but not [discouraged]). The women hidden, as usual. I saw a few from a distance. Not too much confusion. I went to the [*bwaymas*] and observed packing of pottery! Only pots, sago and *nuya*. I couldn't persuade them to get out *bogana sago*. Took a few pictures. Saw Gumawana in the morning for the first time. No trace of magic ceremonies or farewells. Boys go, including even 2- and 3-year-old children. The boats are punted to the promontory where the sails are unfurled (I didn't see this). Came back at 12:30—the Nu'agasi were just leaving—I could not even photograph them. Fatigue. Lay down—closed my mind, and at this moment revelations: spiritual purity. *"Heed kindly other people's souls, but don't bury yourself in them. If they are pure, then they reflect the world's everlasting Beauty, and then why look at the mirrored picture if you can see the thing itself face to face? Or else they are full of the tangled [woof] of petty intrigue and of that it is better to know nothing."* I had revelations (very familiar) of the endless sordid petty threads running from man to man of hatred, intrigue, inquisitiveness. After lunch, still tired; read Kipling; rested. At 4 began to work with Mataora—garden. They lied, concealed, and irritated me. I am always in a world of lies here.—At 6 I learned that the fellows had come back. Boats and Anaibutuna. Marvelous evening. Boats at the promontory. In my boat I enjoyed the view of Gumasila from this side, of Koyatabu and other mountains. Then I rowed around the promontory, the moon hidden behind lacy clouds. I felt I was on the sea 8° lat. and 149°longit. (or something like it) Greenwich. Distinct feeling that next to this actual ocean, different every day, covered with clouds, rain,

wind, *like a changing soul is covered with moods*—that beyond it
there is an Absolute Ocean, which is more or less correctly
marked on the map but which exists outside all maps and outside
the reality accessible to [observation].—*Emotional origin of
Platonic Ideas.*—Came back, sat on the beach. Moonlit night.
White sand, over it dark shapes squat, in the distance the ex-
panse of sea and outline of the hills. In the distance, the sea and
the profiles of mountains. Combination of moods: Baia di Napoli
and Gumawana "from inside." Thought about how to describe
all this for E. R. M. The moon, the sea, the mood. The moon
induces a specific, clearly defined mood, I hum "[Laraisebrue],
and then there was Suzanna, pretty, pale, and virtuous." Expression of feelings, complementary social milieu, imaginary.
Suddenly *I tumble back* into the real milieu with which I am
also in contact. Then again suddenly they stop existing *in their
inner reality*, I see them as an *incongruous yet artistic and*
[savage], *exotic = unreal, intangible, floating on the surface
of reality, like a multicolored picture on the face of a solid
but drab wall.* I came back, Anaibutuna raced with the boys.
Delightful feeling that now I alone am the master of this village
with my "*boys.*"—The moon above the hill makes pale reflections
on the glistening leaves. Supper; I ate slowly, lazily, being tired.
Thought?—Took out the *dinghy* after supper. Gazed at the
stars: S[outhern] Cross—E. R. M. Staś. Atwood (*Semolina
Pudding*); Sirius, Canopus—the two largest stars a "*poor
show*"! Came back, and to bed.

Tuesday 26. Planned excursion to Domdom. Awakened by Tobawona with a fish. Got up, in a hurry to set out for Domdom.—
Then found out that they had no intention of going. Tobawona
in a bad humor, but polite—an excellent informant. Worked until lunch. Then unnecessarily read R & B, and finished a story by
Kipling. Fatigue. In the afternoon *poulo*, but work went very

slowly. Finished at 6; rowed in the dinghy around the island. Very tired. Observed and *assayed:* (1) I consider their secretiveness, reluctance to define their plans (Mailu, Boyowa, here). I catch myself doing this and try to attain "intellectual void." (2) I think—on the occasion of seeing the Koya?—about the value of a dictionary of this language, Samarai *jail, Muvinabayo* in Samarai—*final work of Papuan description—farewell to Sam[arai] & Papua—will it be regretful? Thus all "associations" on lines of definite interest, desire, sentiment. "Thought takes its impetus from life, not life from thought." Or else, thoughts are the drifting floats or the buoys which mark the current & it is not they who direct the current but inversely.— (Next morning I think it over again. Avenarius' * Vitalreihe* [life-series] *even better than Cornelius' Erinnerung von Komplexen* [remembrance of psychological patterns].) *The principles of association by space, time, similarity are just the most external categories, which give hardly any clue at all.*—We go around the promontory and turn eastward. No need for compass because rising moon and setting sun determine [direction. . . .] All attention focused on the island. Mood of "the other side." The shore runs east-west from promontory to promontory, with indentations (bays). The slopes considerably less steep, meadows of *lalang* cover the hills down to the sea, especially in the 2nd bay. Here and there dense jungle in tiers. Two peninsulas like two arms stretched into the sea, covered with *lalang.* Charming, amusing little clusters of dense vegetation nestling in gaps near the shore, at the foot of the *lalang*-covered hills. Joyful feeling of recognition. This island, though not "discovered" by me, is for the first time experienced artistically and mastered intellectually. The moon struggles with the gray light of the misty sunset, when we round the 2nd promontory and glimpse Domdom. Then big waves, and my thoughts bog down in sluggishness and

---

* Richard Avenarius (1843-1896), German philosopher.

nausea. I notice that the stretch between Gumawana and my village is by far the loveliest. Evening; after supper I sit on a chair by the sea, humming waltzes. A moment of fear: have I lost taste for good music? Think of E. R. M. and that I must tell her solemnly that I look upon her as my wife. "The sacramental sacredness of the marriage bed."

Wednesday 27. Day of rest. Tobawona and Silevo have gone somewhere, not a single good informant to be found. Intellectual fatigue because all this week I worked hard. I must make up my mind whether I shall pick Nabwageta or Domdom. In this hole, nothing to do!—In the morning read *Maud Diver*. Photographs, which are *a success*. The novel trashy; I discover gross errors all the time. And yet I read on. *"Engineering of plot; violating of incidents, etc. etc."*—After lunch (episode with spoiled pictures, which improved later), read again. Constantly planning to start letter to E. R. M., but follow line of least resistance. At about 4 took pictures of village, went to the big village. Brudo decided to go. Still feel indolence, intellectual and emotional. Looked at *landscape* and rested ("Rest is one of the most important forms of work"). Chat with Brudo. I notice that he speaks without listening to me (he informs me about what I have to do here, and tells me stories, but doesn't pay attention to my stories, etc.); I fall silent and listen. Stayed too long. Went back by moonlight. Domdom attracts me by its shape more than Gumasila. Back; drank tea; read *Maud Diver*, turned in late. (I don't eat in the evening.)

Thursday 28. Got up late; rested in bed. Yesterday, under the mosquito net, once again fierce, almost religious yearning for E. R. M. Thought about her constantly while reading *Maud Diver*. I decided to settle the issue today: if the Nab[wagetans] go to Boyowa, to go there [Nabwageta] immediately; if not,

first Domdom for two days and then Nab. *pour tout de bon.*
To take care of everything, plans, maps, *census,* to take pictures
of Tovasana and environment.—After breakfast I got ready
and set out at 11. On the trip *glaring light.* I reviewed the
Amphlett material in my mind; then, by way of association,
composed memoir on "Value of Ethnographic Studies for
the Administration." I want to write such a memoir when
I am back.—Main points: *land tenure; recruiting; health
and change of conditions (such as getting them down from the
hilltops)*; above all, *the knowledge of a people's customs allows
[one] to be in sympathy with them, and to guide them according
to their ideas. This point of view of Govt.: a mad and blind force,
acting with uncontrollable force in unforeseen directions. Sometimes acting as a farce, sometimes a tragedy—never to be taken
as an integral item of tribal life. If Govt. could adopt this point
of view, very well. But it cannot.—The final plea: purely
scientific value; antiquities more destructible than a papyrus
and more exposed than an exposed column, and more valuable
for our real knowledge of history than all the excavations in the
world.* Then I rowed a bit; we watched the *poulo.* I was told that
they were going with *bagi* to Boyowa; vexed; at once hatred for
the *niggers* and general discouragement; I even thought of
leaving the Amphletts *altogether,* or settling at Kobayto.—On
arriving, entirely different impression: instead of a tiny village
on the shore of the sea, all life squeezed out from it by its isolation and the emptiness of the immense sea—a large village, pul-
sating with intense life, an important center, many trees, long
row of houses, in bright sunshine. A group of fellows were finishing the sail. I went to Tobwaina. They probably won't leave
before the end of the week. I also tried to speak about ethnographic matters, but without great results. Ate *kamokuki* and
biscuits with coconut. Then sat at the other end and discussed
kula and pots with Tolokouba. Picked a place for the tent,

then went back to Tobwaina. We sailed back; I looked with regret at lovely Gumasila. Decided to write E. R. M., drew up a letter. Roasting of pigeons and fish. Planned trip to Nabwageta. After supper, began letter. I read my previous letter to her (which was not much of a love letter). Then I was so sleepy that I turned in—at 11.

Friday 29. That day moved from Nu'agasi to Nabwageta.* In the morning under the mosquito net—or at night, perhaps, or in the evening—thought of N. S. with regret, wondering what she could give me in the way of love, comparing her with E. R. M. But then I realize again that E. R. M. is the only life's companion for me, and that she can give me incomparably more than anyone else even in love, because our temperaments are compatible.—The sight of syphilitics or lepers in Nab. made a strong and unpleasant impression on me. I thought that if I caught it I'd have to renounce E. R. M. and bury myself away on some tropical island. *I realize* what losing her would do to me and want to write her at once.—After breakfast, the *boys* packed, I wrote. Little sentimentality *re* the removal. My letter not sentimental; rather matter-of-fact, *record of facts.*—At 12 ready for departure (certain apprehension that one or the other might leave me in the lurch at the last moment); the wind is rising, so we wait. The *boys* eat rice; I check on names of houses and other constructions to complete my dictionary.— Then I ate, rested—accidental discovery of cannibalism in Kwatouto and Domdom. (*Old man* asked me: "Do you eat dogs?" "Of course, some dogs and people." "We don't, but Domdom and Kwatouto did.")—At 4:30 we rowed off; afraid they might steal things. Marvelous sunset, which I mentally de-

* The Amphlettans were highly suspicious of other men where their women were concerned, and the men of Gumasila did not want to leave for Boyowa knowing Malinowski was there. He therefore promised to move to the nearby island of Nabwageta when the expedition had left.

scribe to E. R. M. Arrival in Nabwageta. Place looks empty, unfamiliar; somewhat vexed by thought that in a few days they'll leave for Boyowa.—Wrote letter to E. R. M. In my thoughts preparing to work, but some resistance. Slept near a house, but not well (tea). Thought intensely of E. R. M. and suddenly *right into the golden dreams, comes in the leper's face.* —At moments I long, even now, for Melbourne, E. R. M., civilization.—Today accidentally opened this diary and found photograph of N.'s room—and tears came to my eyes.

Saturday, March 30. Yesterday a *pickaninny* woke me, also chickens and little girls aroused me [quacking]: *"Taubada raibaku."* This *beach* shaded by large leafy trees, with a broad view of the sea, has many *Stimmungen* in it.—The rest of day ethnographic work, but it didn't go well. I began *"kabitam"*— copied a few *lagims* and *tabuyos*, and began to ask names: they did not know the names. I asked about *megwa*—they had no *megwa*, no personal *kabitam*, nor any *megwa* used during making of *waga*, or gardens. This irritated me, I went away and began to work with Tom and Topola; it didn't go well either. I felt like stopping and reading a novel. Lunch; read Kipling (very poor); then collected esoteric information about *poulo* and *waila*—whenever I touched upon magic or intimate matters, I felt they were telling lies; this vexed me. At 6 went south for a little walk. Very tired and depressed. Didn't even long for Melbourne. Thought of E. R. M.—would I be happy if she were here? Did some exercises, gazed at the sky with special feeling for S. Cross. When I came back, read *Maud Diver* and ignored the *niggers.*

Sunday, 3.31.18. Last day of the month—complete collapse. In the morning I did nothing. In the afternoon, the *mina*-Dobu [the expedition from Dobu] arrived; I took pictures of the boat and talked with the policeman from Sanaroa. Subjectively: over-all condition such that I need narcotics but I have aversion to them. As usual, my narcotic is a trashy novel. In the morning (was awakened by *conch shell,* a new boat begging for gifts) went to the *beach;* after breakfast I read *Maud Diver.* Finished around 12, and felt so broken and sleepy (in need of arsenic?) that I lay down and dozed until 3 P.M. After lunch, boats—the whole *beach* filled up with people who sat down and chatted, fairly calmly, however. Toward nightfall I set out—still the same fused feelings in regard to the southern point—saw Gumasila and Domdom on one side, and Koyatabu, Yabwaga, and Kwatouto on the other, against a purple cloud. Impress of beauty, thought of E. R. M. and whether we'd be able, together, to wrest beauty of its secret. I am longing for her (moments of longing pierced my screen of sleepy melancholy musing); I felt I wanted her the way a child wants his mother. I thought of Mother, I'd like to see them both together. I also recall *N.** who was always very kind to me and very loyal.—On my way back I inspected the Dobu boats near the shore. Then, during and after supper I discussed *kula* with the policeman and took notes.

Monday, 4.1.18. The "Kayona" arrived; *1st of April "bad luck"—13th day of the Amphletts?*—Wrote letter to Billy, finished and sealed 2 letters to E. R. M.; then watched the rest of the boats sail away. Regret that I didn't pack *lock, stock and barrel,* that I didn't go to Kiriwina. (Today, 4/2, this regret comes back—perhaps I really was foolish, staying here?) Then I came across a fellow—Toyarima; he wanted to see my teeth and he turned out to be an excellent informant. After lunch I read Kipling (a little too long). Then an hour's conversation,

* In the manuscript, this is the small letter *n* in a circle, the symbol used in Part I apparently referring to a woman he had known in Poland.

rather unsystematic. Observed an old woman preparing a meal. The boat and the noise and the water discouraged me and *I retreat (with or without honor?).—Then, I [try] synthetically to look at the natives and I also think about the delight we take in mystical, mysterious things (à propos of Kipling and a little bit also my fright): And I restate my theory of religion—or part of it—over again and also that of social psychology—"the S. Integral of a given psychological phenomenon."—After I come back, I feel that if E. R. M. were here, I would develop it to her and feel stimulated, and then I begin to write it to her. Then, again, I get the old man Yariba and we talk—ending at 10.—I am too tired to write to her, but I think of my problems. —I have also a few nasty mental temptations* (seduction of Miss Mc[. . .]—) but I resist them victoriously.—When and how shall I meet Elsie? At the Station or at the Khuners or when?* I* don't think about it, I just wait, endure, and time flows along beside me.

Tuesday, 4.2.18. In the morning I felt some scruples about not having left on the "Kayona"; the "Itaka" arrived.* I got ready; regret that I had not taken pictures and had not worked on pottery. Joy: I'll be again *in the middle of things,* and lots of material.—I don't waste too much time making up to the white fellows. A bit *seasick* at first, and I don't react intensely to the landscape as we are moving away from the Amphletts.—The whole *romance* of Koyatabu and the Amphletts vanishes.—I sit on the *rigging;* I go downstairs, read Cassidy. Strong feelings about the war, and very pro-British ones, particularly in view of the bad news from France. I think of E. R. M.—will she love me in these unheroic circumstances? Happy at the thought that

---

* The boat was not expected, but the captain, knowing Malinowski was there, stopped to see if he was ready to leave. Otherwise, M. might have missed the arrival of the Dobuans in Sinaketa.

I'll have letters from her. Night falls. Gaze at the stars after anchor is dropped.

Wednesday, 4.3.18. Between Muwa and Yaga, sailing into Trobriand. I look at the green waters of the lagoon, at dark points as though *swimming and shimmering* (?) *over the glassy waters.* At moments, like an emerald blended with a dull amethyst, where dark clouds cast reflections. Mixing with whites in George's house. Then long stretch to Gusaweta. I am nervously excited; once again the lagoon of Oburaku; I think about a letter to E. R. M.; about what I'll do in Gusaweta. Arrival. Few letters. Only one letter from E. R. M.—Letters and presents from N.—like a knife in my heart. I don't read her letters.— I slept well but on Thursday felt rotten. Why does Gusaweta have this bad effect on me? Trip to Kiribi in rain. I went to Sinaketa and read letters; from M. H. W., which "wake me up" (I compose a reply in my mind); then from E. R. M., which is objective, but precious. (This is [poorly] formulated!) Then interview with George who was examining pearls, Mr. Campbell, Raffael (was a little less enthusiastic about him, but he is a fine fellow). Looked at Billy's house. Came back, supper with George, then visit to Raffael, and discussion on "the uniformity of shapes of stone implements." (Plan of an article: In the St. Germain museum with pearl-trader. *"Beku."* Have we all evolved starting from the same point? Were these things *transmitted?* Or did "identical conditions create identical needs"?)—Went back home, wrote letter to M. H. W. Bad night: the animals, dogs, cats, etc.

4.4. Thursday. (Combined with preceding entry.)

4.5. Friday. In the morning, wrote a few letters and had breakfast with George. Around 12 I went over to Kunubanukwa. After lunch went to the village, ate *paku*, talked with the boys, when the Dobu arrived.* I hurried out (and in my hurry didn't take *extra* rolls of film!). Impressions from *kula* (once again feeling of ethnographic joy!). Sitting in Tovasana's boat I looked at the *kula* ceremonies. Raffael watched from the shore. Sinaketa almost like a summer resort with all these *gumanuma* people.— I was engrossed—as an ethnographer—in all the goings-on. At the same time, Friday and Saturday morning I thought of the letters I had to write. Also Raf., whom I like very much and who creates the social atmosphere, is a factor in my "orientation." In the evening I went to see them, and was received hospitably; they asked me to come every evening. Came back very tired; didn't feel up to writing letter to N. S.

4.6. Saturday. In the morning read and wrote letters to N. S., fairly optimistically, though optimism in this matter is a flimsy illusion. Geo. A. left under my nose. We sent a canoe after the "Kayona" with Raffael. Then went to take pictures, and lounged among them. In the evening talked with a fellow from Domdom.

4.7. Sunday. *My birthday*. Again worked with camera; by sunset I was simply exhausted. Evening at Raf.'s; discussion, first on physics; theory of origin of man and totemism in Trobriands. —It is remarkable how intercourse with whites (sympathetic ones, like the Raffaels) makes it impossible for me to write the diary. I fall, confused, into [the way of] life there. Everything is in the shadow; my thoughts are no longer characteristic in themselves, and they take on value *qua* conversation with Raf. And so, on Sunday morning I fumbled around, didn't leave for To'udawada† until 10; then photographed a few boats—and in

---

* Described at length in *Argonauts*, Chapter XVI.

† The most important chief in Sinaketa.

this way passed the time until 12 (made drawings of *lagim* and *tabuyo*, which is very tiring). Then lunch. Around 4 again took pictures on the shore and a few from a boat. Inspected boats. In the evening so tired I almost fainted. Sat with George on the veranda. Arrived fairly late at Raffael's.

4.8. In the morning, without my knowledge, the boats of the Dobuans left. Worked at home with a few fellows on the *kula* question. Then, at lunch time, read Stead. Thought of E. R. M. *by flashes*. (Wondering about political problems in Austr. and Poland; found an item about *poor Tommy* in newspapers; looking at Raf. and his wife, at the naughty caricatures in *Vie Parisienne*—she is the only woman for me, more and more often.) Then, around 4 I worked again; at 5 I went to the village and saw Toula, who was doing *kula*. Then Raffael. Talk about atoms, about electricity, the existence of the soul, competition; with Auerbach leafed through *Vie Parisienne*; he told me anecdote about Lourdes, etc. At night, in bed, I thought very intensely about E. R. M.

Tuesday, 4.10 [*sic*]. All day long very strong feelings for E. R. M. In the evening I longed for her. Thought how I'd see her and press her to my heart; about the happiness of being with her again, *intimement*. Yesterday I wondered whether she was happier in her absolutely monogamous love; I cannot imagine [other women in my past]. To eradicate this, as one eradicates unpleasant and humiliating memories. My everyday reality is permeated with E. R. M. Thought about my marriage, how Marnie would accept it, Leila, the Peck family (continual novelistic fantasies). Same thoughts when I went to bed, and awakening at night. Identity of this feeling with feelings of child for mother (*vide* Freud's theory).

In the morning got up late; planned what I had to take along, etc. Wrote the diary, packed, carried everything to the house, but forgot to inspect the *dinghy!* Rain began to fall. Toula has moved to my veranda and begs. I went to see Raffael. A certain familiarity, sudden, excessive, based on mutual sympathy but insufficient previous acquaintance. They invited me to *déjeuner*. Left at 1. Nervousness because off balance [. . .]. At the same time wanted to think about way of describing *kula* to E. R. M.; read novel and looked at the landscape. Continual *flashes of Sensucht* [longing] for Melbourne, P. & H., and E. R. M. Feeling that being in the house at Gusaweta gives me no time for desperate longing (the Raffaels help a great deal). I began to develop films, felt energetic and wanted to work.— Conversations, during which I tried not to show too much enthusiasm for Raffael. 24 plates in the evening. At night, storm; two plates broken; then three ruined by insects. Unhappy about this.

Wednesday, 4.11 [*sic*]. First half of day in Gusaweta; normal routine: got up late after bad night, had conversations with Bill about photography, etc. Examined films (after breakfast), cleaned camera, finished developing. Washed and shampooed. At 1 ready to leave; rain; wrote E. R. M. All that morning I was energetic, felt well, in love with E. R. M.—In the afternoon, instead of reading novel or idling, I read my old diary. Reflections: I asked myself whether my present life achieves the maximum of intensity obtainable in view of my health and good nervous condition. *No:** I interpreted the doctrine that best work is done during *leisure hours* as doctrine of following line of least resistance, as *taking it easy*. Doubts à la S. I. W. [Stanislaw I. Witkiewicz]—is it worth while to eliminate fruitful sources of inspiration (which every thinker and artist will find by following the line of least resistance)? But it is a fact that when you eliminate one form of inspiration you gain another, and

---

* Underlined in original.

that to eliminate line of least resistance is above all to eliminate *pure* waste of time (reading novels, sitting *extra long* in company, etc.). For instance, my present mode of life: I turn in too late, I get up at irregular hours. Too little time devoted to observation, contact with natives, too much to barren collecting of information. I rest too frequently, and indulge in "demoralization" (e.g., in Nabwageta). I also thought about problems of keeping a diary. How immensely difficult it is to formulate the endless variety of things in the current of a life. Keeping a diary as a problem of psychological analysis: to isolate the essential elements, to classify them (from what point of view?), then, in describing them indicate more or less clearly what is their actual importance at the given moment, proportion; my subjective reaction, etc. For instance, yesterday afternoon: First version: "I went to Sinaketa in Raf.'s *waga*." (I could give hundreds of examples of such versions.) Second version: (a) external impressions; landscape, colors, mood, artistic synthesis; (b) dominant feelings in respect to myself, to my beloved, to friends, to things; (c) forms of thought; specific thoughts, [programs], loose associations; obsessions; (d) dynamic states of the organism; degree of concentration; degree of higher awareness; [resulting] programs.—Concretely: (a) after departure from Gusaweta (I had a comfortable seat, the *waga* was heavy and *stable*), gray and dark blue clouds. Definition of the mood created by the flat *coastline* of Losuya, Kavataria: "afternoon holiday mood and rest" (*a smiling relaxation and promise of changes*); flat and long coastline indented by shallow bays; today *jet-black under the luminous distant clouds and a clear dark blue sky with the characteristic appearance of emptiness— like a blackened-sky effect in an old master.* Then the landscape disappears; I read the diary, sailing between mangroves. Then the green lagoon of Oburaku. Oh yes, Boymapo'u *manche:* the water *dun-colored* with intense violet reflections (the dark-blue of the clouds blending with water). Oburaku lagoon: *mat, pale green, like a naked chrysoprase, on that, the intense violet; above, dark blue clouds and intense goldish green mangroves and other trees*. (b) Feelings for E. R. M. steady, am continually referring to her, but I am above all alone. I am entirely caught up in creative thoughts, seized by a wave of concentration. (c) Clearly defined ideas: the nature of psychology and to what extent introspective analysis modifies psychic states; also, is introspective analysis discredited because it modifies states?— Historical problems (?)—associations: memories of my life in Samarai; memories of Paul and Hedy suddenly come to me out of nowhere. (d) Dynamically, I am in a state of concentration; I resolve not to read novels, to go to bed and get up at regular hours, to write letter to N. S., to write regularly, every day, to E. R. M.; to attain absolute mental faithfulness to her, as well as to aim at achieving "a strong will" in the sense I gave this term previously.

After nightfall, took the boat out, punted for about 45 minutes. Then I sat watching the phosphorescent fish in the water, got two fish out of the boat. Planned trip to Vakuta* and work there. Arrival: Ted gone. Supper with Raf. Reading of [Musset]. My attitude was much more objective than before: I stayed *in my shell* and looked more critically at Raffael, but not without sympathy. Formula: I clearly see differences in our outlook—his ideas which I don't accept, which is *ein überwundener Standpunkt* [a point of view I have left behind]—but I check my impulse to discuss them.

Thursday, 4.12 [*sic*]. All day long I was in a mood of concentration. After writing diary, I worked with Layseta.† After

---

* The Dobuans were expected again in Vakuta—their final destination before sailing home.

† Layseta was a chief in Sinaketa; he had a wide knowledge of magic and had lived in the Amphletts and Dobu.

lunch, read bits of Australian poems *in Memorial for Fallen Soldiers*, and worked with another fellow here on the veranda. Both times on *kula*. At 5, to see Kouta'uya;* spent an hour copying the list of his *karayta'u*. Then at the Raffaels'; talked with natives; *conjuring tricks*. Moral tenets: I must never let myself become aware of the fact that other women have bodies, that they copulate. I also resolve to shun the line of least resistance in the matter of novels. I am very content that I have not fallen again into the habit of smoking. Now I must accomplish the same thing in respect to reading. I may read poems and serious things, but I must absolutely avoid trashy novels. And I *should* †
read ethnographic works.

4.13. We planned lunch together, photography, and croquet. This morning I resolve: before 10 write a few lines to E. R. M. Then 2 hours of preliminary ethnographic work. Describe *kula* for E. R. M. and make list of problems raised by *kula*.—From 10 to 12:45 I looked over notes on *kula* and copied them for E. R. M. Lunch at the Raffaels', taking pictures; I examined pearls. Came back at 3, again busied myself with *kula*, then the *boys* from Kitava came. Went again to see Kouta'uya and worked fairly well despite the sluggishness of these fellows. Then talked with a couple of fellows from Kitava on the beach. Wondered whether it would pay to go with them to Vakuta. Decided I would go.—Evening at the Raffaels'. We discussed the Germans—are they *ahead in science?* We talked about Giligili and Wright, Solomon, and other people from Samarai. Moment of heightened sympathy, when he spoke about *"looking through" a person*. He asked me whether I did this; I said, Of course I do, just like you. Then I mixed lemonade and we drank

---

* Kouta'uya was the second-ranking chief in Sinaketa and played a major role in the *kula* expedition between Sinaketa and Dobu detailed in *Argonauts of the Western Pacific*. He had 116 *karayta'u* [*kula* partners].

† Underlined in original.

[. . .]. Oh yes, also a very personal conversation about Sam's marriage and the influence of Emma.—Went back, wrote E. R. M. At night awakened by storm and nasty thunder. Terribly frightened; for a moment I thought I might never see E. R. M. again and this thought created fear. I thought about C. E. M. and how terrible death must have been for him. My precious, marvelous Elsie.

4.14. Saturday [sic]. In the morning sky overcast, rain. Woke up late; under the netting a tendency to let myself go, as usual, which I mastered. Planned details of excursion to Kitava, and thought about documenting *kula.*—I got ready. Wrote down conversations; *mail* to Samarai; finished letter to E. R. M. At 12:30 went to the village; conversation with Kwaywaya,* Toudawada, & Co. They refused to take me to Vakuta. Lunch at Raffael's; he showed me his *blisters* [blister pearls]. Came back; at 4:30 went out, made drawings of boats until 6:30. Then to Raffael's. We talked about the *natives:* their "specific weight"; their ideas about causes of natural phenomena—he didn't know about *kariyala.* In the evening we talked about suicide *by means of tuva, chagrin d'amour,* etc. Jealousy among natives (a married woman betrayed by husband takes *tuva*—is this suicide out of love?). Then we read *Phèdre.*

Sunday, 4.15 [sic]. Awakened by Vakuta people; the *waga* waiting for me. On the principle that it is better to visit the same place twice, I decide to go to Vakuta for a week.—I packed (unpleasant clash with Ginger *à propos* of termites; I was enraged and punched him in the jaw once or twice, but all the time I was scared, afraid this might degenerate into a brawl). Lunch at Raffael's. He showed me his pearls. I told him about

* Chief of Kitava Island.

my plans for a dictionary. Went to the boat; but felt poorly. Talked a bit with the Vakuta people; but it was raining. Then, tired by talk, read *Lettres persanes*, but I found none of the ideas I was looking for, only lewd descriptions of harems. . . . Night fell, behind Muwa. Arrival in Giribwa around 9. Slept in a new house. Again read *Lettres persanes*. . . .

Landschaftlich [notes on landscape]: After leaving Sina-keta we sailed fairly close to the shore. In spots, tall trees on a bit of beach; elsewhere, jagged, dried *scrub* with the white arms of little boughs cutting across the green in many places—"a disorderly mixture" is a better description. In spots, a low stretch of mangroves, and woods above. In the distance, Kay-leula submerged in water; lagoons on the north shore. On the horizon, Kuyuwaywo, Yaga. From afar, we see [a drawing of the shoreline in the manuscript], as if suspended between sea and sky, Gumasila and Domdom. The overcast gray sky falls like a curtain on the flat shores and shuts them off, turning them into a specific melancholy wilderness. Between Muwa and the shore a long, narrow *karikeda*. The tall trees of Muwa over the narrow stretch of land (weightless shapes, floating rather than set on any foundation) bring to mind the atmosphere of the Vistula; pushing the ship off the sandbar at Susuwa [Beach] —*generic name for a series of shallow bays and forelands*. Then night; I can't make out details but obviously the *raybwag* is close. Water plashing against stone, the shadow grows *more solid and high, instead of the choral croaking of frogs, the first chirping of crickets*. Rain more and more threatening, finally begins to fall. Marvelous points of phosphorescence emerging to the surface of the sea. Giribwa and the fairylike promontory of Vakuta. *The flat belt shown by an island or continent, like the face of a man, hiding and symbolizing his personality. First*

*impression which can never be the real, [to] unveil the whole is
nonetheless provoking and irritating.*

Monday, 4.16 [actually, 4.15]. In the morning, pouring rain. Curious effect: yellow (bright) sand. A group of boats from Kitava,
and on this side, right beside them, on the sand, mats spread out,
huddled bodies of people sleeping or cooking food underneath. All
this glows in deep dull red against the bright green sea with blue
reflections under the gray sky. I took a walk through the little
villages—11 huts and a couple of *bwaymas* scattered pell-mell on
the sand. [I went] toward the sea (my eyes and head ache) ; view
of Kitava; two currents collide against the isthmus and form
little foamy waves. Rain over Kitava. Looked at the bouquet of
trees very tropically merged with the profiles of the rocks on the
opposite shore.—They tell me about a *lili'u* of the fish Baibai.
Then to Vakuta; the clear bottom of the sea. They show me
mythical stones. Headache (seasickness) ; I lay down and dozed.
Shallow muddy waters, mangroves. We enter the *waya* [tidal
creek] floating amid open watery clearings in the mangrove. The
waga passes among the trees. *Headwater pool; wagas* from
Kitava. Headache dominant. Walk; I arrange the house here,
sleep till 6. Walk toward Kaulaka. Planning my work here.
Thought of Melbourne, longed for it. Went back: the village by
gentle moonlight; voices of the people; smoke surrounds the
houses like a cloud and blots out the tree trunks. The tops of the
palms seem suspended in the sky. Mood of return to a human
environment, a peaceful village. Thought of E. R. M., of returning to Melb. [. . .] F. T. G. The mysteriousness of condensed
life; artificial intensity and absurd lighting.—In the evening I
sat with Kouligaga and Petai surrounded by a circle of on-
lookers, and we talked, the light of the lamp falling on the broad
ornamented front of the *lisiga* where K. with his wife sat higher
up. A group of people in *buneyana.*—At night rain, insomnia;

thought of *N.* [circled letter] and Tośka with sensual regret, for that which will never come back. Thought about Poland, about "Polish woman"; for the first time deep regret that E. R. M. is not Polish. But I rejected the idea that perhaps our engagement is not definitive. I shall go back to Poland and my children will be Poles.

Tuesday, 4.17 [*sic*]. Over-all mood: strong nervous excitement and intellectual intensity on the surface, combined with inability to concentrate, *superirritability and supersensitiveness of mental epidermis and feeling of permanently being exposed in an uncomf. position to the eyes of a crowded thoroughfare: an incapacity to achieve inner privacy.* I am on a war footing with my *boys* (i.e., with Ginger), and the Vakuta people irritate me with their insolence and cheekiness, although they are fairly helpful to my work. Still making plans for subjugating Ginger, and still irritated with him. About Elsie I think constantly, and I feel *settled down.* I look at the slender, agile bodies of little girls in the village and I long—not for them, but for her.

Events: In the morning watched the farewells of the Kitava people. After breakfast, it was too noisy here; I went to the village, talked with Samson, Kouligaga, and others. Rain. After lunch (during which I also talked) *kabitam*, I went to the boats, copied the designs; rain abated. Came back, wrote a bit, then went to Kaulaka. Formulated problems, especially those of *kabitam.*—Kaulaka is a poetic village in a long hollow amid palm trees, a kind of sacred grove.—The pleasure of new impressions —unsettled consciousness, where waves of new things, each with its well-defined individuality, flow from all sides, *break against each other, mix, and vanish.* A pleasure like that of listening to a new piece of music, or experiencing a new love: the promise of new experiences. Sat in *Lauriu*, drank *coconut* milk; they told me about *Puwari.*—Went back with Ogisa; clouds threatening;

I walked fast without thinking about anything definite. Four eggs for supper; then again to the village; talked about *kula* with Petai. Sleepless night; continuous rain, nervous excitement, itch in big toe (a new form of psychopathological obsession). . . . I think about E. R. M. a great deal—how we'll make our *grande entrée* at the ball [Under the Rams] (ribbon of the Legion of Honor).

Wednesday, 4.18 [*sic*]. After bad night, awakened by cries about *kovelava*. Boats leaving to fish. Got up sluggishly. The same mood of nervous tension. They brought me a lot of [inedible things] and two decent *utakemas*. Resolved to pick one or two important Vakuta problems and develop them thoroughly. To begin with, *kabitam*. Then, local mythology. Then go over the whole range of similarities, differences, between Vakuta and Kiriwina. I carry out this decision and work well, choosing a couple of the most important questions (in the morning, traditions with Petai, in the afternoon L. T. [*lili'u tokabitam?*] with [. . .]). A couple of first-class informants. Rain pouring all day with one hour's interruption at 11. During lunch (*crab*) did not read. Right after lunch, M'bwasisi* & Co. Around 6, still raining but I feel I must go out; Beethoven melodies flit through my head (*Fidelio Overture*), longing for and thoughts about E. R. M. The *tokabitam* brings me a comb, which overjoys me. In the rain and mud I walked to Kaulaka; associations with similar walks in Zakopane [in Poland, near Cracow]. Yesterday and day before horribly sultry, like the worst days on Oburaku, everything a thick soup of fog, mist, and smoke. Mental excitement, I repress it. Planned new designs for combs. Thought of my ethnogr. work. Planned final letter to N. S. In Kaulaka, bought stones. On my way back planned article "*The New Humanism*," in which I would show that (1) humanistic thinking *as opposed to*

---

* M'bwasisi, the garden magician of Vakuta.

dead-petrified thinking is profound and important; (2) to associate this thinking with the "classics" is a fatal error; (3) I
would analyze the essence of humanism and sketch a new plan in
which living man, living language, and living full-blooded facts
would be the core of the situation, and *mildew, patina, and dust
would not be like a halo on the head of a saint, making a broken,
putrid, dead thing the idol of a whole thinking community, a
community that monopolizes thought.* A man of genius gives life
to these things, but why should not he be inspired to this by life
itself, why should he not take life as the first subject to analyze
and understand, and then with its light to get the other things
unraveled?—To begin with, the joke about the 2 Assyriologists.
—As a corollary, if we want to banish this thing from our
schools, we must banish it from our mature thought first.—Went
back in the evening; strong feeling of contentment with this life:
solitude, possibility of concentration, work, essential ideas; true
existence.—Lying on the bed, I thought about it. Supper, then
wrote E. R. M. I am aiming at a "rhythm," work without
nervous super-tension. Sleepless night again. . . . Dream about
St. Ig. W. and N. S. Feeling of having wronged, deceived her.

Thursday, 4.19 [*sic*]. Fine day; sunshine in spots, some rain.
Got up at 8, intending to write diary and copy loose notes, but
my informants came and I collected information instead of copying. Worked well, without rushing things. At 1 rested, though I
was not tired. Loaded camera. At 3 worked again. *Guma'ubwa
libagwo.*—At 5 went to Kaulaka. A pretty, finely built girl
walked ahead of me. I watched the muscles of her back, her
figure, her legs, and the beauty of the body so hidden to us,
whites, fascinated me. Probably even with my own wife I'll never
have the opportunity to observe the play of back muscles for as
long as with this little animal. At moments I was sorry I was not
a savage and could not possess this pretty girl. In Kaulaka I

looked around, noting things to photograph. Then walked to the beach, admiring the body of a very handsome boy who was walking ahead of me. *Taking into account* a certain residue of homosexuality in human nature, the cult of the beauty of the human body corresponds to the definition given by Stendhal.—View of Kitava: low rocks, covered with lush vegetation blending with the stones and bending over a narrow belt of shallow water, beyond which the sea drops off to a great depth. In the distance Kitava, a dark strip against the gray horizon. The shallow water is of a dull green color, with pink stones in it. Slowly the clouds take on colors, a violet reflection on the surface kills the play of colors at the bottom, everything takes on surface colors and merges into a single dull-red harmony. Earlier I had observed the play of the fishes among the stones, and dolphins outside the reef pursued by some predatory fish. They showed me the [place] near the shore where they catch *milamala*. We talked about it and went back. In the village I sat a moment on the *pilapabile*, and I pawed a pretty girl in the *lauriu*. In Kaulaka we sat and again talked about catching *milamala* and about celebrating *yoba balomas*. Walked back by moonlight, composing in my mind an article on *kula*, and I questioned my companions.—In the tent (at 8:30 eggs and tea) terrible mosquitoes; went to village for a while; back at 10:30; turned in at 11.

General remarks: Work, excellent. But mental attitude toward E. R. M., bad. That lousy girl [. . .]—everything fine, but I shouldn't have pawed her. Then (morning of 4/20) I thought about Lila Peck. At the same time I thought a great deal about N. S., strong guilt feelings. Resolve: absolutely never to touch any Kiriwina whore. To be mentally incapable of possessing anyone except E. R. M. *As a matter of fact*, in spite of lapses, I did not succumb to temptations and mastered them, every one of them *in the last instance*.

Friday, 4.20 [*sic*]. Another day of intensive work, without tiredness or *surchauffage* [getting overheated], physically well and content. In the morning wrote alone and despite everything I felt a little more deserted than when the *niggers* are here.— Got up as usual. On both sides of the gray interior, green walls —on the east weeds of fresh *odila*, on the west a couple of pink palms divide the upper half of the picture vertically: the road lined with [. . .] and in the distance *odila* jungle with cascades of vegetation. Interior: rotten sticks covered with pile of rubbish, and patched in a few places; in the middle Samson's mat; my bed enthroned, the table, a pile of my things, . . . etc.— *Well*, I covered a great deal systematically; around 12 the *niggers* helped me finish *kaloma* and translate the texts. After lunch, Samson came back: Yaboaina, *kaloma libagwo*—I was very tired and I could not think straight. I took a walk . . . along the sandy, stony beach, then walked back. The bonfire cast flickering lights on the pastel-colored background of palms, night fell, Kitava vanished over the distant sea. Once again upsurge of joy at this open, free existence amidst a fabulous (*sic!*) landscape, under exotic conditions (how unexotic New Guinea seems now!), a real picnic based on actual work. I also had the real joy of creative work, of overcoming obstacles, new horizons opening up; misty forms take on contours, before me I see the road going onward and upward. I had the same upsurges of joy in Omarakana—then they had been even more justified, for that was my first success and the difficulties were greater. This may have also been the cause of my joy at Nu'agasi, when suddenly *the veil was rent* and I began to collect information.—By the sea, creative ideas about "*sense of humor, manners and morals*." I came back tired, lay down. Samson offered me his cane. I went with him and he gave me [. . .] information. Also *sawapu*. I came back late and slept well—oh yes, on my way back I went to the pool and delighted in the view of trees, water, and boats by moonlight. It's a pity that I may leave this forever. I want to write about all this to E. R. M. and to remind her that it is just half a year ago we parted.

Saturday, 4.21 [*sic*]. First day of changed clocks. Got up an hour earlier than usual, I was a bit sleepy and depressed, but my health is so good that I worked well notwithstanding, took a long walk to Okina'i, and all day long I thought creatively and intensely. Emotionally, it's rather low tide, and at night under mosquito net, disastrous relapses again: I recalled [Nayore] and G. D., etc. In the morning I moved to the lawn in front of the house and wrote down conversations. Then I hammered away at *libagwo* with my two best informants (Tomeynava and Soapa). Then, under the *bwayma*, lunch and a two hours' rest—didn't read anything, and don't remember what I thought about. Then went to the village, again got Tom. and So. and worked on [GDN], very low pressure; terrified by complications of new rites and need to change point of view. At 6 (new time) went to Okina'i. The road was not too amusing and in spots a strip on the left, fairly big *odila*, a foul stony and muddy path. The new road, the new goal interested me nonetheless. Magnificent view of the lagoon: the sun was setting; compact little clouds on the west. The mountains to the south invisible, towering cottony white cumulus clouds, probably lying on top of the mountain range. A dark mangrove belt in the direction of the *raybwag*—clearly outlined individual trees—*dark and immobile over the moving water, on which colored reflections continually come and go.* Sandy white beaches, just beyond the slimy bottom of the lagoon. I walked along the beach to Okina'i, ahead of the *niggers;* I wanted to be alone with my thoughts: initial intensity—for I feel I still have no specific theme in my mind—Okina'i and Osikweya on the sand—the smooth waters of the lagoon through the gray houses and palms bring to mind the mood in Mailu and on the South Coast. I walked alone beyond Osikweya. Formulated plans for next five months: Vakuta must be given *No. 1 place*. Revise and formulate basic gaps: *Mwasila* magic; *waga megwa; tauva'u* in Vakuta, etc., and then develop all this systematically. Eliminate Capuan* days in Sinaketa and Gusaweta. I must hurry in any case. Working at my present pace I should finish (?) and at all events come back as laden with materials as a camel.—On my way back by moonlight I thought about the letter I had planned to the Carnegie Institute, and my thought deviated to B. Sp. and C. G. S.—"Creative thoughts and filthy thoughts"—avoid the latter! I felt that my thoughts were becoming uncreative and I stopped them—the rest of the way I just looked, and my associations were insignificant. I drank tea in front of the house, the *boys* and *niggers* were in the kitchen. I was flooded with reminiscenses of Italian songs. Thought of E. R. M., P. & H., M. H. W. as audience. "Marie," "Sole," etc.—Then Pida examined the boat I had bought, and I made two important discoveries: the models of boats are an object of *kayasa;* and *Kwaykwaya* (custom of robbing houses of specific kinsmen or others under specific conditions). Walked to the village; the dogs irritated me.—Under the mosquito net, "I burn at two ends"—thought of composing a tango with Olga Ivanova. Then disastrous thoughts—the magic of E. R. M. silenced by a wave of corruption. Fell asleep very late. Pleasant and interesting dreams.—In short, health is A-1, joy of living, existing in these conditions—I completely forget, physiologically speaking, that my conditions here are negative. I am completely under the spell of the tropics, as well as under the spell of this life and my work. For nothing in the world would I read trashy novels, and I think with pity about people who keep taking medicine all the time! Health!!

* Capua: city of ancient Rome noted for luxury.

Sunday, 4.22 [*sic*]. Got up at 6 after six hours' sleep. Sunday:
I went to Tap.—*just another ethn. experience.* Dry cool breeze
—*laurabada.* Thought about E. R. M.—composed letter to her.
Then I wrote—I wrote all day long, in the morning in a hut because of the sun, in the afternoon under the *bwayma.* At 6 I
went to Kaulaka and to the shore where the *wagas* are drawn
up. I was nervously exhausted and excited: I deliberately stopped
my flow of thought, which was sparkling but lacked depth.
Talked with the *niggers* about "the positions" during sexual
intercourse. Magnificent *cove;* sand between two rocks, crowned
with a thicket of pandanus; foaming waves, misty moon. Came
back very sleepy and tired. At home, irritation because of
supposed theft of Kaluenia.—This day is a break in the intensive
work. The letter to E. R. M. is a rather dead, unpolished formulation of my ideas—a duplicate of the diary, not an expression of my thoughts or feelings in relation to my beloved.—I
have *a flash of insight:* physical intimacy with another human
being results in such a surrender of personality that one should
unite only with a woman one really loves.

Monday, 4.23 [*sic*]. Felt rather rotten—inability to concentrate, a bit feverish. Got up at 7, did *not* * at once get to writing diary or working. No spontaneous thoughts or plans come
to mind. I read French newspapers for a while; then I sat,
looked over my papers, and talked with *niggers* a bit. At 12 lay
down, dozed. After 1, lunch with Samson; then *kayaku* in his
house; worked on gardens. In the evening took out boat to lagoon: pleasant feeling of being in an enclosed semicircular area;
thoughts flowing. A certain passive satisfaction; even my longing takes on no specific form. Went back through clearings
drenched in moonlight, thinking of E. R. M., of her presence;
at moments, doubt whether she would bewitch everything as N. S.

* Underlined in original.

did. Then I thought about my departures *à propos* of N. S.
("The Lake"), etc., and about how little music I found in her
company in August 1914, and I reached the conviction that the
only woman I really love is E. R. M.—In the evening sensual
temptations: I saw a woman's body in a certain special position,
in a certain character, curvature—and in my sensual apperception, N. S. corresponds to my emotional longing better than
E. R. M.—Slept well despite 5 mosquitoes under the netting.

Tuesday, 4.24 [*sic*]. Last night and this morning looked in vain
for fellows for my boat. This drives me to a state of white rage
and hatred for bronze-colored skin, combined with depression, a
desire to "sit down and cry," and a furious longing *"to get out of
this."* For all that, I decide to resist and work today—*"business
as usual,"* despite everything.—In the morning, after writing
the diary and a letter, I went to the village, *interviewed* the
policeman, then went to Okina'i, and met Ginger *and Co.* [Hiai]
offered to take me to Sinaketa. Still shaking with anger. After
lunch went to Kaulaka to take pictures. Then to the beach;
clear afternoon with one enormous white cumulus cloud casting
strong reflections on the sea, the thickets of bushes grown together with the rock on the crests of the pandanus. I did not
think of the *niggers* or of the work, I was still depressed by
everything that had happened. I thought a little about tomorrow's *mail*, which, as I supposed, was waiting for me at Sinaketa. Turned in early.

Wednesday, 4.25 [*sic*]. Again irritation. Had to get help from
M'bwasisi to chase after the fellows. At last, after much ado, I
got my things on the *waga*, but I was so angry that I simply
couldn't look at the *negroes*. Read *Lettres persanes* which don't
give me much food for thought, except for a few philosophical
maxims and sociological suggestions. I looked at the landscape:

the water murky at first; the coast, after the beach of Okina'i and Osikweya: little rocks covered with vegetation on small strips of sand. Near Giribwa, the water is clear, on the bright-colored sand rounded lumps of reef (*vatu outcrop*). Beyond Giribwa, the coastline not as rocky and high as I had imagined; a flat *raybwag* rising above the shore, which at some places is even sandy. Then mangroves; Muwa always reminds me of Saska Kempa.* Fatigue; headache; felt *ill prepared to receive the mail.*—There was no *mail;* spent afternoon at the Raffaels', who asked me to stay with them since Billy's house was occupied. Visit to Auerbach. Evening at the Raffaels', *de omnibus rebus,* but we turned in early.

4.26. Got up at 6—we had planned to work on grammar with Raffael. He showed me his enormous *blister* [blister pearl], we chatted, we made plans. Then, for about 2 hours, we did grammar *under high pressure.* During lunch we discussed Napoleon, etc., etc. Then again grammar for about 1½ hours. At 6 I was completely fed up with talking. I ran to Kaulasi, letting the rainy, gray-evening darkness wash over me. My thoughts were galloping. In my mind I kept on talking, explaining, persuading— but not about work, only about trifles. I tried *to divert the stream of associations,* but in vain. Best thing is to stop it altogether. (Types of association: the situation between George and Raffael. I remember all my conversations with Raffael, etc.) In the evening we talked and read fragments of Chateaubriand, Victor Hugo, etc.—Slept badly.

Friday, 4.27 [*sic*]. In the morning rain, dampness, wet weather. Moved to George's. Unable to work: uncomfortable situation, irritated by *boys,* bothered by mosquitoes. At 2½ lunch. Then discussion of—? (Discussions: in the morning about ritual mur-

---

* A well-known rural area outside of Warsaw.

der, in the evening about Freemasonry; regarding the latter, was rather convinced.) In the afternoon worked very poorly until 5; then went to George's; talk with George also exhausts me nervously. Walked to Bwadela. On the whole, these days, aside from the pleasure I take in the new contact with French language and literature, are rather barren.

Saturday, 4.27 (error in dates—4.8-10). In the morning worked on grammar, with Raffael and alone. In the afternoon (late lunch; then, from 3 to 4, boys from Oburaku bought pearls), at 4:30 saw George Auerbach, who received load of betel nuts, then went to Bwadela in a state of nervous excitement. Took a few pictures there and came back very tired. Made notes on the evening landscape in the village. In the evening we read a little, then turned in early.

Sunday, 4.28. In the morning work. In the afternoon did hardly anything; talked with Raffael, looked at dogs and *natives*. Took a short walk to the village, where I talked with Motago'i* (*first-class informant*). Then—

Monday 4.29. In the morning wrote letter to E. R. M. and worked with Raffael. Mrs. Mahoney came by. Wasted the whole day with her. Went to see Auerbach. Conversations: Headon killed Dr. Harse's dog; the doctor sued him. Samarai sympathizes with Headon. Dr. H. is a shark. Mrs. Mahoney wants no *trade;* she has debts, wants to *wind up affairs,* but can't. He is in love with Miss L.—problem: what is she to do about her future?—She tells us about her interventions in struggles among *natives*. This 63-year-old woman, tall, strong, with an ultra-energetic Anglo-Saxon face, constantly using profane language

---

* Motago'i, one of Malinowski's best and most important informants, cited in *Coral Gardens* and *Sexual Life*.

(*damn, blooming*), is quite likable. Went back. R. dejected. Sam had learned from the boys of Kavataria that R. had chased them from the veranda, and that they had gone to George's. Made a row with R. in a letter. R. takes this to heart and reveals *all sorts of things:* S. opens his letters, does not give him enough *vaygu'a,* finds fault with him continually—and in addition to everything else, Emma. I tried to calm him philosophically—but of course it's difficult to be a philosopher when you are peeved yourself. We turned in very late, waiting for letters.

Summary reflections: Since Thursday I have been in a state of utter distraction. I must absolutely stop this. It is caused by too violent and too passionate contact with people, by an unnecessary communion of souls. There is no doubt that the presence of an intelligent fellow with a Parisian background is very important and full of charm for me. But I mustn't make this my *main subject.* We may talk evenings, but should be silent during the day. Same thing with George: I shouldn't be brilliant, shouldn't give him the theory of his brilliancy and ambition. If I let him talk and confined myself to listening, both of us would be better off.

Observations of instincts and feelings of dogs: Raton is in love with "Vilna," follows her, nuzzles her, makes fierce attacks at her, masturbates in the air; she keeps growling and doesn't yield an inch. And yet there is a bitch here that Raton does not even notice. In other words, animals have individual erotic feelings, what [Shand] calls *"sentiments."*

Ethnographical problems don't preoccupy me at all. At bottom I am living outside of Kiriwina, although strongly hating the *niggers.*

Physical comforts: excellent—living on their veranda, food perfect, feel fine except for slight nervousness.

Evenings we read French—Racine's *Phèdre* makes no great

impression on me; Chateaubriand's prose and V. Hugo's poetry,
a considerably greater one. I speak French fairly fluently; I
have no difficulty formulating my linguistic ideas to Raffael.

I don't think much about E. R. M., but all my erotic impulses center on her. Also moments of strong emotional longing
for N. S.

Moral: I must absolutely avoid, under any pretext, quit-
ting my state of solitude as completely as this, which just makes
me fidgety.

Tuesday, 4.30. In the morning worked a little. At 12, letters:
Ivy, then read N. S. with enclosed letter from Robertson; then
Mim, Paul, etc. At last E. R. M.—N. S.'s letters like stabs in
my heart; I decide to write her an absolutely irrevocable letter.
E. R. M.'s letters absorb me fully, but as usual slightly irritated
after reading them. This irritation has kept on until today (am
writing this in the morning of 5.2). Her remarks about deserting the Spencers, Lil., etc., for me, irritate me a little; am
also peeved by what she says about Charles.—In the evening
walked briskly to Kumilabwaga, composing a letter to N. S. In
the evening, harmless conversation with Johnson and Wills, then
wrote letters to C. G. S. and A. H. G.*

Wednesday, 5.1. In the morning, finished letter to A. H. G.,
wrote to Mother: authorizations to act in my name. Then I began to write to N. S. but did not finish. After lunch tried again
to write her, but could not finish, could not even take final decision. Around 6 P.M. went to see Auerbach; tried to avoid arguments and *surchauffage* in my talk with him. We parted in a
friendly way. I left at 8:30. Conversation with R., who told me

---

* Probably Dr. A. H. Gardiner, an archaeologist, who was mentioned in
Part I.

about his plans. Then read E. R. M.'s letters; her personality always fills me with music. I am also a little proud, and a bit jealous of her political interests.

Thursday, 5.2. Spent almost the entire day writing to N. S. and I wrote with great difficulty. Could not write it spontaneously. I formulated it as a problem to be solved. In the last analysis, I must tell her that I am engaged to E. R. M. Now I shall tell her that I will probably be engaged in the near future.—Her letters with expressions of deep, true love; Jeannie's letters, and Mary's, their eagerness to help me find a post, apparently to further my career—all this is very unpleasant, painful. I am extremely attached to her, and I am heartbroken at the thought that she will suffer. I wrote *very kindly*. In fact, I do want to keep her friendship, and confidence, if possible.—I finished the letter at 4. Then I wrote a few lines to E. R. M. At 5 I mailed the letters and went for a walk in a joyful mood, resolving to get to work, and preparing *gardening problems*. In the village some fellow spoke to me about gardens. I intended to work in the evening, but talked and read with Raffael instead. After that I read E. R. M.'s letters until 12.

Friday, 5.3. In the morning worked on language, fairly well. Same thing in the afternoon: finish grammar, to the extent of materials I have at present. Shall have to draw up plan for further work. I have a strong impulse to work. I must analyze the Vakuta and Oburaku material, review the general problems, and more particularly the linguistic ones. At 5 went to the village where I busied myself a bit, but did nothing important. Then a futile chat with George. Then again talked with Raffael; turned in about 11.

Notes: R's child sick. The mother is very beautiful in her apprehension and grief. R. more and more sympathetic; she, too. I feel very much *at home*. At the same time I simply long for Bill.

—Letters from Gardiner and Robertson *buck me up*. I am planning, on returning to England, to form a society or academy of all those who think like Gardiner and me. A kind of humanistic R.S. [Royal Society], *very exclusive and strictly scientific and international. (M.S.H. = Member Society of Humanists.) (Society of Modern Humanism.)*

Saturday, 5.4.18. A day during which I again did a bit of *field work*. In the morning, went to the gardens where I observed the *tapopu;* a bright day, with clouds. Took a few *snapshots*, talked with Nabigido'u, collected a few good [sayings], and worked alone, making observations without writing them down.—I wrote them down in part after I came back. After lunch (from 3 to 5!) with Raffael, we took linguistic notes, with one of the missionary's fellows. Then went to see Johnson and Wills, and to the village where I talked with Motago'i—he is a *1st-class informant*. After supper, sat with the Raffaels; we talked, hummed modern waltzes, read excerpts from *Jocelyn* [by the French Romantic poet Alphonse de Lamartine]. Then I read E. R. M.'s letters, and passages that had almost irritated me *at first* now seem marvelous. In the evening under the mosquito net and in the morning thought about her intensely.

Sunday, 5.5.18. Got up fairly late; rain at night. Today I must write down everything I did yesterday, and then put in a good day's work with Motago'i. In the morning I worked very slowly. The *boys* irritated me, the child was again sick, temp. 105.3°, I was really worried. In the morning began to read *Lettres des femmes*. One of them very *naughty*, got on my nerves. . . . After lunch went to the village. Motago'i was not there. Went back with Gigiuri. We worked near the house; later with Motago'i. In the evening took a short walk, picked a place for the tent. Then, at George's, gramophone; I pawed Jabulona, and had guilt feelings. Went back to Raf.'s where, after supper we talked about Rostand.—Very strong longing for E. R. M., about whom I kept thinking during talk about Rostand. . . . The total lack of "moral personality" is disastrous. For instance, my behavior at George's: my pawing of Jab., dancing with her, etc., is caused mainly by a desire to impress the other fellows: . . . . I must have a system of specific formal prohibitions: I must not smoke, I must not touch a woman with sub-erotic intentions, I must not betray E. R. M. mentally, i.e., recall my previous relations with women, or think about future ones. . . . Preserve the essential inner personality through all difficulties and vicissitudes: I must never sacrifice moral principles or essential work to "posing," to convivial *Stimmung*, etc. My main task now must be: work. *Ergo:* work!

Monday, 5.6.18. Rain, all day long. I was supposed to visit Billy but he did not send me the *waga*. In the morning I wrote down the conversations of the day before, which took time, and which I did slowly, under pressure. After lunch, from 4 to 6, conversation with Motago'i. In the evening, walked to Kaulasi, then we read excerpts from Alphonse Karr [French journalist and writer, 1808-1890] and Lamartine.—I kept yesterday's resolutions: I worked all day, although I wasted a lot of time talking with R. (about the moral value of doctors and other professional people, etc.). Am still subject to petty irritations in my relations with the *boys*, whom I should treat as dogs. During evening walk I tried to concentrate, to gain *"mental body,"* "spiritual power," to be completely inaccessible to external distracting influences, whether of darkness, crowds, or surroundings. To be able to work on the veranda with all the hubbub going on around me. To work slowly, without nervous "pressure" but without real breaks in the flow of my thought. I must try not to waste a single minute in my present work. Now that I have worked out a system for getting the linguistic and ethnographic materials, I must pick out 2 or 3 points—Wawela, Tubowada, Sinaketa—and be content to stick with them. Too much *moving about* won't give good results. *Plan:* Don't rush off to Kaduwaga, but go back to Kiriwina. *Par excellence*, to Tubowada. On the way: 2 days in Omarakana, 2 days in Liluta (try to get out *as much as you can out of* Namwana Guya'u), 2 days in Kabwaku. After return from Kiriwina, by the middle of June, one week in Bwoytalu, then Sinaketa, eventually a few days in Kitava or Kaduwaga.

Evening walk: Mastering my fear of the dark. I walked through a kind of tunnel formed by lighted foliage against a dark background. The feeling that figures were peeping out at me, almost touching me for a specific purpose. Discovery that under certain circumstances it is easier to succumb to "emotional beliefs" than to resist them. It's simply the line of least resistance. *I appercept these things as real and innocuous hobgoblins rather than as "realities (physical) that act on my nerves."*

Tuesday, 5.7. In the morning wrote rough draft of conversations, and it went incomparably better than the day before: I finished at 11 *instead of* 2. Then walk with Motago'i to the *tapopu.* I felt energetic, worked excellently, efficiently despite difficulties (camera, the sun, taking notes *en route*, etc.). Happy moments of love for tropical nature, regret that I must leave eventually, but wishing E. R. M. were here.—Back home I packed quickly and energetically, without headache, etc. Stopped at George's on my way back. I was in a good mood. In the boat, I made plans and wrote them down. The sun set, the banks vanished, and the whole world receded and was submerged in darkness. The little boat on the waves. I gazed at the pale western sky. I was making plans—I was concentrating but could not think systematically.—In Gusaweta I talked with Billy, sorted my papers, felt sleepy. Under the mosquito net thought of E. R. M. as the only erotic possibility. *I almost faint for longing. I love her madly.*

Wednesday, 5.8. Wonderful cool day, on Billy's veranda. Sea rippled, dark; sky light blue with weightless white clouds. The horizon somewhat misty.—In the morning I wrote and copied material. Fine morning: I saw my 5 months as one long, lovely, pleasant and amusing picnic on Kiriwina, and I wished I were again at Omarakana, etc.—While working I tried deliberately to achieve a peaceful, cheerful rhythm, to be able to work, sleep, etc., despite noises, obstacles, etc. Thought about E. R. M., once again concentrating on being faithful to her, on her uniqueness. —The copying didn't go well, I lost a good deal of time looking over papers and sorting them out. At 11:30 went to Teyava with Billy and took pictures there and looked at the *wasi (never go in company)*. Took pictures of women hanging *noku*. I felt a bit vexed by Billy's presence.—After lunch did some more copying and prepared campaign: *children's plays and games.* Went to the village with Teapot. Some difficulty in picking an informant. Tried to master my impatience and anger. Finally one or two good informants emerged. I worked on *games*, sitting under a tree. Brisk walk to Kapwapu. Ran for 2-3 minutes (stitches in my side). Went back, ate, copied notes, then developed photos with Billy; horrible bellyache. Turned in—under the mosquito net longing for E. R. M. Sick or well, I'd like to have her always.

Thursday, 5.9. Resolution. Copy yesterday's things early in the morning. Look over Vakuta material and send for *boys* from Vakuta: *milamala, kayasa.* Load the camera and go to Teyava.

—Characteristic hatred for little George who is unattractive, dirty, willful, and grabs everything, and whose father does not punish him. Right now he is all puffed up and hideous. I want to analyze his urine.—Worked fairly well all day long. In the morning, copied notes and loaded camera; at 11 felt rather poorly, *dawdled*, was tempted to sit down and read (I felt really rotten). But in spite of it did *kukwanebu* with good results. After lunch, finished *kukwanebu*, and at 3:30 went to Teyava and again busied myself with games, getting fairly good results. (I should make a list of games as I go along and try to see them all and take pictures of them.) At 5 went back, ate ham and eggs with Billy. After supper, conversation with a fellow from Vakuta about little boats and *waypulu.*—Then wrote down *kukwanebu.* Thought frequently about E. R. M.—with the feeling that hard work brings me closer to her. A few times successfully resisted temptations while thinking about her. Under the mosquito net, thought very intensely.

Friday, 5.10. At night, gale (I slept well); in the morning, pouring rain, continuous. Gray sky, silvery reflections on the sea, which is *ruffled and purplish*. I felt "enervated": my eyes were smarting, I had a feeling of lightness and high blood pressure, a feeling of emptiness in the region of the heart. No very definite ideas or emotions. I wanted to do a bit of Swedish gymnastics, or to take a long walk. Resolution: if this rain keeps on, you must do a bit of gymnastics. You should finish *all the remnants:* dictionary, Vakuta, *games.* Rain all day long. In the morning, copied texts and completed them with the help of the *boy*. In the afternoon wrote again; didn't feel A-1 all day. In spite of that, worked. At 4 *knock off;* walked to Kapwapu. Tired, I adopt as my maxim: "*one of the most important forms of work is rest*," and I relaxed. In the evening, planned photographs with Billy.—Thought continually about E. R. M.: she is

present in all my thoughts, plans, and feelings. But I don't long
for her violently. I thought a little about my system of behavior
in relation to Sir B. S., in fact I thought about it a fairly long
time. I am also hopeful and ambitious with respect to my work.
Planned letters to Prof. Goddard, Frazer, and Macmillan.

Saturday, 5.11. Bright morning. I woke up a bit tired, aching
(rheumatism or gymnastics?). Today devoted to photography.
—In the morning, after sending Ginger to Raffael (I forgot to
send *cargo* and *ground sheet*), I broke my teeth. Consternation,
followed by a philosophical calm: after all I did live without
teeth for two months—even longer, for I could not use the teeth
until mid-October. Ate breakfast composedly, talked with Billy
about writing to the dentist. I was a bit tense *nevertheless.* At
10 I went to Teyava, where I took pictures of a house, a group
of girls, and the *wasi,* and studied construction of a new house.
On this occasion I made one or two coarse jokes, and one *bloody
nigger* made a disapproving remark, whereupon I cursed them
and was highly irritated. I managed to control myself *on the
spot,* but I was terribly vexed by the fact that this *nigger* had
dared to speak to me in such a manner. After lunch, from 2:30
on, I worked on *kukwanebu,* linguistically. At 4 I took a walk.
I tried to relax, had no stream of associations. Remember: ability to rest is one of the most important elements of work! Without it, there is no steady, fruitful work. I am now so healthy
and in such good spirits that I feel no desire to break the continuity of work by reading novels. I don't even wait for letters
and I don't want the time to go by too fast; I simply live in and
for my work. I can't reproach myself for wasting time, for not
working hard and purposefully.—During my walk I thought
about my *games* project, about how I will describe it to E. R. M.,
and I tried to formulate a few general *points of view.* The only
break I may give myself is a long walk during which I can con-

centrate again on formulating general points of view: (*1*)
Dogma, orthodox version, theology. (*2*) *Reflex phrases, scholia.*
etc. (*3*) *The rule and the reality,* i.e., to grasp how the *niggers*
formulate a given rule, how we would conceive of it, and finally
to give concrete material, with the help of which it can be controlled, etc. etc.

Narrative again: I met women at the spring, watched how
they drew water. One of them very attractive, aroused me sensually. I thought how easily I could have a *connection* with her.
Regret that this incompatibility can exist: physical attraction
and personal aversion. Personal attraction without strong physical magnetism. Going back I followed her and admired the
beauty of the human body. The poetry of the evening and the
sunset permeated everything. I thought about how marvelously
E. R. M. would have reacted to this, and I realized the gulf
between me and the human beings around me. I walked back
home. At supper, sudden *exhilaration.* Then I worked again,
with Marian and Kaykoba. Turned in at 10:30. Irritated by
Ogisa, Marianna, and the *niggers,* who kept chattering. I don't
care a whit about the Govt., but I realize how futile and foolish
such thoughts are.

Sunday, 5.12.18. Again a rainy, windy day. The day before I
had no exercise, and I didn't feel too well: nervous tension *without edge,* impossible really to concentrate. At the same time
headache, pressure behind my eyes like the time two years ago,
before collapse in Nayore.—In spite of it, worked all day,
but not too intensively, and without inner contentment. Moments
of violent hatred for little George, alternating with moments of
almost friendly affection. But his father spoils him horribly. In
the morning, after writing diary, I copied texts, made linguistic
plans, etc. Then I wrote up *tapopu.* All this too slowly and
without concentration. In the evening, after supper, thought

about E. R. M. as I sat alone on the pleasant, cool side of the veranda; I thought about her with calm, happy longing. At moments unpleasant memories: my broken teeth, Sir B. Sp. etc.— "Association of ideas"—*what a futile principle!*

Monday, 5.13.18. Decidedly, I am superstitious: since today is the 13th, I don't dare to plan anything important and I am at bottom convinced that whatever I may begin today will be *cursed and blighted.* I woke up early, thought about E. R. M. *I bring myself round to the knowledge:* physical contact, frenzied self-surrender is valuable only against background of true spiritual communion. E. R. M. is the only woman for whom I have this feeling.—Obscene thoughts pollute and destroy all chance of this true communion.—Although Socrates did not possess the complete truth when he said Γνῶθι Σαυτόν [Know thyself] & *you will be virtuous, yet to cross* [out] *the equation knowledge = virtue, & to say, video proboque meliora* etc. is also false, or at least partially true.*—I dawdled a bit (shaved, shampooed, copied texts), but about 11 we went to the village. I took a picture of a house; then of games and nets. We went back at 1; the *mailbag* arrived. I read letters from N. and [Lady St.] (I just glanced through them, saw they contained nothing dramatic). Then Hedy, Paul, Mim, Anna. Paul as usual fills me with calm contentment—over the fact that he exists. The letter from Mim, very friendly and personal.—Then E. R. M.—as usual something annoys or irritates me in her letters (this time, a panegyric on Mrs. Gilbraith). Only after reading them 2 or 3 times did I recover my balance—all the shadows vanished and I felt the music of her individuality. I was very much dispirited by absence of letters from 4/1 to 4/14. After reading the letters I went to Losuya; I felt strong and walked briskly, I sweated and prob-

* *Video meliora, proboque; deteriora sequor* (I see and approve of the better things; I follow the worse)—Ovid.

ably strained my heart. "30%" was fairly decent, but a stupid
ass as usual. Walked back—this time I did not abandon any of
my personal reserve and the moment I turned my back to him,
stopped thinking about him. Planned letters to E. R. M., to
Mim, and Paul. Night fell, I walked fast without getting tired.
In the evening we developed pictures, I did not feel too well.

5.14. In the morning read N. S.'s letters and once again I felt
sorry for her, and wished I could devote my life to her, console
her, and lighten her illness. But this feeling is not "true," for I
know myself, and I know that I am unable to devote myself etc.,
and that "happiness in a little whitewashed house" is not for me.
Still I am sorry that such marvelous feelings as N.'s are
squandered on me and because of me. After breakfast I wasted
some time examining Bill's new camera and leafing through war
news, magazines, etc. Then I wrote letters. All day long I felt
poorly—dryness and pressure in eyeballs, lack of energy and
initiative, being crushed by things I have to overcome. Every
difficulty, obstacle, break in work irritates me. I don't think
much about E. R. M. *I make up my mind* that she cannot possibly be sick and nothing bad can happen to her. In the afternoon, I wrote her a letter but, so to speak, without personal
contact. Strangely enough, it is more difficult for me to make
personal contact with her than with anyone else. Perhaps because writing to her requires higher and stronger concentration
than writing to anyone else. In the evening I wrote to Robertson, Hunt. I reread and sealed letter to Elsie. Turned in at
10:30.

5.15. Today I feel decidedly better than yesterday, although I
slept badly, and woke up early. Cold wind, not too strong, marvelous southeaster. *Stimmung.* I began to make plans and work
early, with confidence and pleasure. E. R. M. still a bit unclear.

I'll have to write letters to N. S., Mrs. Pat., Mim. In the morning I began to pack and *overhaul* everything, so as to write to B. P. [Burns Phelp] in the evening and to pack things for Omarakana. I packed all morning, after lunch looked over things and dawdled. (At 3 sent Ginger to Omarakana.) Then went to the village with Billy (or did I go alone?). In the evening letter to N. and business letters. Very tired.

5.16. Thursday. Woke up with sore throat and ugly green mucus. In the morning, finished letters, then Billy went to Kiribi; I walked to the village and took a few pictures. After lunch sat and read. At 3 Billy suddenly came back. I looked through papers, then both of us went to the village. We took pictures of *games.* Then I went to a garden and talked with Teyava people *of gardening and garden magic.* Went back at sunset, feeling *feverish.* I wanted to take some medicine, and took Chlorodyne. Had a pleasant conversation with Billy, went to bed. Marian behaved shockingly. I felt sorry for Billy. Thought very intensely about E. R. M.

5.21.18. Stopped writing diary. Got worse and worse. Had fever in the afternoon two days (Friday and Saturday); on Sunday was quite sick. Monday (yesterday) I felt better, but I was still weak and *my nerves play havoc.* I suffered horribly having to live in this pandemonium of children and *niggers;* particularly my *boys* got on my nerves, also Marianna. However, yesterday I shook off my sluggishness, almost the moment I felt better. But today I must take it easy again.

17. Friday. Morning, *okwala;* afternoon, pictures. Slight fever.

18. Saturday. *Tuma.* Felt rotten in the morning. Afternoon, in the village. Fever.

19. Sunday. Quite sick. Read E. R. M.'s letters. Wrote in the evening.

20. Monday. Billy went to Kiribi. I read novel at first, then to work.

Health: I had a violent cold in the head and a sore throat. It didn't go down to my chest, but "crept into my head." Same state of rotten sluggishness as I had in Nayore. I starved myself, recalling Elsie's theory that I may have a septic center in my intestines. A very unpleasant symptom, entirely new pain in the small of my back which passes about half an hour after I get up.

Problems: Scientific interests wane to the extent that I feel rotten. Sunday I was unable to concentrate or to work. Unmastered longing for E. R. M. whose letters I read, feeling immensely close to her.

Emotionally: Melancholy depression, burying myself in inactivity and sluggishness. Not for a moment do I fear an incurable disease—*so much for my optimism,* although the pain in the lumbar region worries me. Could it be the beginning of tabes?

Resolutions: The most important thing is not to surrender to this sluggishness, to *"take it easy." Yes, take it easy, but in work. Work easily, without effort and heroism. Work ought to be for you a matter of course and a matter of play. You ought to love to see your papers round you, plunging into the depths of work. Again, don't get lured by byways, by a stray novel lying about, or, when you want to fast, by some food being displayed on the table. The main thing now is to return to your full working capacity. To this end you must try the hunger cure again and you must not loose one moment of your time on novels etc.*

—I am reading Chateaubriand. Entirely without stuff & stuffing. He lacks the scientific sense, the aspiration to Truth as

the instinct to see things as they are, in opposition to what our fancy would like them to be.

Thursday, 5.23. Yesterday again felt very rotten. In the morning, getting up, excruciating pain in loins. A few minutes after getting up (I almost can't keep lying down, this dull pain tires me so, and usually passes half an hour after I get up), almost had a fainting spell; I felt dizzy and had to sit in a chair. This frightened and demoralized me. Instead of working or writing letters, I again started to read novels. Read Miss Grimshaw, *When the Red Gods Call,* and a novel by [William J.] Locke. I must note a certain progress: after reading these things, today, when I am still very weak and tired, novels attract me as a *"window open on life."* Yesterday in addition to my general guilt feelings, I had specific ones in relation to E. R. M.: I am wasting time, while it is my duty to her and to "our children" to work as hard as possible and to achieve a "position" in relation to myself—to be someone who really accomplished something; *make my mark in this world.* When I feel so rotten in the morning, quiet despair: if I am to be a useless cripple, I will commit suicide or at all events won't marry her.—I want to write her all the time. While reading novel, continually evoke E. R. M. I love her ever more deeply, more truly, more passionately. All silly jealousies and secondary feelings (like regret and feeling of humiliation because of C. E. M., annoyance because of the Gilbraiths, etc.) vanish.

Tuesday 21. Worked fairly well through the middle of day, but at 5 began to read *Poker's Thumb,* and finished it late at night.

Wednesday 22. In the morning, pain, despair, doubts. Felt very rotten. In the morning, Beatrice Grimshaw. In the afternoon, *The Wonderful Year* by Locke.

Saturday, 5.25. Yesterday and day before, health much better. Didn't read novels or waste any time except for the moments I needed to rest. I don't feel a bit strong and I have made no attempt to go out for a walk. Pain in the lumbar region has gone, whether because the weather is warmer, or because I am wearing a truss again in the daytime. The day before yesterday and yesterday I worked, but without great energy or interest. Longing for E. R. M. and Melbourne is still immensely strong. I keep rereading her letters and thinking about my return. I also recall my little room in Grey St., the Library, etc. I am really attached to her and I love her very much. At moments I am frightened by her likeness to Auntie and to Maria C., remembering the way she was during the worst times, last July, August, and September. She is not "the fulfillment of all the potentialities of woman," but I must drop that kind of thing. Yesterday night I had lecherous thoughts about Mrs. C., L. P. and G. D. But I surmounted tendency and the thoughts disappeared of themselves. This morning, after 10 gr. of quinine, which was indispensable yesterday, I felt a bit flabby, and in the morning, instead of concentrating and writing diary, etc., I read the latest Bulletin. But then came the reaction. I must work hard and consistently. Also, I must be interested in my work, and *"faire travailler mon sommeil."*— The natives still irritate me, particularly Ginger, whom I could willingly beat to death. I understand all the *German and Belgian colonial atrocities.*—I am also dismayed by Mrs. Bill's relations with a handsome *nigger* from Tukwa'ukwa (Mukwadeya). Heaven knows what goes on during *supeponi!*—Am awaiting *the next mail* with longing and impatience. *After all* E. R. M. has not written me for the last two weeks. Yesterday I glanced through her letters and noticed that actually they are not *à sa hauteur*. She ought to keep a diary.

Thursday 23. In the morning, wrote E. R. M. Around 11:30 went to Teyava to do *games*, under a tree. In the afternoon (again wasted some time) went to Tukwa'ukwa, trying to get copies of [*koukwa*] from Mrs. Togugua, but without brilliant results. In the evening copied texts with Mrs. Togugua.

Friday 24. In the morning finished letter to E. R. M., which Norman Campbell will take to Saṃarai. Then helped Billy. Around 12 went to *sopiteyava*. [. . .]; then observed and made notes on games. Lunch with Billy. In the afternoon took picture of interior of house. Then strolled to Tukwa'ukwa. In the evening observed *games*.

Friday 24. I feel much better, and am beginning to work. But after writing diary in the morning I felt lazy and dull. Worked with Togugua, but before that read Rivers as a sort of warm-up. This time he seemed much less absurd and, with reservations he himself recognizes, his book doesn't look bad. Reading it stimulated me, and I simply *bubble up with theoretical ideas*. In my case, so far as I can see, the main trouble will be keeping my mouth shut.—After working with Togugua I felt poorly. I lay down and dozed. Then Davis came. I tried to prepare him regarding the Kiriwina *natives*, and to help him, giving him Seligman, etc., and even promising to lend him [Rev. S. B.] Fellowes [the first missionary in the Trobriand Islands]. Although unshaven and wearing dirty pajamas I managed to maintain dignified manner. Walked with him a few steps. With Billy [talked] about Mick, who grumbles about Norman: "*That bl. big cunt of Kaiawato! You've got half a bottle of whiskey, the b.b.c. of K. and dogs and cats.*" N. used up a case of tobacco in 3 weeks, without buying pearls. In the evening went to Tukwa'ukwa, where the Negroes refused to *mwasawa*. Then to Teyava, where Marianna and her court also went. I walked arm in arm with Nopula. To encourage them to play (there was no one on the *baku*), I began to *kasaysuya* myself. I needed exercise, moreover I could learn more by taking part personally. Much more amusing than the little games organized a few days ago in [Nyora]. Here at least there is movement, rhythm, and moonlight; also emulation, *playing of parts*, skill. I like naked human bodies in motion, and at moments, they also excited me. But I effectively resisted all thoughts I would be ashamed of or would fear to disclose to Elsie. I thought about her, as the human body always makes me think about her. . . . Morality consists in a continual struggle, in a continual improvement of the situation and increase of strength. . . .

Tuesday, 5.28. Yesterday was completely fouled up. Day before yesterday, half the day spent taking pictures of *nasasuma* in Tukwa'ukwa.* After resting I worked in the afternoon with Togugua, and had fairly good results, among other things a version of one *silami*. In the evening, somewhat depressed and sluggish; we developed pictures. Almost all of Billy's unusable; I failed to expose three of them. Davy James called on us; he is not very interesting.—Yesterday I was in one of those disastrous moods that make it impossible for me to do any work, to concentrate on anything. In the morning, I did *not*† write my diary. Then I did *not*† put my papers in order. After lunch I read Rivers, which was *laudable*, but I did not read with real concentration. Then made the *round of the villages*. Teyava was empty in the sun; all the fellows had gone to Tukwa'ukwa, so I went there. Sat for a while with Mosiryba, who is worthless as an informant. Came back, and after lunch read novels through the afternoon, having guilt feelings and longing for E. R. M. all the time. I read Conan Doyle's *Poison Belt*; the *Vicar of Wakefield*: it is easy to read 2 or 3 novels a day!—In the evening I watched

---

* Pictures of ceremonies connected with a first pregnancy, included in *The Sexual Life of Savages*, pages 217-31.

† Underlined in original.

Billy *printing* pictures, did Swedish gymnastics on the cool side of the veranda, and went to Tukwa'ukwa. All the time I had a subconscious longing for E. R. M., but in spite of that I scandalously pawed Nopula. . . . I controlled myself on my way back by moonlight, but I must never again indulge in such things.—I decided today, tomorrow, and day after tomorrow, to complete work on *games* and *kokuwa* and *bwaga'u;* also to take a few pictures. After that, to go to Omarakana.—Diagnosis of yesterday's condition: sexual hysteria, caused by lack of exercise. Today again I had (unnecessary!) dirty thoughts about Mrs. [. . .].

Wednesday, 5.29. Yesterday I finally shook off my lethargy. In the morning worked two hours at Teyava; felt very poorly and very nervous, but I didn't stop for a moment and worked calmly, without tension, ignoring the *niggers.* On returning to Gusaweta, I felt so rotten that I assumed I wouldn't be able to work in the afternoon. In spite of that, the discovery of *yagumorobwa* from Kudukway Kela interested me so much that I talked with them from 3 to 5, and then went to Kudukway. I felt sick, feverish—*cure or kill* (I suspected pneumonia). While walking there I could not think of anything; all I did was dully imagine what my return to Melbourne would be like. I did not feel strong enough to walk a hundred paces. But in Kudukway Kela I felt better, and I came back feeling strong. In the evening I felt tired but well—went out to look at the stars shining over the low scrub, and thought about E. R. M. I had ambitious ideas and plans for journalistic propaganda in London (*Westminster Gazette* or *Manchester Guardian, New Statesman*). I tried to master *the mental froth, which accompanies all ambitious plans and thoughts.* Above all I must eliminate greediness, hope of making money, from all my plans for the future. Disinterestedness must be my fundamental virtue, and to this end, poverty, contempt for excess and expensive things. As far as possible I must travel second-class, eat inexpensively and modestly, dress simply. I must not run the risk of selling out for money.

Thursday, 5.30. Yesterday worked well; I felt better, but toward evening, symptoms of sluggishness again. On my way to Teyava, did some Swedish gymnastics, and felt better afterward.—In the morning, diary and letter to E. R. M. Put my papers in order. At 10:30 began to work, showing *Kavilumuyo* to fellows from Bwoytalu and Tukwa'ukwa. The latter (chiefly the policeman and the *tokabitam*) stayed till the end. At 1:30 I drank milk, read a few pages of Goldsmith, and went to Teyava; there, *cricket*. I came back and discussed *koukuwa* with Mrs. Kaykoba, on Billy's veranda. Then a short walk to the Kapwapu *water hole*. I felt strong and healthy—suppressed thoughts about Baldw. Sp., etc. Tried to be alone with nature. I saw a ship—*mail?* What would it bring me? News from E. R. M.? I saw, like a shadow, the possibility of something bad, an accident, sickness. Metaphysical feeling of *precariousness of things*. If she didn't exist, what would I do with myself? Would I be irretrievably broken? She is the ideal wife for me, beyond any doubt. I came back feeling strong and healthy, and I could not be really depressed.—In the evening talked with Bill—about novels, etc. —then *I joined the company in the kitchen.* The naked bodies outlined under the percale, sprawling legs, breasts, etc. aroused me. I shuddered cataleptically [*sic*] a few times, fixing my thoughts rigidly on E. R. M. I always try to reverse the problem: to think about her and about whether men's bodies arouse similar *crude instincts* in her. This pours cold water on me, *and I physically shudder.* Then I sat with Mrs. Togugua and wrote down Saykeulo *megwa.* Took a walk on the road to Teyava and did gymnastics. "I sought solitude": the wind was blowing, the palm leaves crackled, the full moon lit up the trees, its light gliding over the palm leaves and forming shadows. While doing gymnastics, had severe nervous tension; a feeling as if hundreds of arms were coming out toward me from the mixed shadows—I felt that something was about to touch me, jump at me out of the darkness. I tried to achieve a mood of certainty, security, strength. I wanted to feel *alone,** and *impregnable.*

Friday, 5.31. In the morning felt well and energetic. Wrote E. R. M., and diary. Looked over papers and felt snowed under. Went to Teyava with the Kudukway Kela people. There I got mad at some little girls. I tried to chase them away, but they wouldn't go. Went back to the road, under a tree. The *niggers* were getting on my nerves, and I could not concentrate. Came back around 1. At 2:30 went to the *odila* with Togugua, and we worked on *bugwaywo,* but he is a mediocre informant, and I had a hard time. I felt sluggish, wanted to lie down and sleep, at the same time a restlessness in my muscles and nerves. I tried to revive myself and went to Losuya.—Joyous feeling of freedom, intellectual purity, relaxation. Sky covered with little clouds, tropical vegetation. I tried to formulate for E. R. M. the importance of keeping a diary as a means of self-analysis. Then thought about my work on social psychology, which aims at a basically new approach to comparative sociology. Immediately on returning to Melbourne I must address myself to this—will do preliminary work, and will try to enlist E. R. M.'s aid in this task.—On my way back: the strongly unpleasant impression made on me by missionaries: artificiality, cult of superficiality and mediocrity. *Character: "secret society."* In their prayers they mention the *Governor and G. in Council and legislation* (=*practical purposes*); they pray God that their work may be successful, that their army be victorious and good—always

* Underlined in original.

"we," "for us," and utilitarianism. This made me think about religion: this clan spirit; "God" as an institution for mutual help, for erecting a wall between oneself and metaphysical as well as economic dangers. Durkheim's basic idea* is true, but his formulation discredited. Moreover, his point of view is false, because he starts at the bottom, with the Australians. There are *non*religious† societies, *communities* (Canary Islands), as well as religious ones. Religion = degree of cohesiveness in the sense of metaphysical privilege. The principle of "*a chosen people.*" Study the socio-psychological mechanism of this.— My Polish work concerns "mystical thought and action." Religion as a special case = mysticism and cohesiveness. Supplement this!

Saturday, 6.1.18. Yesterday: in the morning felt rather poorly; after writing diary, letter to E. R. M., etc., wrote down *megwa* with Mrs. Togugua; didn't go well. After lunch, began to read trashy novel; finished at 5 (*Revolt* [*against*] *the Fates*). In the evening, guilt feelings, nervousness (gorged myself with crabs), did nothing, fretted. Almost unable to think about E. R. M.— because of guilt feelings and bitter self-reproach. (I shall again record events of each day under their own date, not date of following day.)

6.1.18. In the morning felt poorly, chewing over yesterday's guilt feelings. I decided to take a long walk in the afternoon and to work at Kudukway Kela. In the morning I had finished going over my papers and was ready to start working, when Billy pro-

---

* In Malinowski's review in *Folk-Lore* (Dec. 1913) of Durkheim's *Les Formes élémentaires de la vie religieuse,* he cited the following: "The god of the clan . . . can therefore be only the clan itself. . . ." The review is included in *Sex, Culture, and Myth.*

† Underlined in original.

posed walk to Olivilevi or Tukwa'ukwa. We went. Billy took pictures, I walked about in the village. Then we watched *va'otu*.—
This left me in an excited, unbalanced mood.—I read Rivers;
theoretical work attracts me. I thought wistfully: when shall I
again be able to meditate peacefully in some library and spin
philosophical ideas. I went to Kudukway Kela and decided to
formulate my theoretical ideas. I mixed this continually with
Rivers' criticisms *ad hominem* of Seligman. Thought about formulating this for E. R. M., and was led to the idea of writing
*"Introduction into Comparative Sociology" (Int. to the study
of Comparative Sociology)*, which would differ in tone from
usual textbooks—much freer, more informal, giving *tips and
side views*. Free from the academic *"noncommittal"* and containing many things *sub beneficio inventarii*. Written in a
strong, striking, amusing style. If I must spend one more year
in Melbourne with Paul and E. & Mim, I'll write an outline of
this book and hold a seminar once a week on the subject. This
Introd. must differ from the full treatise, which I must write, too,
and in which I'll develop the basic conception (Tono Bungay*):
"Socio-psychological correspondences" = *The main study is to
understand how ideas (social) & social institutions react on
each other. The study of the mental (which is always individual, differential) becomes objective, consolidated into an institution, & this again reacts on the individual.* It would be a good
thing to write an article of about 100 pages and to publish it in
J.A.I. or in some American journal. At Kudukway Kela, moment
of embarrassment when I sat among *niggers* and did not know
where to begin. Then I took them under a tree and we talked—
results not too bad. On my way back I was tired and couldn't
think intensely. In the evening worked with Togugua, who is very
difficult. Read E. R. M.'s letters. Went under the mosquito net
and had unnecessary lecherous thoughts about E. E. etc.

* Novel by H. G. Wells (1909).

Sunday, 6.2.18. I felt brisk and healthy. In the morning, frightful noises and commotion on the veranda. I took a short walk trying to concentrate. Definition of the foul temper I was in a few days ago: anxiety, waiting for something to happen. Mood of calm and certainty: keeping on with my work, with no unnecessary efforts or breaks; must work steadily, without respite and without *surchauffage.*—Looked over papers, copied. At 10:30 went to Tukwa'ukwa; I got Kaykoba to work with me a good bit on the *bwaga'u.* Intended to go to Kudukway Kela in the afternoon, but I didn't go, read Rivers. At 4 began to work on *bwaga'u* and, despite great obstacles (children and *niggers* yelling and being rowdy on the veranda), I got some work done. In the evening, pouring rain. I sat with Billy; began to look over and copy *bwaga'u.* We talked about Freemasonry, and I tried to convince him that there can be no such thing as Masonic mysteries, that Raffael is a real Mason and that he told me everything there is to be known about Freemasonry. I expressed my contempt for British F. M. I went overboard on the subject. My authoritativeness loses force by being too explicit. One must discuss things *man to man,* not *ex cathedra.*—Turned in at 10. All day long felt fairly well.

Monday, 6.3. In the morning didn't feel very sleepy, *in fact* slept badly, because I'd had no walk yesterday. Got up at 6:30 in a mood for work, but theoretical rather than practical kind. I told myself: I must observe and talk but I must also keep my eyes open and overlook no detail, no *feature.* To this end I must study my material continually, as well as read Rivers and observe the *niggers* and talk with them.—This morning, rain, dampness. I must *overhaul* the phonograph and Viteku must sing for me. I must pack and be ready to go the moment the weather improves. In the morning, violent downpour; I worked on *bwaga'u* until 12, intensively and effectively; I cracked the "nut" and got ready to investigate further and to complete the construction.—At 12 I wanted to go the village, but feeling tired and weak, I decided to rest and take a walk. But it was raining too hard; I went back and *in spite of all* did gymnastics. After lunch, *bwaga'u* again until 4. At Tukwa'ukwa I could not find informants, and I went to Teyava. An hour on the veranda —not the worst. After supper, another half hour. Then I wound up the phonograph, although I could get nothing out of it— Viteku won't sing for me.—I came back, and instead of working (I felt up to it), talked with Billy—our theoretical memories. Then from 9 to 11 wrote down *silami*. Turned in. M., who is a vulgar whore, carried on noisily. I thought about how I'd receive Billy in Melbourne, at Paul's, Ernest's, my in-laws'—once again lack of enthusiasm for the latter.

Tuesday, 6.4. Slept badly, drank too much tea yesterday and took a double dose of iodine. Awakened by some bastard screaming furiously. Thought about E. R. M.—about her silence from 4/1 to 4/14—could something have happened then? Did she betray me—*un piccolo momento di debolezza*—with Paul? Would I reject her? No. I would have no right to. I don't feel that I can or even want to repudiate her. A terrible complication. Strangely enough, this thought increases her sensual charm. Furious upsurge of passion for her. For two days I had been thinking about her continuously, and she attracts me strongly. I think about her as my wife. *De facto* I am married. —Decision: to pack and set out for Omarakana tomorrow. Today is a cold, overcast day, but so far it has not been raining.—I worked all day well, without lapses. In the morning I wanted to finish *bwaga'u*. There were no informants at Teyava. I went to a garden with a group of children: excellent information. Wrote it down when I came back. Then very tired. After lunch began at once to put papers and things in order. Then, from 4 to 5, went

over MS., also notes on Oburaku. Need for physical exercise.
Ran to Olivilevi. General ideas about methodology. Intended to
look over my papers after supper, but Mukwadeya & Co. gave
out a steady stream of interesting details. I did some writing.
Then sat gazing at the southern horizon. There was a cool
breeze. I thought about—E. R. M., of course, and what else? I
tried to relax.

Wednesday, 6.5. Felt rotten getting up. Took calomel and salts,
and refrained from eating. Then felt better. Came across a novel
by Meredith. Went for a little walk, tried to concentrate. Ideas
about method. I analyzed the nature of my ambition. An ambition stemming from my love of work, intoxication with my own
work, my belief in the importance of science and art—eyes
turned to the work do not see the artist—ambition stemming
from constantly seeing oneself—*romance of one's own life;* eyes
turned to one's own form. Read description by Sigismund Alvan,
and this at once gave me courage to go on working. External
ambition. When I think of my work, or works, or the revolution
I want to effect in social anthropology—this is a truly creative
ambition.

Omarakana. 6.8.18. That day (6/5) I worked all morning,
going over my previous notes and making plans for the future.
At 1, Harrison came; I shocked him by my *bad language* and
contemptuous remarks about religion. Tried to learn something
interesting from him. War news—*even this dated*—and Samarai
gossip, the only [. . .]. Then he began to talk ethnography,
and made a few remarks; we spoke about *kula.* Rather negative
impression. He cannot grasp my terminology, contradicts me,
and has stupid, petty *points of view.*—Talk with him gives me
congestion of the brain.—Took a *dinghy* out; this didn't relax
me, either. In the evening, I couldn't do a thing. Next day, in-

stead of fasting, I ate *a heavy curry*, then packed. Finished after 12, but felt completely broken, had to lie down in the afternoon. I felt as one does during a spell of seasickness. Simply a strong migraine caused by congestion of the brain. Once again, the principle: "rest is an extremely important form of work."

6.5. Morning, work. Noon, Harrison. Afternoon, *dinghy*, migraine.

6.6. Packing. Migraine. Read *Capt. Calamity*.

6.7. Sluggish. Got ready. Went to Omarakana. Felt A-1.

6.8. In the morning, felt distinctly tired and weak.

—Friday morning [6.7] it was raining. Struggle between sluggishness and desire to free myself. Finally I got myself going, although I felt very liverish and apathetic. Set out at 1. A certain excitement at the thought that I'd be again in Kiriwina and Omarakana. I drew up plans: How to behave in Omar. in regard to tobacco. What to do, what to work on, etc. Ideas about methods of *field work*. The main principle of my work in the field: avoid artificial simplifications. To this end, collect as concrete materials as possible; note every informant; work with children, *outsiders, and specialists. Take side lights and opinions.*

This morning I woke early (I did not sleep very well and had two horrid . . . dreams. In first one, which was of the Freudian type, feeling of sinfulness, evil, something loathsome, combined with lust—repulsive and frightening. What does it come from? And this feeling of wickedness, which rises to the surface. Then a bit sluggish and I don't know where to begin.

6.25.18.

6.8, 9. Saturday and Sunday felt rotten—did not eat anything.

6.10, 11. Monday (10th) wrote letters (Sunday, *mailbag* from Gusaweta, read in a fever). Monday, read *Patrician.*

Tuesday morning felt well, got up.—[. . .] 2 registered letters.* Sent Ginger—went to see whether he was not stealing *yaguma.* Went into the thicket and burst into tears. Mosquitoes drove me out. On my way to Tilakaywa, went here and there and sobbed. (There are experiences to which memory does not go back.) Then sat in the tent and wrote letter to E. R. M., in which I crystallized my feelings—phrases which rise to the surface of emotions like foam.—Walked to *raybwag* via Tilakaywa. Tokulubakiki† *joined me.*

6.12. Letters to the Stirlings, to N. Walk via Kabwaku, Okaykoda, Obowada.

6.13. Again wrote letters, and again sent Ginger away. Walked alone to Tubowada.

6.14. Read Dostoevsky—glanced through, could not read seriously, afraid to work.

6.15. Read *Jane Eyre.* Began one day and read the whole novel until 3 or 4 at night.

6.16. *Buritila'ulo* in Wakayse-Kabwaku—first things I resume work on.

6.17-24. Period of concentrated work. Almost indifferent in relation to grief. Read novels (excerpts from *Jane Eyre*). Worked intensively. Full of ambition and ideas. Thought about *"New Humanism"*—in my thoughts, went continually back to my schooldays in Cracow. About critique of history. About nature of sociology. Thought a little about E. R. M., but thoughts about her are painful. Living in my present work and impersonal plans for scientific work.—External ambitions keep crawling over me like lice. *F.R.S.* [Fellow of the Royal Society] —*C.S.I.* [Companion of the Order of the Star of India]—*Sir.* Thought about how one day will be in *Who's Who,* etc. etc.

---

* The entry of 6/26 makes it clear that these letters brought news of his mother's death earlier in the year.

† Tokulubakiki, an important informant; Malinowski referred to him as "my best friend" in *The Sexual Life of Savages.*

True, tried to shake it off; to struggle. I know that the moment
I would obtain a title, etc., it would mean nothing to me. That at
bottom I don't believe in, despise distinctions, that I might even
refuse them. At moments, longings for Australia, for Paul &
Hedy, for E. R. M. Thought about N. [circled letter].

6.24. Walked to Kaulagu with Ogisa. Overcome with grief,
I sobbed. Then deep sadness, and fatigue. I feel so strong and
healthy now—and all this is so pointless. I know that if I lost
my eyesight or my health now, I could easily commit suicide.

6.25. In the morning worked calmly, without *surchauffage*,
and took pictures. Then looked over my notes and added to
them. Then went for a walk via Kabwaku, Okaykoda. Very
tired. I sobbed and was very sad. In the evening worked again.
Marvelous moonlit night. Went to Yourawotu; boundless sorrow
and grief submerged everything. I sobbed. By moonlight, etc.,
lecherous thoughts.

6.26. This morning felt I should resume the diary. I went to
Yourawotu. Thought about external ambitions. American plans.
—Also argued mentally with Baldwin Spencer. Aggrieved
thoughts about Mother—hopeless. In the morning worked hard,
but general ideas tired me. At 11:30 went for a short walk. Then
I [*biboduya*] *megwa* with Tokulubakiki. After lunch simply exhausted; I took a nap, sent Ginger to Gusaweta. Then *megwa
bulubwalata*. I may be unable to think, but I can write. Walk
via Kabululo, Kudokabilia, [Kanimuanimuala]. Cloudy, drizzle
on and off.—I was so tired that I was almost asleep as I walked
along. All the time, grief—as if a knife had been thrust into
my heart—despair. Ragged thoughts about my work.—Metaphysical thoughts, hopeless pessimism. "*Warte nur, balde ruhest
du auch*" *—comfort in the thought of mortality. Evil, destruc-

* "Wait a little, soon you too will rest"—the last lines of the Goethe-
Schubert song mentioned in Part I.

tion—during the morning walk I saw a butterfly with colorful wings, and how miserably it perished. The external beauty of the world—a pointless toy. Mother is no more. My life pierced with grief—half my happiness destroyed.—All the time I feel grief and desperate sadness, such as I felt as a child when I was separated from Mother for a few days. I resist it with the help of shallow formulas. I close my eyes—but the tears flow constantly. In the evening I was so tired that I could not do a thing. Shaved. Ate little, slept fairly well.

6.27. Cold day, sky overcast. Worked to the point of complete exhaustion, with excellent technique, i.e., without needless effort. In the morning Tokulubakiki and Tokaka'u from Tilakaywa. Then Tokaka'u alone. After lunch, short talk with Towese'i, then went to observe construction of a big *gugula*, and to Kwaybwaga, where they were roasting *bulukwa*. Then short talk with Tokulubakiki. I felt rotten and wondered whether I should risk a long walk or lie down and sleep.—I went to M'tava, and this did me a great deal of good. When I came back I wrote down *wosi:* writing down and translating 8 *raybuta* couplets took me 2 hours! Read *Papuan Times*, where I was struck by Murray's speech.—Feelings and thoughts: sadness and grief permeate everything. The moment I let myself go, my thoughts go back to Poland, to the past. I know that I have a black abyss, a void, in my soul, and with all the emotional pettiness peculiar to me, I try to avoid the abyss. But my sorrow is intense and deep. I have no joyous thoughts. A feeling of the evil of existence.—I think constantly about the shallow optimism of religious beliefs: I'd give anything to believe in the immortality of the soul. The terrible mystery that surrounds the death of someone dear, close to you. The unspoken last word—something that was to cast light is buried, the rest of life lies half hidden in darkness.—Yesterday during my walk I felt that happiness and joy in living, in their true, complete form, escape me whenever I attempt to get closer to them.—Yesterday, I deliberately shunned ambitious ideas and plans.—During my walk I thought that some day I'd like to meet Anatole France, Wells—will I ever manage this?

6.28. Cold, overcast day. I am continually on the brink of exhaustion, but since I began to take iodine again, there have been no septic symptoms of fatigue, *feverishness*, apathy, mental fog. Now I often have the feeling of being at "the bottom of consciousness"—the feeling of the physical foundation of mental life, the latter's dependence on the body, so that every thought that flows effortlessly in some psychic medium has been laboriously formed inside the organism. I am also aiming at inner economy.—Once again, spent all day in the tent. In the morning, Namwana Guya'u, and I completed translation of his *silami;* after lunch, Monakewo,* Yobukwa'u, and Nabwosuwa; we ate candy, and I finished the lists of *guya'u* wives.—During the break I tried to nap for half an hour, but to no effect.—In the evening, walk to Obweria. Again overcome by grief and despair. No bright, warm, sunny thoughts can now occur to me during my solitary walks. I think of my longing to get out of here—and I go back to my longing to see Mother which now will never be satisfied.—I went for a walk; it was drizzling, night was falling, the damp road glistened in the twilight.

6.29.18. In the morning I went to the *ligabe* in Kwaybwaga and took pictures of the *kalimomyo.*—In the afternoon worked in the tent. In the evening went to Liluta, where a man had died and they were *yawali*-ing. I felt very tired and feared I might col-

---

* Monakewo was an important informant and regarded by Malinowski as a friend. Yobukwa'u was a son of To'uluwa's.

lapse for several days (in the evening I took quinine and aspirin, and today—7/1—I feel fine).—Went back leaning on Monakewo and Yabugibogi.* In the evening read a little (*Jane Eyre*); the moon—I went out and sobbed. Also under the mosquito net.

6.30.18. Sunday. Fine morning; we strolled along the *bukubaku* and we counted *taytu*. After lunch, worked a bit with Tokulubakiki and Tokaka'u, then went to Kasana'i, where they were making a *bwayma*. Then worked with Paluwa,† Monakewo & Co. In the evening went to the [*ibubaku*] and talked with Monakewo about copulation. Then sat and wrote down and translated *Ragayewo*.—Then I went for a walk and again wept.—At night, sad, plaintive dreams, like childhood feelings. I dreamed about Warsaw, about our apartment in the boarding school, about some apartment with a bathroom (Zenia and Staś) in Warsaw. Everything permeated with Mother. Woke up every other minute. By morning drowned in sadness. Went out on the road and wept.—Sudden flashes of understanding, visions of the past. Life pierced with the arrow of grief, guilt feelings, irretrievable things.—Tiny details recollected: the linen Mother gave me when I left. Continual memories and associations. At moments an acute, sweet sorrow—I wept (the luxury of strong feelings). At other moments, true mourning, despair, numbness in grief.—Many things I can't look at—return to Poland, memories of last days, things squandered. Scientific work and plans for the future are the only things that comfort me—but I am carried away by grief at moments, even so.

* Yabugibogi, another son of To'uluwa's, is referred to in *Sexual Life* as "perhaps the most obnoxious waster in the whole community."

† Paluwa was the father of Monakewo; his daughter Isepuna married a son of the chief, and an account of his dowry problems is included in *Sexual Life*.

7.1.18. Half of this accursed year has gone by! Last night, I wondered what I would do if I lost the whole MS.? Will E. R. M. not be taken from me in some way or other?

7.16. For two weeks haven't kept the diary. Throughout that time my health was good, my capacity for work was excellent, and I worked a great deal. In the morning after I got up, the *niggers* would come to *gimwali*. I worked a great deal with Tokulabakiki —great progress in magic and linguistics. During work, I am normally calm, occasionally even cheerful. Sometimes—only in the afternoon—in addition to the words of *megwa*, images from the past emerge.—Italy, the Canary Islands, or other places I visited with Mother. Then I go for a walk. For some time I was calm and lightheaded, then there was an immensely strong resurgence of grief. Every day I went for a walk alone and wept. The whole tone of my life turned gray. Only at moments do I strongly want "to live"—to be with friends, with Elsie, to be in Australia, to write, to be active. Occasionally everything seems so gray that I don't feel any real desire to change my surroundings.—The weather is marvelous.

[From the "retrospective diary":]
7.18.18. . . . *On the theory of religion.* My ethical position in relation to Mother, Staś, E. R. M. Twinges of conscience result from lack of integrated feelings and truth in relation to individuals. My whole ethics is based on the fundamental instinct of unified personality. From this follows the need to be the same in different situations (truth in relation to oneself) and the need, indispensability, of sincerity: the whole value of friendship is based on the possibility of expressing oneself, of being oneself with absolute frankness. Alternative between a lie and spoiling a relationship. (My attitude to Mother, Staś, and all my friends was strained.)—Love does not flow from ethics, but ethics from

love. There is no way of deducing Christian ethics from my theory. But that ethics has never expressed the actual truth—love your neighbor—to the degree actually possible. The real problem is: why must you always behave as if God were watching you?

7.18.18. The weather is marvelous—the sky is overcast almost all the time. Since 7/1 there has been no rain; it is cold, I wear warm clothes.—Every small detail reminds me of Mother—my suits and my linen which she marked. I count the dates from January 29. Memories: Cracow, boarding school, and Warsaw. I think—but [. . .]—about going back to Poland, meeting Auntie, Mrs. Boronska, Mrs. Witkowska. My time at the gymnasium; I recall Szarlowski and other teachers, but Sz. most vividly of all. Planty [public gardens in Cracow], morning moods, going back home. At times I see Mother still alive, in a soft gray hat and a gray dress, or in a house dress, or in a black dress, with a round black hat.—Again frightening thoughts: death, a skeleton, naturalistic thoughts interwoven with pain in the heart. My own death is becoming something infinitely more real to me.—Strong feeling—to go to Mother, to join her in nothingness. I recall things Mother used to say about death. I recall the countless occasions when I deliberately cut myself off from Mother, so as to be alone, independent—not to have the feeling that I am part of a whole—furious regrets and guilt feelings.—Our last moments together in London—our last evening spoiled by that whore!—I feel that if I had been married to E. R. M., I would have behaved very differently.—Mother's last words, what she would have told me about her feelings, fears, hopes. I never was open with her, I never told her *everything*. Now, had it not been for this accursed war, I might have given more in my letters than I had been able to give her in person.—At moments I feel that this is only the death of "something" within me—my ambitions and appetites have a strong hold on me and tie me to life. I shall experience joy and happiness (?) and success and satisfaction in my work—but all this has become meaningless. The world has lost color.—All the tender feelings of my childhood come back: I feel as when I had left Mother for a few days, returning from Zwierzyniec with Father. —I go back in my thoughts to Anna Br.—how utterly everything has vanished from my life!—Staś's betrayal, and N.S. Truly I lack real character.

/\/\./\/\ AN INDEX OF NATIVE
TERMS by Mario Bick

THESE DIARIES cover periods of time Malinowski spent in the
Port Moresby area, the Mailu area, and the Trobriand Islands,
and shorter stays in Woodlark Island and the Amphletts. He
seems to have used four languages in his field work: Motu in
the Port Moresby and Mailu areas, Mailu, Kiriwinian and
pidgin. My research suggests that native terms from some of
the other islands, particularly from Dobu, also occur in the
diaries.

The diaries were written in Polish with frequent use of
English, words and phrases in German, French, Greek, Spanish,
and Latin, and, of course, terms from the native languages. One
of the main jobs in preparing the Index was to sort out this
linguistic melange, a task considerably complicated by the fact
that Malinowski's handwriting was difficult to read. Often, in
the case of half-legible words, it was not clear which language
they were from. If more of these words can be identified, the
definitions will be included in future printings.

Since I was unfamiliar with the native languages used, a
second problem arose from the need to separate the native terms
referring to places and individuals from those which appear in

the common vocabularies. I therefore compiled three lists: place names (complicated by the inclusion of place names from Australia and Europe which were not always immediately identifiable as non-Melanesian); personal names (many of the people mentioned in the diaries were European, and Malinowski often referred to them by nicknames or abbreviations); and native terms.

I identified place names with the help of a number of maps from the following publications:

Bronislaw Malinowski, *The Natives of Mailu, Transactions and Proceedings of the Royal Society of South Australia,* 39:494-706, 1915 (plate 26)

———, *Argonauts of the Western Pacific,* London, George Routledge, 1922 (pages xxxii, 30, 50, 82)

———, *The Sexual Life of Savages in North-Western Melanesia,* New York, Halcyon House, 1929 (page xxix)

———, *Coral Gardens and Their Magic,* 2 vols., London, George Allen and Unwin, 1935 (figure 1)

National Mapping Office, "Map of the Territory of Papua and New Guinea," compiled and drawn for the Department of Territories by the National Mapping Office, Department of the Interior, Canberra, Australia, 1954

H. A. Powell, "Competitive Leadership in Trobriand Political Organization," *Journal of the Royal Anthropological Institute,* 90:118-145, 1960 (page 124)

W. J. V. Saville, *In Unknown New Guinea,* London, Seeley Service, 1926 (end map)

C. G. Seligman, *The Melanesians of British New Guinea,* Cambridge, Cambridge University Press, 1910 (end map)

Many personal names were identified in standard reference works, in Malinowski's own works, in the Saville and Seligman works cited above, and in the following:

Raymond Firth (ed.), *Man and Culture: An Evaluation of the Work of Bronislaw Malinowski*, London, Routledge and Kegan Paul, 1957

Gavin Souter, *New Guinea: The Last Unknown*, New York, Taplinger, 1966

The inclusion of obscure book and magazine titles, as well as authors' names, added to the complexity. Many of these were identified through standard reference guides. The fact that Malinowski was a known devotee of plays on words (Firth, *op. cit.*, pages 10-11) added another peril to the identification of some terms, leaving a number of these identifications open to question. Lastly, the sketchiness of the diaries in some places made it difficult to use context as a means of identification of terms.

There are few good dictionaries and grammars of the native languages used in the diaries, and all of them were not available to me (for a recent listing of all linguistic sources for the area, see H. R. Klieneberger, *Bibliography of Oceanic Linguistics*, London Oriental Bibliographies, Vol. I, London, Oxford University Press, 1957). I was, however, able to cull from Malinowski's Mailu report a glossary from the native terms that are liberally sprinkled throughout. This glossary served as the basis of the identification of Mailu terms along with the Saville work previously cited and the following:

Peter A. Lanyon-Orgill, *A Dictionary of the Mailu Language: Edited and Enlarged from the Researches of the Rev. W. J. V. Saville and the Comte d'Argigny*, London, Luzac, 1944

W. J. V. Saville, "A Grammar of the Mailu Language, Papua," *Journal of the Royal Anthropological Institute*, 42:397-436

Motu terms were identified with the help of the following:

B. Baldwin, *English to Motuan and Kiriwinan Vocabulary*, typescript

W. G. Lawes, *Grammar and Vocabulary of Language Spoken by the*

Motu Tribe (*New Guinea*), 2nd edn. rev., Sydney, Charles Potter, 1888

For the Kiriwinian terms, I depended primarily on Malinowski's ethnographic reports (those previously cited and *Crime and Custom in Savage Society*, London, International Library of Psychology, Philosophy and Scientific Method, 1926), the Powell work previously cited, and Mr. Baldwin's unpublished vocabulary, which I received only near the end of my labors, as well as other works on the Trobriand Islands that contain Kiriwinian vocabulary):

L. Austen, "Procreation among the Trobriand Islanders," *Oceania*, 5:102-113, 1934

———, "The Seasonal Gardening Calendar of Kiriwina, Trobriand Islands," *Oceania*, 9:237-253

———, "Megalithic Structures in the Trobriand Islands," *Oceania*, 10:30-53

———, "Native Handicrafts in the Trobriand Islands," *Mankind*, 3:193-198

B. Baldwin, "Usituma! Song of Heaven," *Oceania*, 15:201-238

———, "Kadaguwai: Songs of the Trobriand Sunset Isles," *Oceania*, 20:263-285

Bronislaw Malinowski, "Classificatory Particles in the Language of Kiriwina," *Bulletin of the School of Oriental and African Studies*, 1:33-78

———, "The Primitive Economics of the Trobriand Islanders," *The Economic Journal*, 31:1-16

———, "Lunar and Seasonal Calendar in the Trobriands," *Journal of the Royal Anthropological Institute*, 57:203-215

———, *Magic, Science and Religion and Other Essays*, Glencoe, The Free Press, 1948

Dr. H. A. Powell provided invaluable assistance in identifying some of the Kiriwinian terms I had been unable to translate, and in confirming some of my translations (Powell personal communications). Seligman's classic (previously cited) and Fortune's (Reo Franklin Fortune, *Sorcerers of Dobu*, New York, E. P. Dutton, 1932) also provided information on a number of terms used from Dobu and other islands of the area.

Since so many different sources have been used in the preparation of this Index, it is not surprising that variations in spelling and orthography have occurred. A further problem came from the fact that, while he was writing the diaries, Malinowski himself was in the process of learning the languages from his native informants, who of course could only give him the sound of a word, which he then transcribed in the English alphabet. He found that the natives throughout the area made virtually no distinction between the sounds of *r* and *l*, or *s* and *t;* instead, they ordinarily used an intermediate sound—respectively, *y* or *ts* (the Slavonic *c*)—and when pressed for a careful pronunciation would perhaps say *r* on one occasion, *l* on another. Malinowski himself, writing in Polish, often used *w* and *v* interchangeably, and *i, j,* and *y*. Wherever the words could be verified in Malinowski's published work, his final decision as to spelling has been used; in the case of unidentified words and conjectures, an attempt has been made to spell them exactly as they appear in the manuscript, in the hope that readers familiar with this area may recognize many of them.

In addition to Malinowski's Mailu report, another interesting report on this people is Saville's *In Unknown New Guinea* (previously cited). The main works by Malinowski on the Trobriands are *Argonauts of the Western Pacific, Crime and Custom in Savage Society, The Sexual Life of Savages, Coral Gardens and Their Magic, Magic, Science and Religion* (all previously cited) and the following:

Bronislaw Malinowski, *Myth in Primitive Psychology*, London, Psyche Miniatures, gen. ser., no. 6, 1926

———, *Sex and Repression in Savage Society*, London, International Library of Psychology, Philosophy and Scientific Method, 1927

Other publications on this area include the Baldwin publications and the Austen cited before with the following additions:

L. Austen, " 'Botabalu': A Trobriand Chieftainess," *Mankind*, 2:270-273

———, "Cultural Changes in Kiriwina," *Oceania*, 16:15-60

Powell's work is the first anthropological restudy of the Trobriands since Malinowski. His reports on his research can be found in the previously cited work and in *An Analysis of Present-Day Social Structure in the Trobriand Islands*, Ph.D. Thesis, University of London. The main work on Dobu is Reo Fortune's, cited above. A summary of recent research on the Motu area can be found in Murray Groves, "Western Motu Descent Groups," *Ethnology*, 2:15-30, 1963. The best historical study of New Guinea during the period of Malinowski's research can be found in the Souter book previously cited.

Lastly, evaluations of Malinowski's work and the most complete bibliography of his writings can be found in the book edited by Firth. Other evaluations are included in the following:

George H. Fathauer, "Trobriand," in David M. Schneider and Kathleen Gough (eds.), *Matrilineal Kinship*, Berkeley, Univ. of California Press, 1961, pages 234-269

Max Gluckman, "Malinowski—Fieldworker and Theorist," in Gluckman, *Order and Rebellion in Tribal Africa*, New York, The Free Press of Glencoe, 1963, pages 244-252

E. R. Leach, "Concerning Trobiand Clans and the Kinship Category 'Tabu,' " in Jack Goody (ed.), *The Developmental Cycle in Domestic Groups*, Cambridge Papers in Social Anthropology No. 1, Cambridge, Cambridge University Press, 1958

Marguerite S. Robinson, "Complementary Filiation and Marriage in the Trobriand Islands: A Re-examination of Malinowski's Material," in Meyer Fortes (ed.), *Marriage in Tribal Societies,* Cambridge Papers in Social Anthropology No. 3, Cambridge, published for the Dept. of Archaeology and Anthropology at the University Press, 1962, pages 121-155

Other critical and biographical discussions of Malinowski can be found in:

H. R. Hays, *From Ape to Angel: An Informal History of Social Anthropology,* New York, Capricorn Books, 1958, pages 313-328

Abram Kardiner and Edward Preble, *They Studied Man,* Cleveland, World, 1961, pages 160-186

Robert H. Lowie, *The History of Ethnological Theory,* New York, Rinehart, 1937, pages 230-242

J. P. Singh Uberoi, *Politics of the Kula Ring: An Analysis of the Findings of Bronislaw Malinowski,* Manchester, Manchester University Press, 1962.

In explaining the problems of preparation of this Index and the sources used, I hope that the reader may have a degree of tolerance in judging the results.

I would like to thank the Rev. B. Baldwin of St. Therese's Presbytery, Moonah, Tasmania, for permission to use his vocabulary. I would particularly like to acknowledge with gratitude the unselfish help of Dr. H. A. Powell of the University of Newcastle. His prompt and extensive identification of many Kiriwinian terms, as well as his kindness in providing me with Mr. Baldwin's vocabulary manuscript, added greatly to whatever value this Index may have. In this assistance he was without the aid of the diary manuscript and was forced to rely totally on my correspondence with him. Any errors in the Index are solely my responsibility; whatever reliability the Index may have is to a large degree thanks to his assistance.

∧∨∧

amuiuwa: a type of canoe made by the people of Woodlark Island and used throughout the Massim area; also called *vaga*

aura (Mailu): a patrilocal, patrilineal clan; this is equivalent to the second meaning of *dubu*

babalan: a type of native curer, or medicine man, frequently also a spirit medium

badina (Motu): the root or cause of a thing

bagi: heavy necklace of ground shell discs

bagula: garden

baku: large open space in the center of Trobriand villages, surrounded by a ring of dwelling huts and an inner circle of yam storehouses; the chief's houses stood in the *baku*, and part was used as a dancing ground; another part was formerly used as a burial ground

baloma: the spirit or soul of a man which leaves his body after death

bapopu: a form of the verb *popu*, to defecate

bara: a dance performed in the Mailu area that came from Kerepunu in Hood Bay, popular in Papua at the time; generic name of a group of dances introduced to the Mailu from areas to the west

bara'u: a male practitioner of sorcery

beku: large, thin, polished ax-blades, used in the *kula* exchange

bobore: Mailu outrigger war canoe; each belonged to an individual clan

bogana sago: sago, an edible starch which is a staple in the Pacific islands, extracted from the pithlike center of the *boga* palm *bora'a:* pig

boroma (Motu) : pig

bulubwalata: a form of evil and malicious magic; sometimes used to injure the garden of neighbors, sometimes used to send pigs into the bush, or to estrange wives and sweethearts

bulukwa Miki: a European type of pig known as Mick's pig, first introduced into the islands by Mick George, a Greek trader; the pigs are valued highly—one will bring 5 to 10 native pigs in exchange

buritila'ulo: a competitive display of food, held between two villages

bwaga'u: a sorcerer who practices the most prevalent form of black magic; there are usually one or two in each village

bwaybwaya: coconut, in the stage of its growth when the flesh is a sweetish jelly

bwayma: Trobriand storehouse, sometimes with a sitting shelter or platform. See *Coral Gardens* for a complete description.

dadoya: flood, or pond

damorea: the most popular women's dance of the Southern Massim area; held during the *maduna* ceremonies and frequently danced for pure entertainment

dayma: digging stick, the main garden implement

dogeta: doctor

dubu (Mailu) : clan clubhouse; also the general word for clan and subclan

eba: mat made of pandanus

gagaia (Motu) : sexual intercourse

gaigai (Motu) : snake

gedugedo: possibly *geguda,* unripe crops; or *gedageda,* ache

gimwali: barter, as distinguished from exchange of gifts

giyovila: chief's wives

gora: taboo, general term; also warning signs on places or things telling people what is taboo *guba* (Motu) : wind gusts ; (Mailu) rain

gugu'a : workaday implements and household goods

gugula : a heap ; a food display piled into a heap

gumanuma : foreigners ; in some contexts, white men

gunika (Motu) : inland

guya'u : chief (generic term) ; high rank

gwadi : children generally, male or female, until maturity

haine (Motu) : woman, female

hiri : trade expeditions between the Motu of Port Moresby and tribes of the Papuan Gulf

iduhu (Motu) : tribe or family

ilimo (Motu) : a tree from which canoes are made

ivita : may be *iviati,* warm

iwalamsi : they cry or call (verb form of *walam*)

kabitam : skill, expertise, craft

kadumilagala valu : the points where a road strikes the village

kaiona (non-native, probably adapted from Police Motuan) : good-by, farewell

kala koulo kwaiwa'u : mourning practiced by the kin of the bereaved (for example, by the brother of a widow ; during the mourning period, the brother would not speak the name of either the dead man or the widow)

kalimomyo : garden arbor constructed of poles and yam vines in which family sits to clean yams

kalipoulo : large seaworthy canoe used for fishing expeditions in the Trobriands

kaloma : small circular perforated discs made from spondylus shell, which are made into the necklaces used in the *kula ;* the *kaloma* decorate almost all articles of value or artistic finish in the *kula* district

kara (Motu) : conduct, custom, habit ; *kara dika,* bad custom

karayta'u : an overseas partner in the *kula*

karikeda : fenced path between garden sites

kariyala: the portent associated with each form of magic

kasaysuya: a round game, similar in form to ring-around-a-rosy, with chanted ditties that become more ribald as the game progresses

katoulo: an indisposition from natural causes, or recognized as the result of natural causes by the natives, but felt to be a fertile base for the application of sorcery by a sorcerer

kaulo: vegetable food, generic term

kavikavila: probably, lightning

kayaku: a gathering to discuss business or just socialize; the village council before the new gardens are started

kayasa: entertainments, including competitive, obligatory dancing and amusements in which women take part, not held in the dancing season; also contractual enterprise

kayga'u: the magic of mist, used for safety at sea

kaylasi: fornication; an illicit sex act such as adultery

kaytaria: the magic of rescue at sea

kekeni (Motu) : girl

keroro (Motu) : a tree

kibi (Motu) : shell trumpet

kivi: to gather

koya: hill or mountain

kuku (Motu) : tobacco

kukwanebu: fairy tales

kula: the famous trading cycle between Melanesian communities described in *Argonauts of the Western Pacific*

kurukuru (Motu) : long grass used for thatching; see *lalang*

kwaykwaya: custom

kwila: penis

lagilu: lagiala, immediately; or *ligabu,* pour, spill

lagim: the two decorated transversal boards enclosing the well of the canoe at both ends *lakatoi* (Motu) : a ship; a native vessel made by lashing three or more large canoes together

lalang: a long grass, used for thatch and for making paper, typical of second-growth incursion after clearing of primary forest

laurabada (Motu) : southeast trade wind season

lava lava (imported Polynesian-Fijian) : waistcloth

ligabe: garden during harvest

lili'u: the real or important myths of the Kiriwinian natives

lili'u Dokonikan: a tale about Dokonikan, the most prominent ogre of Kiriwinian folklore

lili'u tokabitam: a myth about an expert carver

lisala dabu: one of the series of mortuary rituals following the death of a woman in which her female subclan kin distribute skirts and skirt materials to the female subclan kin of the widower, who help him undertake the mourning rituals

lisiga: chief's hut

loa (Motu) : walking about

lugumi (Motu) : *oro'u*

maduna (Mailu) : the annual ceremonial feast, the main event in native social life

maire (Motu) : mother-of-pearl in a crescent shape

masawa: large seagoing canoe

megwa: magic, generic term; magic formula

milamala: annual festival and return of the spirits, during the season and month in which the Trobriand Islanders enjoy the peak of prosperity; also, a name for the *palolo* worm, which comes up at a certain full moon and is used in fixing the date of the festival; the worm's arrival is sometimes connected with the arrival of the spirits

mirigini (Motu) : north wind

momyapu: papaya

mona: taro pudding

monikiniki: the system of *mwasila* in South Boyowa; much of it was also used in Kiriwina

mulukwausi: flying witches

mwasawa: to have fun, to sport; here, dancing for fun as against serious occasions

mwasila: magic performed on arrival at destination of *kula*, designed to induce generosity in the host partners

nakaka'u: widow

nakubukwabuya: an adolescent girl

nanama: female mourning helper

nasasuma: pregnant woman

noku: a plant considered by the natives to be an inferior form of nourishment, eaten only in times of famine

nuya or *luya:* coconut

oba'ua: small axes made of conus shell

obukubaku: apparently some part of the *baku*

odila: the bush, as opposed to cultivated areas

ogobada'amua: name of the *gauma* (big net) owned by the Mora'u, a subclan of Mailu

okwala: a ritual conducted so that small yams might grow

oro (Mailu): hill

oro'u (Mailu): large double canoe with crab-claw sail, considered the best seagoing canoe of the region

paku: medicated leaves

pandanus: screw pine, with leaves which are put to many uses in the area—dishes, for example

pilapala: thunder or thunderbolt

poulo: fishing expedition

pwata'i: large prism-shaped receptacles for food produce filled with smaller *kuvi* (large yam), and topped with betel nut and sugar cane *rami:* grass petticoat worn by women

raua: a dance, imitating a dog, performed at the *maduna;* of secondary importance among the dances performed at the ceremony

raybwag: coral ridge running around the island; it holds small patches of fertile soil which remain covered with jungle

rei (Motu) : grass

sagali: ceremonial distribution of food

samarupa: design of shell-disc necklaces used by women

sapi: the weeding, or sweeping clean, of gardens

saykeulo: pregnancy robes, two long mantles and two skirts, worn during pregnancy and just following the confinement

sihari (Motu) : mistress (in *The Natives of Mailu*; in Malinowski's copy of the Motu vocabulary, there is this marginal note in his handwriting: "*sihari*—custom of sitting on the girl's knees.")

sihi: perineal band, a belt covering the thighs and adjacent parts of the body

silami: illness and disease, generic term

*soba:,*face-painting

so'i: a ceremonial feast, in general similar to the *maduna,* held by the people of Bona Bona

sopi: water; also probably water hole; *sopiteyava* may be the creek or a water hole at Teyava

soulava: necklace of spondylus shell discs, one of the main articles exchanged in *kula*

supeponi: a game similar to hide-and-seek played by the Trobriand natives

tabekusi: sink, capsize

tabuyo: ornamental prowboard

tainamo (Motu) : mosquito net

tanawagana: chief or "boss"

tapopu: taro gardens

tapwaropo: prayers, missionary style

taubada raibaku: taubada (Police Motuan), a term of address used for white men; *raibaku,* possibly a childish term meaning to lie abed; the phrase seems to be an exhortation to get up

tauva'u: evil anthropomorphic beings who come from the southern islands and cause epidemics

ta'uya: conch shell blown like a trumpet for many ceremonial purposes

taytu: yams

tobwabwa'u: a male mourner wearing mourning soot

toea (Motu) : white armshells

tokabitam: skillfulness in general; or, the tradition of skilled craftsmen; or, expert carver

tomakava: an outsider; often used among Trobriand Islanders in speaking of the relationship of a father to his family (see *The Sexual Life of Savages*)

tona gora: taboo sign set up before feast to insure a plentiful supply of coconuts

tova'u: see *tauva'u*

towamoto: hot vegetable dish with peppers

towosi: garden magician

tselo: a minor dance held at the *maduna* ceremony

Tuma: the spirit land of the Trobriand Islanders, an island northwest of Boyowa

tuva: a creeper whose roots supply poison for fish

ula'ula: food offering as payment for magic

unu'unu: body hair, regarded by the Trobriand Islanders as ugly and kept shaved; also growth on yam tubers and on the back of leaves

ura (Motu) : wish, desire

uri: taro

usikela: a variety of banana

vada: sorcerer

vaga: Woodlark canoe (see *amuiuwa*) ; also an alternate spelling of *waga*

vai: marriage (general term)

valam: alternate spelling of *walam*

va'otu: a "present of inducement," offered by a village boy to a girl in a visiting party from another village; acceptance means the girl accepts the boy as her lover for the night

vatu: boulder attached to bedrock

vatuni: main spell of Omarakana garden magic

vayewo: possibly a kind of food or fish

vaygu'a: native valuables important in demonstrating and maintaining status

veyola: kindred

vilamalia: magic or ritual of plenty, performed for food

waga: in the Trobriands, all kinds of sailing craft, general designation; also, large built-up canoe

walam, walamsi: a cry or call

Waribu: a field of thirty plots, owned half by the Burayama subclan and half by the Tabalu subclan (To'uluwa's subclan)

wasi: the exchange of vegetable foods for fish between the coastal and interior villages

waya: inlet, tidal creek

waypulu: festivals of hair dressing

waywo: native mango

wosi: song, singing

Yaboaina: possibly Yabowaine, Dobu supernatural being

yaguma: pumpkins

yamataulobwala: meaning uncertain; *yamata* means to care for, to look after; *tau* is the word or prefix for man, male; *bwala* is some kind of house or other structure

yavata: winds and weather of the northwesterly monsoon

yawali: a wake

yoba balomas: the driving away of the ancestral spirits of the dead at the close of the *milamala* festival

yoyova: witches

CPSIA information can be obtained
at www.ICGtesting.com
Printed in the USA
FFOW02n1410310717
38370FF

/\\/\\/\\ A DIARY IN THE STRICT SENSE OF THE TERM

Facsimile page from Trobriands diary, beginning with entry for April 22, 1918

⋀⋀⋀ A DIARY IN THE STRICT SENSE OF THE TERM by Bronislaw Malinowski ⋀⋀⋀⋀

WITH NEW INTRODUCTION

PREFACE BY VALETTA MALINOWSKA
INTRODUCTION BY RAYMOND FIRTH
TRANSLATED BY NORBERT GUTERMAN
INDEX OF NATIVE TERMS BY MARIO BICK

Stanford University Press
Stanford, California

Stanford University Press
Stanford, California
Text © 1967 by Valetta Malinowska
Introduction © 1989 by Raymond Firth

Originally published by Routledge and
  Kegan Paul, 1967
Reissued, with a new Introduction, by
  the Athlone Press, 1989
Reissue first published in the United States of
  America by Stanford University Press, 1989

Printed in U.S.A.

Cloth ISBN 0-8047-1706-0
Paper ISBN 0-8047-1707-9

Original printing of this edition 1989
Last figure below indicates year of this printing:
03 02 01

This book is printed on acid-free paper.